T0314300

HARVESTING STATE SUPPORT

JAPAN AND GLOBAL SOCIETY

Editors: AKIRA IRIYE, *Harvard University*; MASATO KIMURA, *Shibusawa Eiichi Memorial Foundation*; DAVID A. WELCH, *Balsillie School of International Affairs, University of Waterloo*

How has Japan shaped, and been shaped by, globalization – politically, economically, socially, and culturally? How has its identity, and how have its objectives, changed? Japan and Global Society explores Japan's past, present, and future interactions with the Asia Pacific and the world from a wide variety of disciplinary and interdisciplinary perspectives and through diverse paradigmatic lenses. Titles in this series are intended to showcase international scholarship on Japan and its regional neighbours that will appeal to scholars in disciplines both in the humanities and the social sciences.

Japan and Global Society is supported by generous grants from the Shibusawa Eiichi Memorial Foundation and the University of Missouri–St. Louis.

Editorial Advisory Board

Frederick R. Dickinson, University of Pennsylvania
Michael Donnelly, University of Toronto
Joel Glassman, University of Missouri–St. Louis
Izumi Koide, Shibusawa Eiichi Memorial Foundation
Gil Latz, Portland State University
Michael A. Schneider, Knox College
Patricia G. Steinhoff, University of Hawaii at Manoa
Patricia Wetzel, Portland State University

For a list of books published in the series, see page 269.

HANNO JENTZSCH

Harvesting State Support

Institutional Change and Local Agency in Japanese Agriculture

UNIVERSITY OF TORONTO PRESS
Toronto Buffalo London

© University of Toronto Press 2021
Toronto Buffalo London
utorontopress.com

ISBN 978-1-4875-0854-8 (cloth)   ISBN 978-1-4875-3847-7 (EPUB)
ISBN 978-1-4875-2592-7 (PDF)

Japan and Global Society

Library and Archives Canada Cataloguing in Publication

Title: Harvesting state support : institutional change and local agency in
    Japanese agriculture / Hanno Jentzsch.
Names: Jentzsch, Hanno, 1983–, author.
Series: Japan and global society.
Description: Series statement: Japan and global society | Includes bibliographical
    references and index.
Identifiers: Canadiana (print) 20200411039 | Canadiana (ebook) 20200411063 |
    ISBN 9781487508548 (cloth) | ISBN 9781487538477 (EPUB) |
    ISBN 9781487525927 (PDF)
Subjects: LCSH: Agriculture and state – Japan. | LCSH: Local government –
    Japan. | LCSH: Farms – Japan. | LCSH: Agriculture, Cooperative – Japan.
Classification: LCC HD2093 .J46 2021 | DDC 338.1/852 – dc23

University of Toronto Press acknowledges the financial assistance to its
publishing program of the Canada Council for the Arts and the Ontario Arts
Council, an agency of the Government of Ontario.

Canada Council   Conseil des Arts
for the Arts   du Canada

Funded by the   Financé par le
Government   gouvernement
of Canada   du Canada

Contents

Figures

Abbreviations

ABL	Agricultural Basic Law
AC	Agricultural Committee
ALL	Agricultural Land Law
ar	are, measure of area, 100 square meters, or 1/100 hectare
DPJ	Democratic Party of Japan
GATT	General Agreement on Tariffs and Trade
gentan	*gentan seisaku*, Rice Acreage Reduction Policy
ha	hectare, measure of area, 10,000 square meters, or 100 ares
JA	Japan Agriculture, Organization of Agricultural Cooperatives in Japan, abbreviation referring either to the Organization of Agricultural Cooperatives as a whole or to local cooperative branches
JA Zenchū	*Zenkoku Nōgyō Kyōdō Kumiai Chūōkai*, Central Union of Agricultural Cooperatives in Japan
JA Zennō	*Zenkoku Nōgyō Kyōdō Kumiai Rengokai*, National Federation of Agricultural Cooperatives in Japan
LDP	Liberal Democratic Party
MAFF	Ministry for Agriculture, Forestry, and Fisheries
MIC	Ministry of Internal Affairs and Communication
NBL	New (Agricultural) Basic Law, replaced the ABL in 2000
Nōkyō	*Nōgyō Kyōdō Kumiai*, abbreviation referring either to the Organization of Agricultural Cooperatives as a whole or to local cooperative branches; renamed JA in 1992 (see above)
OECD	Organization for Economic Cooperation and Development

PRIMAFF	Policy Research Institute of the Ministry of Agriculture, Forestry, and Fisheries
PSE	Producer support estimate, measure used by the OECD to calculate total support for agricultural producers
SMD(-PR)	single-member districts (and proportional representation), mode for lower house elections in Japan, first used in the general election in 1996
SNTV(-MMD)	single non-transferable vote (in multi-member districts), mode for lower house elections in postwar Japan, 1947–93
TPP	Trans-Pacific Partnership
URAA	Uruguay Round Agreement on Agriculture
VofC	varieties of capitalism
WTO	World Trade Organization

Foreword

University of Toronto Press, in cooperation with the University of Missouri–St. Louis and the Shibusawa Eiichi Memorial Foundation of Tokyo, has launched an ambitious new series, "Japan and Global Society." The volumes in the series explore how Japan has defined its identities and objectives in the larger region of Asia and the Pacific and, at the same time, how the global community has been shaped by Japan and its interactions with other countries.

The dual focus on Japan and on global society reflects the series editors' and publishers' commitment to globalizing national studies. Scholars and readers have become increasingly aware that it makes little sense to treat a country in isolation. All countries are interdependent and shaped by cross-national forces so that mono-national studies – those that examine a country's past and present in isolation – are never satisfactory. Such awareness has grown during the past few decades when global, transnational phenomena and forces have gained prominence. In the age of globalization, no country retains complete autonomy or freedom of action. Yet nations continue to act in pursuit of their respective national interests, which frequently results in international tensions. Financial, social, and educational policies continue to be defined domestically, with national communities as units. But transnational economic, environmental, and cultural forces always infringe upon national entities, transforming them in subtle and sometimes even violent ways. Global society, consisting of billions of individuals and their organizations, evolves and shapes national communities, even as the latter contribute to defining the overall human community.

Japan provides a particularly pertinent instance of such interaction, but this series is not limited to studies of that country alone. Indeed, the books published in the series will show that there is little unique about Japan, whose history has been shaped by interactions with China,

Korea, the United States, and many other countries. For this reason, forthcoming volumes will deal with countries in the Asia-Pacific region and compare their respective developments and shared destinies. At the same time, some studies in the series will transcend national frameworks and discuss more transnational themes, such as humanitarianism, migration, and diseases, documenting how these phenomena affect Japan and other countries and how, at the same time, they contribute to the making of a more interdependent global society.

Lastly, we hope these studies will help to promote an understanding of non-national entities, such as regions, religions, and civilizations. Modern history continues to be examined in terms of nations as the key units of analysis, and yet these other entities have their own vibrant histories, which do not necessarily coincide with nation-centered narratives. To look at Japan, or for that matter any other country, and to examine its past and present in these alternative frameworks will enrich our understanding of modern world history and of the contemporary global civilization.

Akira Iriye

Acknowledgments

This book concludes almost ten years of research on agriculture in Japan. It began entirely unintentionally when I first came to Japan with the organization Willing Workers on Organic Farms in February 2010. Six months of work and travel took me to rural and semi-urban areas throughout Japan, from the vineyards in the Kōfu Basin in Yamanashi Prefecture to the sugarcane fields on the tiny island of Tokunōshima to the rice and black bean fields in Hyōgō Prefecture and back. I met many different people along the way, very few of them full-time farmers (let alone organic). As a student of East Asian politics, I was intrigued by the significance of agriculture for everyday life on the one hand, and the small-scale, fragmented, and often nonprofessional agricultural production structure on the other hand. Wherever I went, I noticed the presence of an organization called JA (Japan Agriculture), the powerful, but not necessarily popular organization of agricultural cooperatives. Ever since this journey, people, products, practices, peculiarities, and politics of Japanese agriculture have never ceased to fascinate me.

This project would not have been possible without the support of a long list of institutions and individuals. I want to thank the DFG Research Training Group "Risk in East Asia" and the Institute for East Asian Studies at the University of Duisburg-Essen for sponsoring me as a PhD candidate. The Institute of Social Science at Tokyo University and the German Institute for Japanese Studies in Tokyo (DIJ) kindly hosted me during two phases of field research in 2013. Between 2016 and 2020, the DIJ and its director Franz Waldenberger provided me with the perfect work environment to continue my project as a post-doctoral researcher. Over the years, I have published on aspects of institutional change in the Japanese agricultural sector, including farmland reforms, the local origins of national farmland consolidation policies, and hamlet-based collective farming. I am grateful to Taylor and

Francis (Jentzsch 2017a), Oxford University Press (Jentzsch 2017c), and Pacific Affairs (Jentzsch 2020a) for permission to reuse parts of this material in this book.

During and after my research project, Karen Shire provided me with concise and constructive criticism, challenged me to sharpen my arguments, and offered plenty of academic, personal, and practical advice, all of which I am deeply grateful for. I am equally indebted to Robert Pekkanen, who shared insightful advice and supported my career in many ways. I also want to extend my gratitude to the two anonymous reviewers, whose comments and critique have helped me immensely to improve the manuscript; to David Welch, the editor of the Japan and Global Society series at University of Toronto Press; and to Daniel Quinlan, who helped me to navigate the peer review process. I am grateful to Ian MacKenzie for shepherding the manuscript through copyediting, and to Janice Evans for managing the production process. Isaac Gagné, Steffen Heinrich, Barbara Holthus, Nicole Freiner, Daniel Kremers, Aaron Kingsbury, and Pauline Debanes commented on parts of the manuscript and helped me to improve my arguments and my writing. I also received invaluable practical and emotional support from other friends, colleagues, and lunch partners, who always had an open ear and words of encouragement when I needed it: Sonja Ganseforth, Torsten Weber, Ronald Saladin, Nora Kottmann, Till Knaudt, Alison Lamont, Connor Malloy, Itō Kaori, and Tomonori Akashi. I owe special thanks to Kostiantyn Ovsiannikov, who put together the figures in chapter 6, and to Professor Gōdo Yoshihisa for sharing his expertise and his views on the secrets of the Japanese agricultural sector. And I am deeply grateful to my many respondents in the field, who were willing to go out of their way to share their knowledge, their views, their work life, and in some cases even their homes with me.

Finally, this book would not have been possible without the support of my family. My partner Olga endured the countless small and larger crises surrounding this project, and patiently reminded me of what was most important. Our first son Wanja – born in 2012 – grew up with me working on this book. Whenever he noticed the logo of JA during our drives through the Japanese countryside, he would tell me to "go in and tell them you are writing a book about them." This book is for Wanja.

HARVESTING STATE SUPPORT

PART ONE

Introduction: Institutional Change in Japan's Agricultural Sector

One morning in late October 2013, I assisted a group of farm workers harvesting a small plot of adlay[1] in Hikawa Town, Shimane Prefecture, in western Japan. For the most part, this meant standing by and handing tools every other minute, as the harvester continued to break down. "No wonder it gets stuck," one of the men commented. "This field is more weeds than adlay." The men worked for a local agricultural company called "Green Support." They harvested the plot as a service for a small hamlet-based collective farm. I asked if the collective farm itself could expect any gains from the harvest, given that they also had to pay for Green Support's service. "Not in terms of selling the product," the man replied casually. But to receive a certain subsidy, the collective farm had to ship at least some adlay, he explained. "It does not matter how much and which quality." I had just witnessed an element of Hikawa's elaborate local subsidy machine in action. Since 1970 an ever-evolving rice production control scheme has required Japanese rice farmers to idle a certain share of their paddy fields each year or divert the land to other crops to stabilize the rice price. Paddy field diversion is incentivized by subsidies. Yet many small, aging farm households in Japan are either unwilling or unable to grow anything but rice, and thus cannot utilize their land in the most (subsidy-)productive way. In Hikawa, the local administration and the local agricultural cooperative created a comprehensive system to organize land use and rice production control. Small farms outsource some or all tasks associated to paddy field diversion to large, professional cultivators, including Green Support. The incoming subsidies are then distributed between landowners and cultivators. In a sense, the workers on the small plot were harvesting state support rather than adlay.

The episode reveals one detail of a comprehensive institution-building process through which local actors in Hikawa – the agricultural cooperative, the local agricultural administration, and farmers them-selves – have (re-)interpreted Japan's changing regulatory framework of agricultural support and protection. As I kept digging deeper into the social and normative foundations of this local process, and the con-siderable differences from other localities, I became intrigued by the question of how local agency and the local institutional landscape affect the outcomes of national agricultural reform. This book argues that gradual institutional change in the Japanese agricultural support and protection regime is best understood through the local lens.

Chapter One

Japan's Agricultural Support and Protection Regime

Only days after the difficult adlay harvest, the television in Green Supports' meeting room aired the decision of the Japanese government to fade out the longstanding rice production control scheme in 2018. The decision represented another step in agricultural reform, in the course of which state control over the rice price eroded, and harvesting state support has become more difficult for small rice-farming households, which have been the main beneficiaries of agricultural support and protection throughout the postwar era.

At the tail end of a prolonged decline, the agricultural sector made for little more than 1 per cent of the Japanese GDP in 2016 (Trading Economics 2020). Yet its economic significance has long been outweighed by its political importance. A multifaceted and notoriously generous agricultural support and protection regime has been a central building block of the country's postwar political economy (George Mulgan 2000). For much of the postwar era, a combination of rice price support, import restrictions, and exclusion of corporations from buying and using farmland prevented the emergence of large-scale industrial farming, and instead created and sustained an agricultural production structure dominated by small-scale household farms, the majority of which engaged in part-time rice farming. As the agricultural support and protection regime grew into an instrument to redistribute the benefits of economic growth to the structurally weak rural and semi-urban peripheries, it also came to constitute a crucial institutional element of Japan's fragmented postwar welfare state (Estevez-Abe 2008), and thus of Japan's "nationally embedded, non-liberal capitalist economy" (Streeck and Yamamura 2003, 2) as a whole. The emergence of the agricultural support and protection regime is closely linked to the longstanding dominance of the Liberal Democratic Party (LDP), which was based in no small part on catering to the electorally overrepresented rural voters. The mutual dependence between (part-time) rice farmers and the LDP was sustained and exploited by Nōkyō (*Nōgyō Kyōdō Kumiai*, since 1992 called JA, or Japan Agriculture), Japan's powerful umbrella organization of agricultural cooperatives. With a membership that included virtually all farm households, Nōkyō became a powerful interest group, a crucial partner for the LDP in elections, an influential actor in agricultural policy-making, the main executive agent of the state for carrying out agricultural policies, and a potent economic player – in short, a political and economic giant unknown in other capitalist democracies (Bullock 1997). With regard to the economic salience of the farm sector, however, the agricultural production structure that Nōkyō had helped to build and maintain became increasingly critical as a result of the inefficient and highly subsidized overproduction of rice by small, aging part-time farm households (George Mulgan 2000; Sheingate 2001).

Gradual Change and an Ongoing Crisis

Japan's economic structure has come under strong pressure to liberalize since the early 1990s, which triggered a remodeling of the postwar political economy as a whole (Vogel 2003; Kushida, Shimizu, and Oi 2013; Lechevalier 2014). Amidst this process, the agricultural support and protection regime became one of Japan's toughest political battlegrounds. Following incremental steps toward liberalization of agricultural trade throughout the 1980s, Japan's accession to the WTO in 1994 signaled the end of the isolation of the sector from the world market. Electoral reform in the same year and administrative reforms challenged the established alliance between the Ministry of Agriculture, Forestry, and Fisheries (MAFF), Nōkyō, and incumbent LDP "farm politicians" – creating opportunities for agricultural reform.

More than two decades on, the results have left advocates of market liberalization and defendants of the postwar regime equally disappointed. Although agricultural support in Japan has been declining, it remains high in international comparison, at about three times the OECD average (OECD 2017). Meanwhile, the notorious structural problems of the sector – farmland fragmentation, low productivity, and an aging workforce – have prevailed, especially for rice farming. Rice remains the most politicized crop in Japan and the dominant form of agricultural production, despite its economic inefficiency (Yamashita 2015a). In general, farms in Japan are still remarkably small, about 1.6 hectares on average (2.2 hectares including Hokkaido), compared to

16 hectares in the EU, and almost 180 hectares in the United States.[1] The share of the primary sector in the national GDP has halved from 2.4 per cent in 1990 to 1.2 per cent in 2014 (Statistics Bureau of Japan 2016). Net output of the sector has decreased by more than 30 per cent between 1990 and 2011 (Tashiro 2014b, 15). Apart from rice, where production remains curtailed by the state, many other agricultural products are far from meeting domestic demand. Japan has the lowest food self-sufficiency ratio of all industrialized nations (Statistics Bureau of Japan 2016). Despite this critical situation, the share of abandoned farmland has been increasing to more than 10 per cent of arable land by 2014 (MAFF 2016a), and the farmland utilization rate decreased to 91.8 per cent (down from 138 per cent in 1956; see Hisano, Akitsu, and McGreevy 2018, 291). As of 2016, around 65 per cent of those engaged in agriculture were older than sixty-five, and the large majority of them was older than seventy (MAFF 2016a); many of their small, scattered plots will become available soon.

Change or Stability in the Agricultural Sector?

Although the agricultural support and protection regime has not broken down, it has not been static. Institutional pillars of the postwar era have been removed or replaced, resulting in a less comprehensive and more ambiguous regime. Gradual liberalization in the domestic rice market since the mid-1990s ended direct state control over the rice price. Instead of universal price support, the government introduced targeted support for a designated group of more business-oriented "bearer farms" (referred to as *ninaite* in Japanese) to consolidate the production structure. Structural reforms have also fostered incorporation of household farms and deregulation of farmland access for general corporations. The share of land in the hands of designated "bearer farms" has grown quickly since the mid-2000s, reaching 52 per cent in 2014, indicating the onset of structural change in the farm sector, driven not least by a small but growing number of large-scale, diversified corporate agri-businesses (MAFF 2016a).

On the other side of the spectrum, small-scale, part-time rice farmers face more complicated access to state support. Many aging farmers are neither willing nor able to adapt to the policy incentives for business-oriented agriculture, and rather drop out of commercial farming altogether. Moreover, the once seemingly unattainable organization of agricultural cooperatives has come under increasing pressure during the reform. At the same time, this process has shifted risks and responsibilities on continued access to state support and consolidating the production structure from the central state to local cooperatives, administrations, and ultimately farmers themselves.[2] Thus, despite the striking persistence of a "peasant-like" agriculture (Hisano, Akitsu, McGreevy 2018), Japan now also displays clear signs for the onset of market-oriented entrepreneurship, diversification, and scale-enlargement – that is, the developments that have marked the neoliberalization of agriculture around the globe (Hisano, Akitsu, and McGreevy 2018; Tashiro 2014b; Sekine and Bonanno 2016).

Other analysts have highlighted the persistence of the agricultural support and protection regime. In George Mulgan's metaphorical words, the "overwhelming impression" of the policy process until the mid-2000s "is of a pack of cards being reshuffled to produce a different 'hand,' but the 'game' itself remains very much in progress" (2006b, 180). A decade later, analyzing the run-up to the 2016 JA reform, George Mulgan argued that the "tripartite" agricultural policy-making of LDP farm politicians, the MAFF, and the cooperative organization showed signs of erosion, but also resilience (George Mulgan 2016). Despite the Abe administration's proactive push for structural reform in the agricultural sector since 2014, Honma and George Mulgan (2018) still find that overly strict farmland regulations and intervention in the rice market continue to hold the sector back. Failure to fully break resistance of the postwar agricultural establishment (most importantly the cooperative organization JA) against more radical reforms in a market-oriented agricultural sector has often been raised as the reason for the structural crisis of the sector (George Mulgan 2003; Honma 2015; Yamashita 2015a, 2015b, 2009; Harada 2012; Freiner 2018). Real change, so the narrative of the proponents of liberalization goes, is still to come.

The Agricultural Support and Protection Regime as a Case to Understand Gradual Institutional Change

In general, the verdict on whether change or stability best describes the trajectory of the support and protection regime seems to depend on the respective viewpoint. On the one hand, the Japanese farm sector is far from being "liberalized." On the other hand, however, holding the trajectory of the support and protection regime against an ideal of "real" market liberalization risks overstating its resilience and conceals the impact of more than two decades of agricultural reform – and indeed liberalization – that was outlined above. This points to an intriguing conceptual problem: the literature on Japan's agricultural support and protection regime lacks a theoretical concept that can capture institutional change beyond the simplistic image of path dependency versus institutional breakdown. Herein lies the link to a crucial theoretical challenge in institutional change in advanced political economies: the need to develop a dynamic and variable conception of institutional change without disruption. Against this background, this book does not treat Japan's agricultural support and protection regime as an example of institutional stability. Rather, it finds in it an ideal case to advance the theoretical toolset for a more fine-grained analysis of gradual institutional change.

The Argument in Brief

To move beyond the dual picture of change and stability, this book takes a *local* perspective on the trajectory of Japan's agricultural support and protection regime. It treats it as a "macro-institution," "composed of many component rules and practices that are themselves institutions," which are not necessarily formal (Hall and Thelen 2009, 9). Beyond the realm of macro-level policy-making, institutional change in the agricultural support and protection regime is also shaped at the interface between formal rules and local social network ties, (farmland) norms and practices. At this interface, local actors – including farm households, local cooperatives, local administrations, or emerging agri-businesses – translate the increasingly ambiguous agricultural regulatory framework into distinct local interpretations. Building on in-depth field research, the book shows how local actors resort to hamlet-level norms and practices (e.g., regarding the exchange of land use rights or collective cultivation) and community ties to construct distinct local interpretations of the national reform process. Analyzing and comparing these local interpretations also reveals factors that affect (and potentially limit) how such local institutional agency plays out. In some localities, incumbent actors such as the local cooperative branch have managed to create and enforce local interpretations of the national reform process that reflect their own, defensive interests. Yet, the potential for comprehensive defensive local agency is increasingly curtailed, e.g., through boundary changes that reduce the local social embedding and thus the influence of local co-ops. Where incumbent local actors such as local JA lack the abilities to enforce their interpretations of national policies, the "neoliberal" aspects of the national reform process are amplified.

Beyond the case, the analysis also moves forward the ongoing theoretical debate on the pace and the character of institutional change in (formerly) "non-liberal" capitalist economies such as Japan. This debate has already contributed to a more dynamic understanding of gradual, non-disruptive processes of institutional change. Yet, the ways in which local actors respond and adjust to policy changes, and the role of traditional norms, practices, and social ties for these local acts of institutional renegotiation have so far been underplayed in the literature. The local perspective reveals the dynamic ways in which informal institutions shape broader processes of institutional change. Further, it draws the attention to the specific conditions under which local acts of institutional renegotiation unfold.

Chapter Two

Toward a Local Perspective on Gradual Institutional Change

Theorizing on how, when, and why institutions change has been a weak spot of neo-institutionalist theory. Across their different onto-logical and epistemological foundations, rational-choice, sociological, and historical approaches alike have mostly been pinned to the no-tion that institutions are principally stable, self-reproducing, or even self-reinforcing social phenomena, and will thus change only through exogenous shocks. This has supported a dichotomous understanding of institutional change, marked by a sharp distinction between long phases of path-dependent institutional stability and brief periods of radical shifts, or even breakdown.

The neo-institutionalist stability bias has come under attack from many directions, including the field of comparative political economy.[1] Analyzing the variegated and contested trajectories of the institutional arrangements shaping the "varieties of capitalism," a number of authors have argued that the long-held analytical focus on institutional stabil-ity and exogenous shocks has obscured explanations for – and even the recognition of – more gradual agency-driven institutional "change without disruption" (Streeck and Thelen 2005b, 4).[2] In contrast, the lit-erature on endogenous institutional change conceptualizes institutions as inherently ambiguous and subject to constant contestation. As such, they neither provide unchallenged guidelines for behavior nor always create an equilibrium in which compliance is the best (i.e., "rational") choice for all actors involved (Mahoney and Thelen 2010b, 10).[3] Since "social rules are never perfect," actors find leeway to strive for change "in the gaps or soft spots between the rule and its interpretation and the rule and its enforcement" (13). From this perspective, "there is nothing automatic, self-perpetuating, or self-reinforcing about institutional ar-rangements" (8) – rather, both stability and change are closely related results of constant institutional agency. Consequently, institutional arrangements can change from within, and without wholesale break-down, such as the accumulated result of micro-level agency, or driven by actors' ability to build and maintain (social or political) coalitions in order to alter or at least subvert certain rules.[4] This approach has profoundly contributed to the understanding of gradual deregulation and liberalization in advanced political economies, including Japan (Streeck and Thelen 2005b; Hall and Thelen 2009; Vogel 2005; K. Tsai 2006), and incremental institutional change in general (Mahoney and Thelen 2010a).

Shifting the Analytical Focus to the Local

While proponents of endogenous institutional change have convinc-ingly argued that the "normal, everyday implementation and enactment of an institution" leaves space to strive for its gradual change (Streeck and Thelen 2005b, 11), the practical details of *how* actors interpret and eventually alter institutions have remained mostly unexplored.[5] This gap is not least a matter of perspective: most of the literature on grad-ual (endogenous) institutional change takes the form of broad historical narratives, with the nation state as the main unit of analysis. In contrast, this book shifts the focus to the concrete processes through which local actors make sense of changing formal rules, how they interpret these rules, and eventually translate them into local practices, thereby ech-oing recent calls from several fields to recognize seemingly mundane, everyday processes and actions to understand institutional stability and change.[6]

I argue that this shift to the local is especially fruitful because institu-tional change in advanced political economies typically takes the form of highly contested, multifaceted, and often inconsistent processes that tend to increase institutional ambiguity instead of steering toward clear-cut liberalization. Japan provides a case in point in this respect. Over the past decades, the trajectory of the political economy has been marked by the interaction of "old" and "new" institutions (both formal and informal), and significant discrepancies in the pace and the inten-sity of liberalization across policy fields (Vogel 2005; Kushida, Shimizu, and Oi 2013; Lechevalier 2014). Beyond Japan, variegated and multifac-eted institutional change in advanced political economies has spurred a vivid theoretical debate on how to make sense of the "internal cap-italist variety" in what once appeared to be coherent national "varie-ties of capitalism" (Thelen 2012, 2014; Röper 2017; Jackson and Sorge 2012; Hall and Thelen 2009). Moreover, incremental deregulation, lib-eralization, and privatization often go hand-in-hand with shifting risks and responsibilities from the central state to local actors, both private and public.[7] The local perspective allows for a better understanding of how, by whom, and in which social and normative contexts changing macro-rules are (re)interpreted – that is, how actors construct defense mechanisms against new competition or expand their freedom beyond formal restrictions – and how these local processes shape the pace and the direction of institutional change as a whole.

The Local as a Level of Analysis

The analytical key to capture local institutional agency is to avoid indistinct concepts of the "micro-level" and the respective actors. Accordingly, this book addresses the "local" not as a homogenous (and thus vague) level of analysis, but as a juxtaposition of distinct institutional arenas – local agricultural regimes – within the same macro-level regime. (Historical) institutionalist analysis in general and in comparative political economy in particular has typically analyzed macro-level institutions as a homogenous "single-action space," most likely within the confines of a nation state. Arguably, this notion has supported the deterministic character of neo-institutionalist thought (Crouch and Voelzkow 2009b, 1). In contrast, recognizing and analyzing sub-national "institutional heterogeneity" has been identified as a way to uncover the underlying conflicts and frictions, and thus endogenous sources for institutional change or resilience.[8] Sub-national institutional arenas (such as local economies, administrative divisions, or regions) offer the analytical space to uncover variations within the same macro-institutional context, the potential breeding ground for institutional innovation from within (Crouch and Voelzkow 2004a, 2009a). Working in the opposite direction, the outcomes of national institutional change have been shaped by sub-national counter-movements. For example, when the Mexican coffee market was hit by a "neoliberal shock" in the early 1990s, national reforms provided political incumbents on the sub-national level with opportunities for "reregulation." National liberalization was thus followed by new, diverse local forms of market governance (Snyder 1999).

Local Institutional Arenas

There are many ways to delineate the boundaries of such sub-national institutional arenas, ranging from administrative units (e.g., prefectures, municipalities) over geographical formations (e.g., regions, valleys, basins), socioeconomic formations (e.g., local economies), to informally bounded socio-spatial formations (e.g., neighborhoods, communities, natural villages). This book focuses on local agricultural regimes, the boundaries of which roughly correspond to municipalities and/or agricultural cooperative districts.[9] Regardless of the actual local arenas in question, a key advantage of focusing on such relatively narrow socio-spatial contexts is that informal institutions – social ties, norms, and practices – appear in the spotlight.

Researchers have often associated neighborhoods, villages, or similarly narrow socio-spatial formations with distinct sets of social network ties and, closely related, certain norms, values, and practices.[10] Social networks in particular have been found to be "spatially structured, as both cause and effect" (Johnston and Pattie 2011). In order to understand social networks as informal institutions, they need to "represent a stable and recurrent pattern of behavioral interaction or exchange between individuals or organizations" (Ansell 2006, 75). For this precondition, narrow spatial contexts provide particularly fertile ground. Local social networks affect the distribution of power and resources in and across such narrow contexts in many ways.[11] Social networks and norms interdependently affect each other within the spatial context they operate in: norms, practices, and identities are disseminated via local social networks, but also reinforce the social ties in the respective localities (Clemens and Cook 1999, 451; North 1990). For example, frequent social interactions within a narrow local context (typically reinforced by multiple levels of connections made in schools, clubs, or the church) shape spatially concentrated patterns of partisan alignment in the United States (Gimpel and Lay 2005).

The distinct social and normative underpinning of a certain local institutional arena also contributes to differences in how macro-level processes manifest locally. For example, Glassmann (2004) analyzed how a particular "local industrial regime" in Germany has reacted to the pressures of globalization by intensified cooperation within a locally confined inter-firm network, including large, small, and medium-sized enterprises. In India, distinct local informal institutional settings across villages have shaped local variants of agrarian change (Harris-White, Mishra, and Upadhyay 2009). In China, Tsai (2007) has shown that the embedding of local officials in "solidary groups" within the village's boundaries can create local informal "institutions of accountability" for said officials to allocate public resources according to the interests of the village community as a whole. These institutions emerge in particular where the political-administrative and the social-normative boundaries in a given village overlap tightly. Because the quality of these informal institutions of accountability varies across villages, so does the performance of local officials in providing their jurisdictions with public goods – affecting not least how the broader process of decentralization has played out in China.

Analyzing the specific character of, and the differences between local institutional arenas thus provides the opportunity for a more nuanced view of how informal phenomena such as local social ties, norms, and practices affect the trajectory of broader processes of institutional change. From this perspective, informal institutions emerge as variables that underlie distinct, spatially bounded (i.e., local) *variants* of a (changing) macro-institutional configuration – such as through supporting or inhibiting certain actors (and groups of actors) to construct and enforce their interpretation of changing formal rules. Importantly, for the purpose of this book, such local institutional arenas are of analytical interest only in relation to other, similar local arenas – or in other words: as local variants of a pattern that differs in quality, but not in principle. Focusing on these local variants and their underlying social and normative foundations opens up the analytical space for a more dynamic conceptualization of informal institutions and their role in institutional change.

Toward a Dynamic Concept of Informal Institutions and Institutional Change

It is widely acknowledged that informal institutions shape institutional change.[12] Prominent calls to enhance our understanding of the role of informal institutions in explaining the outcomes of political reform (Helmke and Levitsky 2004, 2006) have spurred a growing body of literature. Many of such studies focus on regime change in post-socialist and developing countries, which provide insightful test cases for what happens if new – and often weak – political and economic institutions meet the informal remains of former (non-democratic) regimes.[13]

In advanced market economies, however, informal institutions have remained "consigned to the analytic margins" (Azari and Smith 2012, 37).[14] In the literature on gradual institutional change in advanced political economies, informal rules and norms tend to be subsumed as elements of multifaceted institutional arrangements (e.g., Hall and Thelen 2009), or as the social and normative embedding of "regimes" (Streeck and Thelen 2005b). While this embedding is assumed to be reflected in the trajectories of broader institutional arrangements, it has rarely been the focus of the analysis.[15] Streeck and Thelen (2005b, 10–11) have explicitly limited their research agenda on those norms and sanctions that are formalized, thus also excluding "informal norms sanctioned by community disapproval."[16] This is not least because such informal rules are typically seen as more or less immune to agency. For Streeck and Thelen (2005b, 10), only formal rules can "change by decision," while informal institutions change "by cultural evolution" or erosion – a view they share with sociological neo-institutionalism, which highlights the impact of norms on behavior "beyond conscious scrutiny," and thus beyond the reach of human agency (Zucker 1991). Accordingly, informal institutions are typically pictured as reactive and "slow-moving" (Roland 2004, 116–17) – for example, in generational pace – and thus "lagging behind" formal change (Estrin and Mickiewitz 2010).

The inertness associated with informal institutions has strongly influenced how they have been analyzed in institutional change: they are typically ascribed a passive role, obstructing, constraining, or even compromising the outcomes of formal institutional change. Yet, as Tsai (2006) has argued concisely, this notion has limited our understanding of the informal dimension of institutional change. In contrast, a more dynamic perspective on informal institutions can prove analytically fruitful for analyzing endogenous institutional change. For example, the trajectory of market reforms in China has arguably been shaped through "adaptive informal institutions." Confronted with a "myriad of [formal institutional] constraints and opportunities," micro-level actors forge "an institutional reality of their own" by devising "informal coping strategies" (K. Tsai 2006, 118) – the creation and eventual political adoption of which has been shaping reform in China from within and below.

Informal Institutions as Dynamic Resources in Local Institutional Arenas

The local perspective offers an opportunity to refine this notion. In narrow socio-spatial contexts, even seemingly obsolete traditional social norms and rules appear far less static, but rather ambiguous and contested, and thus "targets for renegotiation," as Knight and Ensminger put it (1997). How such renegotiations turn out is a matter of which actors hold "superior bargaining power" vis-à-vis other actors regarding the "proper" enactment of a certain social norm in a given context (Knight and Ensminger 1997, 1998). As will be shown in more detail over the course of this book, such local acts of (re)interpreting, reviving, or adapting social norms and practices can also hold concrete political relevance. Under certain circumstances, seemingly traditional social norms can provide the foundation to construct local regimes that help local actors to defend themselves against macro-level policy changes. Yet in other local contexts, such acts of institution-building do not (or only partially) occur, opening up maneuvering space for local challengers to take advantage of the changing regulatory framework. The local perspective thus allows us to analyze social norms and practices as they emerge as flexible resources for actors to construct distinct local interpretations of a (changing) regulatory framework, and thus shape broader processes of institutional change. It adds empirical substance to the notion that actors constantly and creatively recombine institutional elements to produce change in "unusual" (Crouch 2005, 3) or "syncretic" ways (Berk and Galvan 2009). Moreover, the local perspective highlights factors that support or inhibit such local institutional agency, including the disruption of local socio-spatial boundaries.

Institutional Change in Japanese Agricultural Support and Protection through the Local Lens

On the basis of the discussion above, this book seeks to understand institutional change in Japan's agricultural support and protection regime by examining how the changing regulatory framework is translated into local practice. The following chapter lays out the basic findings and arguments presented throughout the book.

At the center of the empirical analysis is the consolidation of farmland in the hands of the designated "bearer farms" – the core objective of national agricultural policies since the 1990s, and an important element of structural change in the agricultural sector. Importantly, while the share of land held by "bearer farms" has roughly doubled over the 2000s, the definition of what a "bearer farm" is – and thus the criteria for preferential access to state support – has remained strikingly vague. It includes a broad range of different forms of agricultural production, from hamlet-based collective farms over expanding business-oriented household farms to the small but growing cohort of large-scale, diversified corporate agri-businesses (see chapter 5 for details). The local perspective reveals not only the factors that inhibit or support consolidation of the production structure, but also illuminates which types of "bearer farms" emerge in a given locality, and how these farms relate to the local branches of the cooperative organization JA – typically considered the main defendant of the postwar regime – and the respective local administration. It thus allows for detailed analysis of the consolidation of the production structure as a matter of renegotiating the agricultural support and protection regime. To capture these local acts of renegotiation analytically, this book conceptualizes the "local" in the agricultural support and protection regime as a juxtaposition of distinct institutional arenas, or *local agricultural regimes*, which produce different local manifestations of the changing support and protection regime.

The argument is developed through in-depth analysis of a core case – the local agricultural regime in Hikawa Town – in comparison with evidence from several other localities. Data were sourced in two main phases of field research in Hikawa Town / Izumo City (Shimane Prefecture, March, September–December 2013) and in the Kōfu Basin (Yamanashi Prefecture, March–June 2013) through participatory observation, semi-structured interviews with farmers, cooperative officials, and members of local administrations, countless informal conversations, and analysis of documents such as administrative presentations, statistics, reports, maps, etc. Additional data were gathered through document collection and interviews with local officials, representatives of local cooperatives, and farmers on several field trips in 2013, on a follow-up visit to Hikawa in July 2017, through regular follow-up visits to the Kōfu Basin, and several field trips to other localities throughout 2017–19.[1] The local analysis is nested in a detailed review of the postwar trajectory of the agricultural support and protection regime until the second Abe administration (2012–20), and an analysis of the effects of cooperative mergers since the 1990s and municipal mergers in the mid-2000s.

Farmland Consolidation in Hikawa Town

In many ways, Hikawa – a town in the northern part of Shimane Prefecture in western Japan – reflects the overall development of agriculture in postwar Japan. Within the overlapping boundaries of the town and the local agricultural cooperative JA Hikawa, the local agricultural sector became dominated by small-scale, part-time paddy field farming in the decades following postwar land reform. Consequently, Hikawa was also not spared from the demographic pressure of a rapidly aging farming population, and the political pressure to consolidate the agricultural production structure since the mid-1990s. Yet, when I first came to the town on a three-day research trip in March 2013, I was presented with what appeared to be a strikingly successful local implementation of the national agricultural reform. Over the 2000s, Hikawa's agricultural sector saw a remarkable consolidation of the production structure in line with the major national policy objectives. The share of farmland under the management of "bearer farms" was far above the national average in 2013, and further increased to 79.2 per cent in 2017 (Hikawa Town Agriculture and Forestry Office 2017), which put Hikawa's farmland consolidation rate in the top 10 per cent of Japanese municipalities.[2] Farmland was also utilized more efficiently than in national and prefectural comparison (Izumo City 2013). Meanwhile, virtually no land had fallen idle in Hikawa. These results set Hikawa apart from the national development, and even from neighboring localities – including Izumo City, the municipality Hikawa has belonged to since a merger in 2011. Consolidation of the agricultural production structure in Hikawa thus provides a particularly productive case to investigate the deeper causes behind different local manifestations of national reform, in that it reveals more information on the underlying processes and actors' roles than a typical case.[3] In September 2013, I returned to Hikawa and Izumo for three months of intensive field research.

Harvesting State Support in Hikawa

Upon closer look, farmland consolidation in Hikawa was far more than a case of successful policy implementation. It also reflects a distinct local *interpretation* of the national reform process. The main driver behind farmland consolidation in Hikawa is a public corporation called the Hikawa-chō Nōgyō Kōsha (or Kōsha, for short),[4] which was jointly founded by the town government and the local JA Hikawa in 1994. Since the early 2000s, the Kōsha has been acquiring land use rights from retiring farmers and allocating them to designated "bearer farms." As a result, large-scale (corporate) farms in Hikawa enjoy good access to relatively well-connected plots of land and the full array of national support policies, but are also constrained in their economic freedom by strong public control over the farmland market and their integration into a local scheme to organize rice production control – that is, they are less independent entrepreneurs than extended arms of the local agricultural administration. Meanwhile, the Kōsha system has allowed for quick and comprehensive responses to national reforms. For example, an important feature of farmland consolidation in Hikawa is the strong promotion of hamlet-based collective farms, which occupy about 40 per cent of the land used by "bearer farms" (Hikawa Town Agriculture and Forestry Office 2017). This kept a relatively large number of small, aging farm households under the umbrella of state support when subsidization became more exclusive in the mid-2000s. In this sense, beyond raising efficiency, the Kōsha system has also been *harvesting state support*. More generally, the local agricultural regime in Hikawa has produced a highly selective interpretation of the national reform process: it has emphasized land use efficiency through a successful redistribution of farmland toward "bearer farms," while at the same time muting the more market-liberal aspects of the same reform process. As one consequence of this development, JA Hikawa has retained – if not strengthened – its role as the economic and political ordering force of the local agricultural sector.

Noticeably, the Kōsha system has remained strictly locally confined. In neighboring Izumo City, no coherent public instrument to redistribute farmland has emerged. As farmers grew older and the agricultural reform process gained momentum over the 2000s, many farms in Izumo retreated from commercial farming or gave up their land entirely. The surplus land was not absorbed by expanding farms as smoothly as in Hikawa. Consequently, the share of abandoned land increased sharply between 1995 and 2010 (JA Izumo 2010, 16). Designated "bearer farms" in Izumo City (excluding Hikawa) held 42.5 per cent of the active farmland in 2017, which is less than in national average (Izumo City 2017). Compared to Hikawa, professional agri-businesses in Izumo face a more complicated access to farmland, but fewer constraints on their entrepreneurial freedom.

Local Agricultural Regimes in Comparison

Despite its distinct characteristics, the local agricultural regime in Hikawa shares basic features with other local agricultural regimes throughout Japan. Like in Hikawa (an autonomous municipality between 1955 and 2011), the jurisdictions of municipalities and the local branches of the agricultural cooperative organization have typically displayed remarkable territorial overlap and organizational cooperation throughout the postwar era. Together, they have bounded the local arenas within which the emerging agricultural support and protection regime was enacted. Cooperative mergers since the 1990s and municipal mergers in the 2000s have partly disrupted these boundaries in many localities, the consequences of which will be addressed in more detail below. Yet the cornerstones of local agricultural regimes are still more or less constant, defined most importantly by the national laws and regulations on subsidization, farmland use, or production control. The key actors and their formal competencies are similarly constant – apart from farmers and the local agricultural cooperatives, these include most importantly the agricultural offices of local governments, and agricultural committees. The latter are formal bodies that oversee farmland issues on the municipal level, while the former are, inter alia, in charge of devising local programs to identify and support "bearer farms."

Farmland Consolidation as a Contested Political Process

In each local agricultural regime, consolidation of the agricultural production structure is a contested political process in which local actors are entangled in risks, opportunities, and potentially conflicting preferences. For farm households, giving up their land means giving up a potential additional source of (old-age) income, and not least letting go of a lifestyle that has been a part of their family history for generations (Freiner 2018). Many aging landowners do not give up farming voluntarily, and tend to have an interest in transferring the rights to use their land (or parts of it) to relatives or trusted members of the community (K. Yoshida 2015). For expanding agricultural entrepreneurs, on the other hand, accumulating high-quality, well-connected farmland is the foundation of their livelihoods, not least because farmland consolidation and professionalization are opportunities to obtain the full array of state support. Yet access to suitable land is constrained by (non-economic) factors that will be addressed in more detail below. Local governments can be assumed to have an interest in implementing national agricultural reforms, not least because emerging "bearer farms" also secure a continued flow of subsidies and public investment to the jurisdiction. Throughout the postwar period, local governments have relied heavily on the respective local co-ops as the local executive agents of national agricultural policies (George Mulgan 2000), and they typically still do. Local branches of JA thus face a particularly complicated situation. On the one hand, promoting consolidation of the production structure falls within their long-held responsibilities. The cooperative organization is by no means opposed to the redistribution of farmland to "bearer farms" per se, in that preventing further agricultural decline is not least a means to save their raison d'etre (Esham et al. 2012). On the other hand, however, consolidation also constitutes a risk for local JA, and the cooperative organization as a whole. Expanding agricultural entrepreneurs are more likely to develop direct marketing strategies, or engage in professional contract farming with external agri-food corporations, i.e., to operate outside the cooperative framework (Ōizumi 2018). Deregulation of farmland access for non-agricultural corporations in 2009 has created further potential competition for the cooperative organization – including through large corporations investing directly in agricultural production. At times the interests of local co-ops and local governments might overlap – such as in promotion of subsidy-productive hamlet-based collective farming (see chapter 10). Yet local governments have also welcomed external investments in struggling local farm sectors (Sekine and Bonanno 2016). Moreover, they also have an interest in supporting emerging local "bearer farms" who operate independently from (or even opposed to) JA. Against this background, exerting a certain level of control over consolidation of the local agricultural production structure and binding expanding "bearer farms" to the organization are vital goals for local cooperatives and their most important clients: (part-time) household farms with an interest in securing their land and access to state support.

Local Agricultural Regimes between Organization and Disorganization

I argue that far beyond the increasingly ambiguous regulatory framework itself, the risks, constraints, opportunities, and preferences of the respective local actors, and thus the ongoing farmland consolidation itself is shaped by the specific institutional context of the respective local agricultural regime. As the case of Hikawa/Izumo illustrates especially well, this can result in distinct local manifestations of the changing support and protection regime, which differ along a functional dimension (consolidation of the production structure by designated "bearer farms") and a political dimension (the extent to which these farms remain attached to – and under control of – incumbent actors such as the local JA).[5] I argue that these differences can be expressed on a spectrum between "organization" and "disorganization." This categorization borrows from Höpner (2007), who identifies organization as a specific dimension of "non-liberal" forms of capitalism. Organization constrains economic actors in their economic decisions "by institutionally sanctioned collective interests." As such, it goes beyond coordination, which refers to strategic cooperation patterns between economic actors in order to reduce transaction costs. While coordination follows a voluntaristic logic, organized economic action pertains to a "Durkheimian" understanding of institutions as "phenomena sui generis" which "force the individual to act in view of ends that are not strictly his own." Organization is thus marked by strong solidarity and normative goals that go beyond the aim of individual profit maximization (5–10).

When we translate this abstract conceptualization to the level of local agricultural regimes in Japan, organized local agricultural regimes such as Hikawa display relatively high control over farmland consolidation on behalf of the local agricultural administration and/or the local branch of JA. This facilitates more efficient consolidation of land in the hands of the types of farms that national policies define as the future "bearers" of the agricultural sector. At the same time, however, these emerging farms are subject to relatively high public/cooperative control, thus constraining their economic freedom. As a result, they tend to act as "quasi-public infrastructures" (Höpner 2007) rather than independent entrepreneurs. Less organized local agricultural regimes lack public-cooperative control over farmland consolidation, which means that expanding (corporate) farms have less favorable access to connected plots of farmland and state support. This leaves farms with more freedom for independent entrepreneurship but can also entail a high share of aging farm households retreating from commercial farming without a designated successor for their land, and thus an (impeding) increase of abandoned land. The extent to which local agricultural regimes lean toward organization or disorganization thus affects not only farmland consolidation itself, but also if and how the major beneficiaries of the postwar support and protection regime – local JA and small household farms – are able to adapt to an increasingly hostile political and socioeconomic environment.

The Social and Normative Foundations of Local Agricultural Regimes

Importantly, the organized local agricultural regime in Hikawa is not indicative of the overall direction of institutional change in Japan's agricultural support and protection regime. Rather, a mix of agricultural decline, land loss, and eroding control of local co-ops over a limited number of innovative (corporate) entrepreneurial farms such as in neighboring Izumo City seems to be the dominant mode in which this process is taking shape. Yet Hikawa is also not the only local agricultural regime on the organized end of the spectrum. Moreover, there are other local agricultural regimes that display high levels of farmland consolidation but fall short of coherent public/cooperative control over it. Several local manifestations of national reform will be introduced in chapter 6. Beyond the examples discussed in this volume, other studies have analyzed cases of communal cooperation between hamlets, local governments, and agricultural co-ops as local strategies to alleviate pressures of changing agricultural policies in times of an aging workforce and (impeding) farmland loss (Tashiro 2006, 2009; Taniguchi 2009).

An eclectic array of potential (exogenous) factors affect how and to what extent the local agricultural production structure is consolidated, some of which will be briefly discussed in chapter 6. Yet analysis of the trajectory of the local agricultural regime in Hikawa in contrast and comparison with supporting evidence from other localities reveals that the organized consolidation of the local production structure during the 2000s is the result of protracted local institution-building, which rests upon the integration of what I call *village institutions*.

Village Institutions

Village institutions are the social and normative foundation of local agricultural regimes. They include unwritten rules of how and by whom farmland should be used, maintained, and exchanged, and social practices such as cooperation on machinery use, irrigation, or rice production control. They further include local social network ties, which affect, inter alia, the local distribution of resources, information, and power between farmers, local officials, and local JA.[6] Such local social network ties are treated as institutions in that they embody reciprocity as a stable and recurrent concept. For example, fieldwork showed that farmers exchange labor, machinery, information, etc., with the expectation that the favor can be returned at any time, but not necessarily in the same "currency," and potentially by other members of the same local network.[7] Both dimensions of village institutions are interrelated, in that local social network ties also carry norms and practices regarding farmland use.[8]

Historically, village institutions revolve around the farm hamlet, today officially referred to as "agricultural settlements," or *nōgyō shūraku* in Japanese (MAFF 2016a). The hamlet is arguably the most important institution shaping agricultural production and social life in the history of rural Japan. Over the centuries, hamlets have created and enforced rules on land use, irrigation, cooperation, and other domains of social life (Fukutake 1980; Jussaume 1991; Haley 2010). Although the socioeconomic changes over the postwar period have opened up and altered hamlet relations, hamlets have remained viable social units in rural and semi-urban Japan, with functions that far exceed the realm of agriculture.[9] One reason for their continued relevance is the persistence of small-scale household farming over the postwar period (Hisano, Akitsu, and McGreevy 2018). Moreover, hamlets were integrated into postwar local administrative and cooperative structures (Fukutake 1980). The (overlapping) constituencies of local co-ops and postwar municipalities thus have provided arenas in which the institutional legacy of hamlet ties and norms became intertwined with state regulations on farmland use, subsidization, rice marketing and production control, and public investments in the agricultural infrastructure. The same boundaries also offered opportunities for local social ties to emerge beyond and across hamlets, as agriculture declined as the main source of income, and socioeconomic heterogeneity increased within hamlets and local agricultural regimes. Meanwhile, governments, farmers, and national-level policy-makers still resort to traditional patterns of (hamlet-level) cooperation as the natural way to organize irrigation, rice production control, or – in hamlet-based collective farms – even agricultural production itself. Thus hamlets and hamlet-level norms and practices have been submerged into broader sets of village institutions – the ambiguous, contested, and at times contradictive social and normative foundations of local agricultural regimes (see chapter 7 for details).

Village Institutions and Local Institutional Agency in the Changing Agricultural Support and Protection Regime

Chapters 8–10 analyze how village institutions shape institutional change in the agricultural support and protection regime, as state policies increasingly emphasize farmland consolidation and corporatization. Regarding farmland consolidation, unwritten rules on the use and maintenance of farmland affect how farmland use rights are exchanged. Expanding farmers still access land mostly via social ties within and beyond hamlet boundaries, and between farmers and the respective agricultural administration/local co-ops (K. Yoshida 2012, 2015). One consequence of this social mode of farmland transfers is that expanding "bearer farms" typically have highly fragmented holdings. Moreover, this mode is increasingly limited to prevent land loss and abandonment, as the land of absent or deceased owners falls outside local channels for farmland transfers – creating problems that recent state policies to facilitate farmland transfers have been unable to resolve. In Hikawa, in contrast, village institutions were comprehensively integrated into the local agricultural regime, such as via the *shinkōku* system,[10] a long-standing feature of local governance that has formally integrated all hamlets into the local agricultural administration. This provided the foundation for creating and enforcing the exchange of farmland use rights through the Hikawa Nōgyō Kōsha in the 2000s (see chapter 8). The Kōsha system has also facilitated public-cooperative control over the types and entrepreneurial activities of emerging "bearer farms" in Hikawa. Analysis of the role of emerging "bearer farms" in other local agricultural regimes, both less organized and more organized than Hikawa, shows that public-cooperative control over farmland transfers is linked to control over the activity and the roles of emerging "bearer farms" (see chapter 9). Evidence on the proliferation of hamlet-based collective farms completes the picture. Hamlet-based collective farming is a particularly subsidy-productive form of farmland consolidation that potentially includes small-scale farm households. Hamlet-level norms and practices serve as the social and normative basis for founding and managing collective farms. Moreover, hamlet-based farms typically emerge alongside local social ties between hamlets and respective local JA and/or agricultural administration, which, for example, convey information on how to apply for state support. In some localities (including Hikawa), integration of village institutions into the local agricultural regime has supported a proliferation of hamlet farming through the local cooperative/administration, which contributes to a subsidy-productive interpretation of national reform that includes aging, small-scale farm households, instead of crowding them out (see chapter 10).

The pace and direction of institutional change in agricultural support and protection is shaped by the ways in which local actors have (re)combined the local social and normative landscape with the increasingly ambiguous regulatory framework into concrete local institutional interpretations. The integration of village institutions can provide the social and normative foundation to construct and enforce organized local interpretations of national reform, thus allowing for subsidy-productive farmland consolidation, but constraining entrepreneurial farmers in their aspirations to be emancipated from their local co-op and seek new marketing strategies and (corporate) partners.

Boundary Change: Limits of Local Institutional Agency

This leads to a crucial question. While the case of Hikawa illustrates the *potential* of local institutional agency to create organized interpretations of national reform, many (if not most) other localities have taken different paths. Why? The evidence from Hikawa points to the significance of stable socio-spatial boundaries for building and enforcing organized local agricultural regimes. During the 2000s, the boundaries of most postwar local agricultural regimes were disrupted by two processes beyond agricultural politics: financial liberalization accelerated the merger of local cooperatives after the 1990s, and fiscal decentralization resulted in a wave of municipal mergers between 2002 and 2006. Both disrupted the postwar overlap of municipal and cooperative boundaries and created much larger, socioeconomically and geographically more heterogeneous local agricultural regimes. Even where municipalities and cooperatives merged more or less in sync, the social and spatial distance between hamlets, local cooperatives, and administrations increased during the 2000s, while agricultural reform gained momentum. Meanwhile, Hikawa Town retained its municipal autonomy until 2011, and JA Hikawa remained independent until 2015, thus allowing the local co-op and agricultural administration to develop the Kōsha system within stable socio-spatial boundaries. Evidence from other local agricultural regimes on the organized end of the spectrum supports the significance of stable socio-spatial boundaries during the 2000s. Boundary change has thus quickened the pace of agricultural reform by reducing the "bargaining power" (Knight and Ensminger 1998) of incumbent actors such as the local co-ops to create, enforce, and maintain organized local responses to national reform. This has political implications, in that boundary change has reduced the potential of the cooperative organization and small-scale rice farmers to defend themselves against the neoliberalization of Japanese agriculture. It also has functional implications, in that boundary change has further undermined the prospects of governing consolidation of the agricultural production structure in the hands of "bearer farms" – not least because national agricultural policies have continued to shift responsibilities for this task to the local level, despite declining organizational abilities of local governments and local co-ops. The latter leads to a pessimistic outlook for the potential of these reforms to solve the structural crisis of the Japanese farm sector (see chapter 11).

Village Institutions as Dynamic Resources

Finally, the book offers a more nuanced perspective on the role of village institutions in agricultural support and protection regime. Traditional rural social organization has been recognized as an important element of the agricultural support and protection regime before. Most importantly, its social embedding in the hamlet provided the foundation of the cooperative organization's rise to political and economic power (Bullock 1997; George Mulgan 2000). While it is generally acknowledged that rural social organization has been subject to socioeconomic change throughout the postwar period (e.g., George Mulgan 2000, 309–15), these changes have rarely been the focus of the literature on agricultural politics. Even relatively recent studies still resort to the social structure in rural communities to explain the persistence of phenomena such as the "farm vote" or the cooperative's ability to discourage farmers to defy the co-op and seek new entrepreneurial strategies (Bullock 1997; George Mulgan 2000; Horiuchi and Saito 2010; George Mulgan 2006c; Freiner 2018). Consequently, our understanding of the role of rural social organization in the support and protection regime has remained vague – as an eroding, but still tangible factor that obstructs agricultural reform.

In contrast, village institutions are dynamic resources for local actors to adapt to national agricultural reform. For example, hamlets can revive and reinterpret agrarian norms and practices when they see a reason to do so, such as obtaining access to a new form of state support. Moreover, the way in which village institutions have been integrated into local agricultural regimes shapes local responses to national reform. This is not to deny that agrarian norms and practices have eroded. Yet, beyond these broader shifts, the role of village institutions in the agricultural support and protection regime is also shaped by local institutional agency. Such local agency, however, is more likely to take hold within stable and relatively narrow socio-spatial boundaries – conditions that have become increasingly rare over the 2000s as the result of cooperative and municipal mergers.

The Structure of the Book

In the remainder of the book, the argument is developed as follows. Part 2 (chapters 4–5) provides a longitudinal perspective on the postwar trajectory of the Japanese agricultural support and protection regime from the postwar period until the second Abe administration (2012–20), including a detailed review of agricultural reform since the mid-1990s. Part 3 (chapters 6–7) introduces local agricultural regimes and differences in how reforms since the mid-1990s have been implemented and interpreted. Despite these differences, part 3 argues that local agricultural regimes also share similarities by taking a historical perspective on the postwar formation of local agricultural regimes and village institutions. Part 4 (chapters 8–11) further analyzes how the integration of village institutions into local agricultural regimes contributes to local differences in redistribution of farmland use rights, large-scale farms and their role within the local agricultural regime, and local proliferation of hamlet-based collective farms. The final chapter in this part argues that boundary change has diminished the capacity of local actors to create and enforce defensive local responses to agricultural reform. Part 5 (chapters 12–13) discusses implications of the findings for the trajectory of the agricultural sector in Japan, and argues that a local perspective on institutional agency can contribute to a better theoretical understanding of gradual deregulation, liberalization, and structural reform beyond the case, and beyond Japan.

PART TWO

Japan's Agricultural Support and Protection over Time

The public and the scholarly images of Japan's agricultural support and protection regime have been informed most significantly by its shape in the late 1980s, when rurally backed LDP politicians, the organization of agricultural cooperatives, and the Ministry of Agriculture formed a seemingly unbreakable phalanx to support and protect a hopelessly inefficient army of small-scale part-time rice farmers at the expense of consumers, export-oriented Japanese companies, and the opposition parties. Yet this image is misleading, in that the agricultural support and protection regime was not static until the late 1980s and did not retain its shape thereafter. The following two chapters trace the regime's evolution from postwar land reform via construction of the "agricultural welfare state" (Sheingate 2001) from the 1960s onwards, up to the rise of growing domestic and international pressure since the late 1980s, and the ensuing agricultural reform, in which the institutional pillars of the postwar regime have been altered or replaced. Neither institutional breakdown nor stability accurately captures the trajectory of this regime. It has been remarkably stable in that extensive agricultural support and protection have survived major shifts in the surrounding institutions – including electoral reform in 1994, which had been expected to be a fatal blow for the alliance between the LDP, the MAFF, JA, and the farmers it represents. Yet it has been undergoing a transformation in the instruments and the targets of state support, the liberalization of commodity markets, and the position of the cooperative organization. Institutional change in the agricultural support and protection regime is thus constant, and – especially over the past two decades – has introduced increasing ambiguity.

Chapter Four

Postwar Evolution of
Support and Protection

We enter the evolution of the agricultural support and protection re-gime at the end of the Pacific War. This is mostly a practical decision, so that the subject does not become too broad. However, the postwar agricultural support and protection regime was not built on an insti-tutional tabula rasa. It evolved through juxtaposition of prewar insti-tutional legacies and new institutional elements on the one hand, and integration of the agricultural sector into the postwar political economy on the other. As farmers became part of the social coalition underlying the LDP's prolonged spell as the ruling party, the agricultural support and protection regime grew into an institutional complement of Japan's postwar model of "non-liberal capitalism." The small-scale, part-time production structure (especially in rice farming) allowed for absorp-tion of rural labor to fuel Japan's postwar economic expansion, while agricultural support and protection emerged as an instrument to re-distribute the gains of this economic growth to the less developed but electorally over-represented peripheries.

Land Reform, the Owner-Cultivator Principle, and Local Control over Farmland

The basis for the small-scale, household-based, and non-corporate production structure that became typical of Japan's postwar agricul-tural sector was laid with land reform (1947–50),[1] which was devised and executed under the Supreme Command of Allied Forces. Beyond redistributing arable land, reform was designed to dismantle the land-lord system and create a new class of small "owner-cultivators." By 1950, the share of land cultivated by tenant farmers had dropped to 10 per cent, and the number of farm households that owned more than 90 per cent of the land they cultivated rose to 3.8 million, or 61 per cent of all farm households (Dore 1984, 176). Subsequently, the 1952 Agricultural Land Law (ALL) cemented the "owner-cultivator principle" as the premise for the structure of the Japanese agricultural sector, that agricultural land "shall be most appropriately owned by the cultivators hereof" (McDonald 1997, 58). To secure farmland ownership and use in the hands of a relatively homogenous group of private smallholders, selling, leasing, and converting farmland was put under strict control of state authorities. Leasing was originally restricted to one hectare, and only farm households could legally lease land. As rapid urbanization and a shrinking agricultural workforce put increasing pressure on the farmland system, maximum holding sizes were given up in 1962 and tenancy regulations were softened from the 1970s onward.[2] Fueled by rural outmigration and a lack of agricultural labor, farmland leasing (formal and informal) became widespread and remains the dominant form of land exchange. However, despite this development, and in sharp contrast to countries like the United States and Britain, corporations remained excluded from the agricultural sector (57) until very recently, as a defining feature of Japan's postwar support and protection regime. Against this background, deregulation of corporate farmland access is a crucial and contested issue in agricultural reform (see chapter 5).

Land reform and subsequent farmland legislation installed oversight over farmland issues largely at the local level. As will be explored more extensively in chapter 7, the principle of "local self-governing" of farmland (Tashiro 2014a, 8) resonated with pre-existing forms of rural social organization. The Agricultural Land Law stipulated that local elected bodies – so-called agricultural committees (nōgyō iinkai) – should oversee regulations on municipal farmland use, transfer, and conversion. With the onset of rapid urbanization, overseeing the conversion of farmland to other purposes became a significant responsibility of these committees (McDonald 1997, 66). Local zoning competencies became a focal point of "farmland gambling" as land prices rose in the 1980s. Another core task of the agricultural committees was to collect information on farmland use, ownership, and leases in farmland registers (nōchi kihon daichō). Strikingly, these registers lacked a solid legal basis until very recently (Gōdo 2014a). Moreover, the Japanese central state itself does not have a comprehensive cadastre.[3] Thus, information on farmland became highly fragmented and localized. In the "absence of any effective system of control over land-use planning nationwide" (Iwamoto 2003, 233), the principle of local self-governing of farmland issues has contributed to the fragmentation and loss of farmland that hampers consolidation of the production structure today (see chapter 7 for details).

Food Control System and (Re)Birth of Nōkyō

While the ownership structure was transformed with the land reform, the Occupation authorities decided to uphold the Food Control Law of 1942, under which farmers had to deliver production quotas to government agencies (Sheingate 2001). This decision was made against the background of severe food shortages after the end of the Pacific War, which rendered organizing food production and distribution an urgent and complex task. To stabilize food supply, the Occupation authorities reinstalled the system of agricultural cooperatives in 1947, which had been disbanded as a result of their role in the fascist regime. The "resurrection" of the cooperatives under the name of Nōkyō (Sheingate 2001, 152) marked the birth of the organization that was to become the "linchpin" (K. Yamashita 2009) in agricultural support and protection. Nōkyō took over responsibility for the collection and distribution of foodstuffs, mainly rice. By 1950, it already handled 90 per cent of the staple foods.

The postwar agricultural cooperatives received a new, voluntary, and democratic legal basis with the Nōkyō Law in 1947. In practice, however, the cooperatives inherited facilities, resources, and members from their organizational predecessors, in which membership was compulsory. Already by 1950, 80 per cent of farm households had joined Nōkyō, and by 1970 virtually all households belonged. Strong membership and internal organizational stability were further supported by the fact that the cooperative organization integrated preexisting forms of rural social organization on the hamlet level (see chapter 7 for details). As a result of its institutional legacy and local social embedding, membership in the cooperative organization was de facto "semi-compulsory," despite the new, democratic principles stipulated in the Nōkyō Law (George Mulgan 2000, 213). On the one hand, this enabled the cooperatives to fulfill the tasks associated with the collection of rice from millions of small-scale producers, and its comprehensive distribution. On the other hand, it became an enormous advantage over every other farmers' group. The almost all-encompassing membership base served as Nōkyō's "prime organizational resource" to expand its political and economic power (211).

Nōkyō was set up in a three-tiered system, mirroring Japan's public administrative divisions. At the local level, farmers joined the multi-purpose cooperative (*sōgō nōkyō*) operating in the respective village, town, or city.

These local co-ops eventually covered a wide range of businesses and services, most importantly banking, marketing of agricultural products, purchasing of fertilizers, machinery, etc., mutual aid, and agricultural guidance, but also political, cultural, and social activities.[4] Moreover, Nōkyō's local branches served as local executive agents of agricultural policies and typically developed close relations – functional as well as personal – with local authorities. The territorial organizational logic of the local co-ops, their all-encompassing service provision, as well as the "functional complementarity with government administration" set Nōkyō apart from "Western-style agricultural cooperatives, which tend to be specialized by operation or by commodity producers" (George Mulgan 2000, 214).

On the prefectural level, Nōkyō was organized in federations, divided by function – that is, banking federations, economic federations, mutual aid federations, and other special-purpose federations. Nationally, this structure was duplicated.[5] Among the most prominent national federations, Nōrinchūkin is the national banking arm of the agricultural cooperatives, Zenkyōren is the national mutual aid federation, and Zennō is the national economic federation, handling, inter alia, the cooperative rice trade. In 1954, an amendment to the Nōkyō Law stipulated that central prefectural and national unions be created. This was the birth of the national central union Nōkyō Zenchū (called JA Zenchū since 1992), which came to act as Nōkyō's political headquarters. With the central unions, the cooperative organization gained a strict vertical hierarchy, through an auditing system that put local co-ops under Zenchū's control (Gōdo 2015; George Mulgan 2000, 60–4). The central unions were granted "legal authority" to engage in agricultural political activities (*nōsei katsudō*) and the right to formulate "proposals to administrative authorities on matters concerning the cooperatives" (George Mulgan 2000, 63). Only one year later, Nōkyō's role in food control was consolidated with an amendment to the Food Control Law (Sheingate 2001, 156). Subsequently, Nōkyō's political arm became regularly involved in the influential advisory councils of the MAFF, and emerged as a major political actor in the agricultural sector (153).[6] Next to specialized LDP politicians and the MAFF, the cooperative organization became the third element of an "institutionalized policy sub-government" dominating agricultural policy-making (George Mulgan 2005). Meanwhile, it utilized its handling of enormous sums of government transfers to expand its business scope (Sheingate 2001, 153; Bullock 1997). By the mid-1950s, Nōkyō had thus obtained a triple role as a major actor in political decision-making and implementation, chief collector and distributor of staple foods with an interest in high rice prices, and a powerful pressure group representing virtually every farm household in Japan.

Nōkyō's rise to become a political and economic giant was hardly a matter of deliberate institutional design. First and foremost, the decision to reactivate the cooperative structures and the Food Control Law was necessary to mitigate the food crisis in the early postwar years. Food security provided stability for the ambitious and risky land reform, with which the Occupation authorities pursued political goals that reached far beyond redistribution of arable land (Hayami 1991; Bullock 1997). Land reform was aimed to create political stability by establishing a democratic but conservative (i.e., non-socialist) peasantry (Dore 1984; McDonald 1997; Kawagoe 1999). From the perspective of the Occupation authorities, the "re-politicization" (Kelly 1990b) of farmers as the rural foundation of postwar democracy was indeed a success.[7] Previously influential leftist farmers' unions lost their main cause after the reform – and stood no chance to regain influence as the political alliance between Nōkyō and the LDP solidified (Babb 2004). However, the subsequent trajectory of the agricultural support and protection regime vividly illustrates the notion that "institution builders 'can never do just one thing' in the sense of creating institutions that have the intended effects and only the intended effects" (Pierson 2004, cited after Thelen 2004, 33).

Constructing the Agricultural Welfare State

Between 1950 and 1960, a large share of the new class of owner-cultivators still struggled to secure their livelihood as farmers. While rural incomes rose in the 1950s, increasing input costs and living expenditures put pressure on the smallest holdings in particular, and many farm household members were forced into supplementary day labor (Dore 1984). Meanwhile, the labor input for cultivating small rice paddies remained very high. By the late 1950s, the relative productivity of farming and rural household incomes had fallen behind (Hayami 1991). Reconstruction and industrialization in urban and urbanizing areas absorbed tens of thousands of low-wage laborers annually (Fukutake 1980; Matanle, Rausch, and the Shrinking Regions Research Group 2011). Strikingly, however, Japan's economic take-off and the accompanying decline of agriculture as the main source of household income did not entail the transition to large-scale industrial farming. Instead, it signaled the starting point for construction of an "agricultural welfare state" (Sheingate 2001), which rendered small-scale, part-time rice farming a lucrative household strategy under the influence of the emerging alliance between Nōkyō and the LDP.

Electoral Rules and National Decision-Making

This alliance was reinforced through the postwar electoral system. Between 1947 and 1996, lower house elections were held under a single non-transferable vote in multi-member districts (SNTV-MMD) system. Each electoral district was represented by an average of four seats (Rosenbluth and Thies 2010). SNTV-MMD systems require large parties to coordinate votes and candidates in order to gain the maximum seats with minimum votes per candidate. They are thus associated with personalized campaigning, weak party profiles, and intra-party factionalism, as well as the strong influence of (local) interest groups and pork-barrel politics.[8] In elections for the Japanese lower house, roughly 10–15 per cent of the votes were usually sufficient to win a seat. Under this system, the agricultural cooperatives functioned as an "adept political force at the grass-roots" (Sheingate 2001, 154). On the basis of its comprehensive membership, Nōkyō was often able to mobilize a stable group of voters for a certain candidate, such as by issuing recommendations.[9] Personal electoral supporter groups (*kōenkai*) of candidates specializing on the "farm vote" also relied on cooperative ties (George Mulgan 2006c; Krauss and Pekkanen 2011). The social embedding of local co-ops amplified the salience of Nōkyō as an electoral partner (George Mulgan 2000; Horiuchi and Saito 2010).

Through Nōkyō, farmers became crucial members of the broad social coalition that backed and profited from the postwar dominance of the LDP (Bullock 2003). Beyond supporting party candidates, active or retired Nōkyō executives also used the mobilization capabilities of their organization to run for office themselves (Sheingate 2001, 154). In 1966, 200 Diet members of the LDP alone had an agricultural background, and more than half of them were under the strong influence of the cooperative organization. Even more strikingly, lawmakers with an agricultural background still made up more than half of all Diet members in the late 1980s, despite the declining role of agriculture in the Japanese economy (George Mulgan 2000, 477–83). This constellation underpinned the informal agricultural "sub-government" consisting of Nōkyō, the "tribe" of LDP Diet members with agricultural ties and the MAFF. MAFF officials "parachuting" into second careers as politicians[10] or former Nōkyō officials running for Diet seats reinforced the policy network. Influential lawmakers also typically had well-established connections to organizations affiliated with the MAFF

(475–7). Such sub-governments occurred in many other policy fields beyond agriculture (Johnson 1995; Curtis 1999), illustrating how the support and protection regime was deeply embedded in the workings of the postwar political economy as a whole.

The Agricultural Basic Law, Rural Public Works, and the Rise of Part-Time Farming

Issued in 1961, the Agricultural Basic Law (ABL) provides an excellent example of how the emerging LDP-Nōkyō nexus shaped the evolution of the support and protection regime. The ABL aimed to reduce the growing gap between rural and urban incomes and to develop agriculture as an industry. Yet the way in which these objectives should be addressed was contested. The MAFF argued for consolidation – an agricultural industry carried by fewer members, but large-scale farmers would increase efficiency and release large parts of the massive rural labor force[11] to fuel Japan's industrial growth. The LDP and Nōkyō, however, prioritized the goal of raising agricultural incomes to the level of other industries (George Mulgan 2000, 29–30). Eventually they prevailed. In 1960, Japan introduced a system of rice price support under which the rice price was calculated using a formula that valued wages for family labor at non-farm wage rates (Hayami 1991, 91). The rice price began to rise steeply (see figure 4.1). As the main collector and distributor of staple food, Nōkyō profited massively from this development – and drove it forward, such as by organizing massive annual "rice price rallies" in Tokyo. Increasingly dependent on the electorally overrepresented rural voters, the LDP was eager to fulfill these demands (George Mulgan 2006b, 31).

Under the Agricultural Basic Law, part-time farming became a lucrative and increasingly popular strategy for land-owning households.[12] With little pressure to enlarge farm sizes or leave agriculture altogether, the number of farm households remained relatively high, while the share of income generated from farming decreased significantly. By 1975, 62.1 per cent of all farm households were "type-2 part-time households," i.e., households in which household income was predominantly generated by off-farm employment (see figure 4.2).[13] Pluriactivity became a source for rural prosperity (Kelly 1990b). In fact, the total income of farm households constantly exceeded the income of non-farm households from the 1970s until very recently (Kimura and Martini 2009, 24).

The rise of part-time farming was further fueled by mechanization and extensive land improvement. The pace of agricultural restructuring rose significantly with a spending program in 1957 and the subsequent

Figure 4.1. Producer Rice Price Development in Postwar Japan

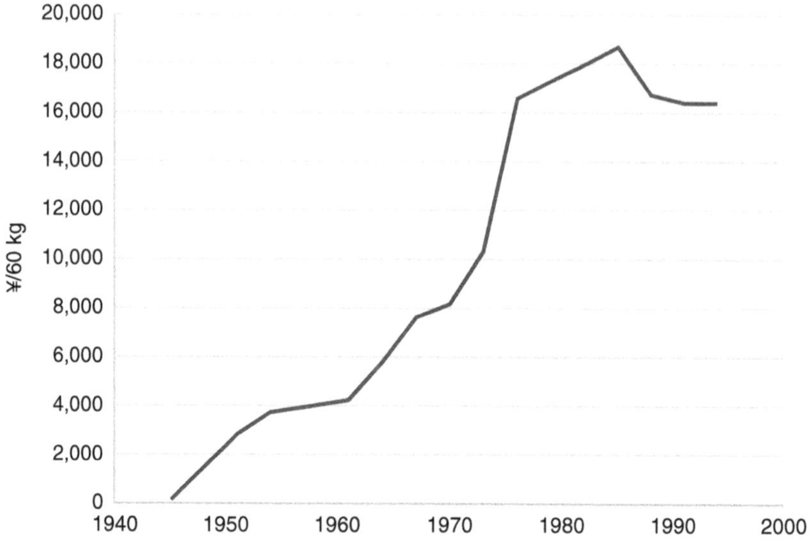

Source: Data provided by H-JA1.

Agricultural Basic Law (George Mulgan 2006b, 40). Large areas of (plain) land were reconstructed into rectangular plots of 30 by 100 meters. By the end of the 1970s, more than one-third of the land was improved in this way (George Mulgan 2006b). Irrigation systems were modernized with the construction of large-scale dams and concrete irrigation channels (Latz 1989; Kelly 2007). Public works grew into the largest item in the MAFF budget and a major source of influence for the ministry (George Mulgan 2006b). In a sense, land improvement and mechanization were the distorted remains of the original "efficiency objective" of the Agricultural Basic Law, in that they decreased the labor input for growing rice significantly – albeit with the effect that landowners could cultivate their small plots as a side-business on weekends and holidays (Kelly 1990b, 2007).

The land improvement boom also tied the agricultural sector to another crucial element of Japan's postwar "conservative coalition" – the construction sector. The allocation of land improvement projects emerged as a highly valuable political asset for LDP politicians, who were eager to direct government funds to rural electorates beyond the farmers alone. Rural areas received a disproportionally high share of the public works budget. A quota system issued by the LDP in 1963 required all projects to involve small, local construction companies

Figure 4.2. Increase in Share of Part-Time Farm Households, 1955–75

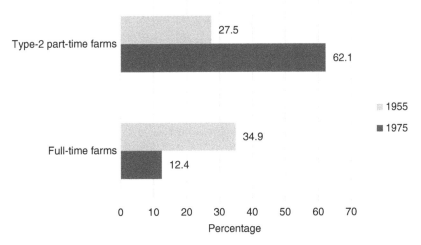

Source: Jussaume (2003, 211).

(Estevez-Abe 2008, 146–7). Construction thus became a major source for state-sponsored off-farm employment in rural areas.[14]

Taking a broader perspective, under the ABL the agricultural support and protection regime was transformed into an element of the fragmented postwar Japanese welfare state. Welfare provision in postwar Japan was marked by relatively low state expenditures but extensive reliance on "functional equivalents" (Estevez-Abe 2008). Rural public investments as a state-funded alternative occupation opportunity for part-time farmers, and agricultural support and protection as a means to turn farming into an additional source of income have been two prolific supplements for direct welfare provision. Both were particularly valuable political goods under the SNTV electoral system (5). In this context, the agricultural support and protection regime came to represent an important institutional complement to Japan's model of capitalism as a whole.[15] The rapid economic growth associated with state-led "developmentalism" (Streeck and Yamamura 2003) has been produced mostly in the metropolitan centers along the Pacific Coast. Similarly, the most prominent features of the Japanese model – especially lifelong regular (and male) employment in large corporations – are to a certain extent "metropolitan" phenomena as well (Matanle, Rausch, and the Shrinking Regions Research Group 2011). While large corporations provided their (male) workforce with comprehensive social security, subsidization and public investments bolstered social security – and indeed prosperity – in rural areas. And while the rise of part-time farming meant that the pluriactive rural population was at least partly available for the rapidly growing non-farm labor market, price support and public works projects redistributed the benefits of rapid economic growth to the less dynamic peripheries (Francks 2000; Kelly 1990b; Jentzsch 2020a).

Rice Production Control and De-agriculturalization

Already over the course of the 1960s, it had become apparent that extensive rice price support undermined the viability of the agricultural sector itself. Millions of small household farms produced rice in abundance. The ever-rising rice price strained the national budget and prevented diversification, or at least adaption to a steadily declining rice demand (George Mulgan 2006b). Yet, under constant electoral pressure of the well-organized farm vote, neither cutting the government price for rice nor abolition of state procurement seemed an option for the ruling LDP. Instead, in 1970 the government introduced an instrument to curtail the acreage for rice production. Originally introduced as an "emergency scheme," the so-called *gentan* remained in place to become a key instrument for agricultural subsidization and rice price intervention.[16]

The *gentan* set annual target rates of paddy land to be idled or diverted to other crops, for which farmers received compensation and support payments. The amount of land under this program increased from 337,000 hectares in 1970 to more than one million hectares in 2004 (H-JA1). The *gentan* reinforced rice as the most politicized crop in Japan[17] and established a similar position for the major diversion crops, including wheat, soy, starch potato, and barley. The annual target rates were set by the government's Food Agency, but in practice were allocated and overseen by the local cooperatives – although this role (and the *gentan* as a whole) lacked a solid legal foundation until 1995 (Gōdo 2013). Nōkyō's ubiquitous membership and its close ties with farm hamlets and local administrations made it the most capable partner to implement the difficult task, which was especially unpopular among full-time rice farmers. As the main rice collector, the cooperative organization itself had a strong interest in maintaining a high rice price.

With the introduction of the *gentan*, the agricultural support and protection regime increasingly fueled the structural crisis of the agricultural sector. With little or no pressure on part-time farmers to give up their land, the agricultural production structure remained small, fragmented, and dominated by the costly overproduction of rice. Many

Figure 4.3. Japanese Rice Marketing System, 1970–94

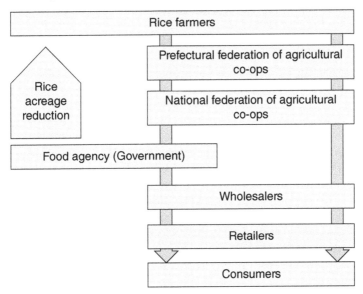

Source: Adapted from Gōdo (2013).

landowners kept growing rice half-heartedly while waiting for an opportunity to sell their land profitably for urban use (Gōdo 2007). Part-time farmers with little or no economic interest in agriculture came to dominate the cooperative membership, thus also reinforcing Nōkyō's interest in maintaining the part-time, small-scale production structure (George Mulgan 2000, 250–5). While the agricultural sector declined, Nōkyō's political power yielded regulatory benefits that allowed it to expand its business activities (Bullock 1997). For example, Nōkyō paid only the cooperative enterprise tax on its earnings, instead of the significantly higher corporate tax rate, and remained exempt from the Anti-Monopoly Law (George Mulgan 2000, 207–8). The cooperative national insurance federation enjoyed regulatory benefits and the back-up of the local cooperative system, through which it could "harvest" customers to become the largest insurance group in Japan. Regulatory privileges also provided Nōkyō's banking operations with competitive advantages (C. Smith 1988a). With its broad range of services, Nōkyō could attract millions of associated members. In the late 1980s, it had a membership of eight million households, a group much larger than the shrinking farm population. In urban areas, many local co-ops lost their connection to farming and practically turned into banks, insurance providers, and real estate developers (C. Smith 1988a; Ishida 2002).

Growing Pressure and Adjustment of the Food Control System

Meanwhile, the original core function of the Food Control system and the cooperative organization – to provide a stable supply of staple food – eroded. By the 1980s, the agricultural support and protection regime thus entered a phase of adjustment. Confronted with the growing deficit of the Food Control Agency, the government raised subsidies for rice marketed outside the government rice channel to decrease the direct state expenditures for rice purchases. From 1987 onward, the consumer price even exceeded the producer price. With this adjustment, "the burden of price support [was shifted] to consumers where the costs of producer rice price support was more 'hidden'" (George Mulgan 2006b, 45), while public control over the collection and distribution of staple food further declined.

Far beyond the eroding food control system, it became increasingly obvious during the 1980s that the agricultural production structure was not only cost-intensive and inefficient, but also unsustainable as the result of a rapidly aging workforce and a lack of successors. Urban consumers became increasingly critical of their price burden, and their criticism was fueled by a number of scandals surrounding the food control system in the early 1990s. Internationally, Japan's secluded farm sector had come under scrutiny during negotiations for the General Agreement on Trade and Tariffs (GATT). Domestic advocates for liberalization – from the corporate and the political world – exploited the international pressure and growing public criticism to push for structural reform (C. Smith 1988b; George Mulgan 2006b; Davis 2004). Domestic and international pressure coincided with major shifts in the postwar political economy. In 1993, the LDP lost its grip on the government for the first time in thirty-eight years. A coalition of eight parties used the exclusion of the LDP from government to attack the SNTV-MMD electoral system, which was eventually abolished in 1994 (Krauss and Pekkanen 2011). In the same year, Japan joined the World Trade Organization (WTO), which required substantial adjustments of agricultural support and protection policies, including partial liberalization of agricultural imports (Davis and Oh 2007). In the light of these developments, the Food Control Law was repealed in 1994. For many observers, the postwar agricultural regime had reached its breaking point.[18] Yet, instead of breaking down, the agricultural support and protection regime entered ongoing contested renegotiation.

Gradual Change and Increasing Institutional Ambiguity in Agricultural Support and Protection

More than two decades after direct state control over rice prices was abolished with the repeal of the Food Control Law in 1994, the agricultural sector is far from being "liberalized." Although overall support to producers has been declining steadily, it made for 47 per cent of gross farm receipts in 2016, which is still about three times more than the OECD average (OECD 2017; see figure 5.1).[1] Meanwhile, the structural problems of an aging workforce, high production costs, farmland fragmentation, and dependency on food imports are by no means resolved. This is particularly true for rice production, which still dominates agricultural land use, despite its shrinking economic role (Yamashita 2015a; Honma and George Mulgan 2018).

A closer look, however, reveals a gradual departure from the "anti-corporate," all-inclusive, and welfare-oriented character of the postwar regime.[2] Since the late 1980s, the share of total support to agriculture (as measured by the OECD) in the GDP was more than halved, from 2.3 to 1.1 per cent in 2016 (OECD 2017). Even more importantly in the context of this book, state support became distributed differently, and under new conditions. Compared to the days of universal price support, the main profiteers of the postwar regime – small, part-time rice farms – have less comprehensive access to subsidies, while promotion of corporate farming has become the key policy objective. Meanwhile, JA (as Nōkyō has been called since 1992) faces unprecedented political pressure and new competitors, and it struggles with organizational restructuring. Agricultural reform went hand-in-hand with shifting responsibilities in order to realize structural change and to distribute state support to local actors. In sum, the agricultural support and protection regime has grown increasingly ambiguous, which – to preview the argument that concludes this chapter – has left local actors with maneuvering space to shape its transformation.

Figure 5.1. Development of Producer Support Estimate in Japan, OECD

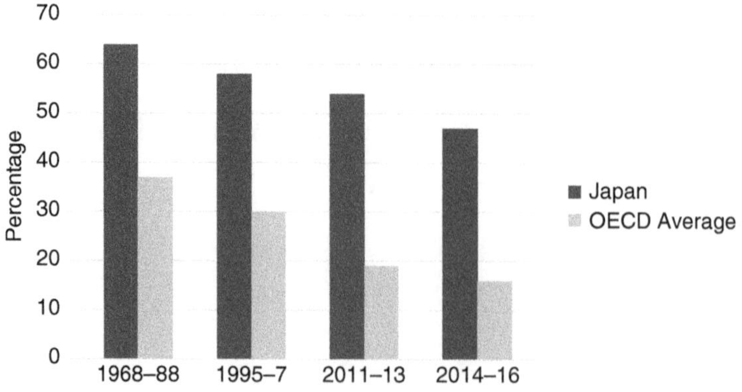

Source: OECD (2014, 2017).

Agricultural Policy-Making in a Changing Political Economy

The gradual change of the postwar agricultural regime occurred in the context of major shifts in the political economy, including most importantly electoral reform in 1994 and centralization of political decision-making. Two other developments have received far less attention in the literature on agricultural politics, but have also profoundly affected the trajectory of the support and protection regime: financial deregulation has forced many local co-ops to merge into larger districts since the early 1990s; and fiscal decentralization caused a wave of municipal mergers in the mid-2000s. The impact of these developments will be discussed separately in chapter 11.

In 1994, the postwar electoral system was replaced with a mixed parallel system of single-member districts and proportional representation (SMD-PR), followed by reforms of party financing and campaigning rules. The reforms were expected to bring more party-based campaigning and reduce personalized voting, as both the PR element and the SMD provide incentives to appeal to the "median voter" instead of catering to local support groups and sectoral interests like agriculture or construction.[3] However, the LDP's quick return to power reduced the disruptive potential of the reforms (Rosenbluth and Thies 2010). Moreover, institutional features often identified as "rational" responses to the SNTV system – such as personal local support organizations – have proven strikingly adaptive after 1996.

Many candidates could retain their highly personalized local support base. In the new single-member districts, candidates can rarely afford to ignore sectoral interests completely. Personal ties to local co-ops remain valuable assets for politicians' support organizations (Krauss and Pekkanen 2011). In fact, smaller districts have allowed some politicians to concentrate on agricultural interests *even more* in the elections following the reform, thus moderating its immediate impact on agricultural politics (George Mulgan 2006c). JA has also adapted to the "nationalization" of elections that came with proportional representation. Both the LDP and its main competitor throughout the 2000s, the Democratic Party of Japan (DPJ), have tackled agriculture with intensity (Scheiner 2013). As the disparity between urban and rural votes was not fully erased, catering to rural interests remained a promising strategy (Feldhoff 2017). In fact, the DPJ beat the LDP in the lower house election in 2009, not least by making a broad appeal to all farmers, who were disappointed by the reform course under the Koizumi administration. The DPJ's rise to power implied a deterioration of the relation between Nōkyō and the LDP and the increasing heterogeneity of the farm vote (Kawamura 2011). Yet, in the subsequent 2012 elections, JA managed to rally the farm vote behind the LDP again (George Mulgan 2013). In the campaign for the 2014 election, the party carefully appealed to the interests of JA and to independent voters alike – a "bait-and-switch" tactic to prepare the ground for the JA reform (Maclachlan and Shimizu 2016b). Subsequently, the LDP further reduced its dependency on rural voters. In the snap elections in 2017, the party displayed a more balanced electoral appeal, including urban voters (George Mulgan 2017). While the farm vote still has the potential to decide elections, at least in rural constituencies, the shrinking number of farmers is bound to further undermine its power.

Centralization of decision-making challenged the postwar dominance of elite bureaucrats, interest groups, and LDP "policy specialists." Since the 1990s, reforms strengthened the prime minister and the Cabinet vis-à-vis the bureaucracy.[4] Prime Minister Koizumi (2001–6) was especially eager to exploit the new leadership instruments.[5] He initiated far-reaching neoliberal reforms, including postal privatization (Maclachlan 2011), fiscal decentralization (Song 2015), and not least agricultural reform. Yet, even under Koizumi, agricultural policy-making remained influenced by LDP policy specialists, JA, and the MAFF (George Mulgan 2006a, 11). After forming the government in 2009, DPJ tried to block JA from direct access to policy-making (George Mulgan 2011), but its efforts were hampered by resistance from the administration and repercussions of the triple disaster on 11 March 2011, in the aftermath of which the LDP regained the government. The Abe government (2012–20), however, was unwilling to reinstate the established mode of decision-making, and instead strengthened the role of the Prime Minister's Office in formulating agricultural reform. As a result, the agricultural policy triangle showed clear signs of deterioration, as illustrated, for example, by the initiative to reform JA, which, inter alia, reduced the central unions' control over the local cooperatives (Tashiro 2018; George Mulgan 2016).

Taken together, the continued interaction between old and new rules in the electoral system and the decision-making process provides a powerful explanation for the "straying,"[6] at times inconsistent course of agricultural policies since the 1990s. Just as the ongoing transformation of the Japanese political economy as a whole is marked by the "syncretic" interaction between new institutions emerging on top of and often parallel with old rules, and the gradual reformulation and reinterpretation of institutions under new "terms of trade" (Kushida, Shimizu, and Oi 2013), the agricultural support and protection regime has been changing gradually without breaking down entirely.

The New Basic Law: An Ambiguous New Constitution for the Agricultural Sector

A crucial building block in this process is the New Agricultural Basic Law (NBL), which replaced its postwar predecessor as the constitution of the agricultural sector in 2000.[7] The New Basic Law caught up with political developments that had shaped reform since the early 1990s and set the course for the increasing ambiguity of the support and protection regime. At its "reformist core" the NBL provided a solid legal basis for liberalization of the market for agricultural products, which had gained momentum since the Food Control Law was abolished in 1994 (George Mulgan 2006b, 126). On the other hand, the NBL has also embraced the notion that the effects of market liberalization should be counterbalanced by state support and intervention. For example, the law puts heavy emphasis on enhancing Japan's food security, which has arguably served as a rationale for continued subsidization and protection from international competition (118). Similarly, the commitment to promote "stable farm management" has justified price stabilization and public investment in the agricultural infrastructure (116). As for how state support is allocated, however, the NBL legislated the shift from the postwar mode of price support to (crop-specific) direct income support and compensation schemes that are in line with WTO regulations (97; Kimura and Martini 2009; Tashiro 2014b). The NBL also embraced "multifunctional" agriculture, which links agricultural production to environmental protection and improvement of the rural living environment in general. This resulted in new subsidy schemes like the 2000 "Direct Payments for Hilly and Mountainous Areas" and the 2007 "Farmland and Water Protection Payment," which comply with WTO standards, but also guarantee ongoing public transfers to rural and semi-urban areas (Gōdo and Takahashi 2012, 20).

A key objective of the NBL is consolidation of agricultural production in the hands of a group of larger, more business-oriented, and potentially more efficient "bearer farms," or *ninaite* in Japanese.[8] As such, the NBL picked up on a concept from the "New Policies" in the early 1990s. In principle, the "bearer farms" category excludes neither household farms nor part-time farm households. It can also include hamlet-based collective farms (*shūraku einō*), which are groups of (small) farmers who pool their land for collective cultivation (George Mulgan 2006b; Honma 2010). While the NBL embraced the notion of more targeted, and potentially more exclusive state support for designated "bearer farms," it has also perpetuated the ambiguity of the "bearer farms" concept. For example, the NBL upheld the notion of the household as the core unit in Japanese farming, but also explicitly called for incorporation of "bearer farms" as businesses (George Mulgan 2006b, 121).

In the years after passage of the NBL, the question of the extent to which state support should be granted *exclusively* to designated "bearer farms" became contested between defenders of support and protection (most importantly JA and conservative farm politicians) and advocates of a more market-based production structure. In this context, it is important to note that the responsibility to identify and nurture "bearer farms" moved to the local level, including the local branches of JA (George Mulgan 2006b, 77; Honma 2010, 152–3). More generally, shifting risks and responsibilities to the local level defined policy-making under the New Basic Law.

Rice Market Liberalization and the Changing Role of Production Control

This shift is also apparent in the changing role of rice production control after the opening of the rice market. Replacing the postwar Food Control Law, the 1995 Staple Food Law reduced the role of government-purchased rice to stockpiling and established new legal marketing channels. Direct state control over prices was abolished, including the highly politicized rice price, which was the main instrument of state support in the postwar era. Yet the state did not give up control over the rice price entirely. Instead, the role of rice production control – in combination with prohibitive border tariffs – was expanded to maintain the rice price and to allocate state support. After twenty-five years without a stable legal foundation, the Staple Food Law "was the first written law that stipulated" the rice acreage reduction program *gentan* (Gōdo 2013). The task to implement rice acreage reduction was officially assigned to local co-ops, local governments, and Food Agency officials (George Mulgan 2006b, 97).[9] The opening of the rice market subjected the cooperative organization to economic competition in rice purchasing, storage, and marketing, not least from large farmers themselves. Further, de-politicization of the rice price determination undermined JA's role as the voice of Japanese rice farmers (91–7). Yet formalization of the *gentan* also reinforced the role of JA in the support and protection regime. Many new rice collectors that emerged under the Staple Food Law were in fact local cooperatives (Gōdo 2013). As further rice market reforms were gradually introduced, the target rates for rice acreage reduction were increased to prevent overproduction. Subsidies for the main diversion crops – for example, wheat, soy, rice for animal feed, or starch potatoes – grew accordingly to compensate farmers for the income gap vis-à-vis rice. Producers had to participate in rice production control to be eligible for state support (Honma 2010, 102–12). In 2004, the Food Agency – a relic from the postwar Food Control system – was dissolved, and the marketing channels established under the Staple Food Law disappeared, together with "almost all regulations on rice marketing" (Gōdo 2013). The target rates for rice acreage reduction were replaced by target rates for rice production.[10] The task to distribute and oversee the quota moved to farmers and farmer organizations (in practice, local JA), while the government merely supplied the necessary supply-demand information and approved the distribution plans.[11] Thus, the central government further outsourced responsibility for maintaining the rice price to self-organizing farmers and local co-ops (George Mulgan 2006b, 160; Kimura and Martini 2009, 57).

While the domestic rice market was gradually liberalized, rice imports remained limited, despite the WTO accession in 1995. Fixed import quotas and a prohibitive tariff rate have greatly softened the effects of the formal "opening" of the rice market (Lewis 2015). Still, in the wake of decreasing domestic demand, the combination of domestic production control and border protection did not prevent fluctuation and decline of rice prices. While fluctuating prices hit commercial farms in general, small part-time farms are particularly vulnerable, because they tend to lack the machinery, labor force, and the skill to grow

Figure 5.2. Producer Rice Price (¥/60 kg), 1994–2016

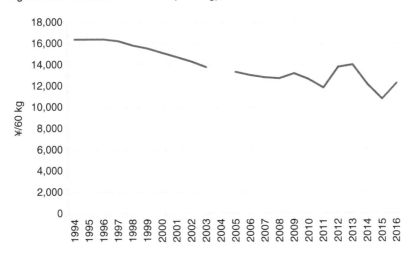

Sources: H-JA1 (1994–2003); data from 2005–16, sourced from Organization to Secure a Stable Rice Supply (n.d.); no data for 2004.

anything but rice, which means they have less access to the expanding subsidies for crops like wheat or soy. Consequently, many small part-time farms dropped out of the rice production control program (and often also commercial farming, see below). In 2014, only about 1 million of Japan's 2.4 million hectares of paddy fields were subject to rice production control (Honma 2015, 104). Control of the rice price and state support have thus grown less comprehensive.

Toward Exclusive Subsidization (and Back)

The gradual departure from the postwar model of uniform price support for all (rice) farmers[12] was further amplified from the mid-2000s onwards, when the allocation of subsidies – including the schemes associated with rice production control – was linked with more pronounced structural reform policies. In 1992, the "New Policies" had introduced measures to promote consolidation of the agricultural production structure in the hands of a designated group of "bearer farms." The concept was formalized in 1993 with the "certified farmer scheme," under which household farms, agricultural production corporations, and hamlet-based collective farms could apply for special support like low-interest loans and infrastructural support if they met certain requirements for a professional and stable farm management. During the 1990s, the "certified farmers scheme" was employed mostly to justify *additional* state support (George Mulgan 2006b, 78).[13] In the mid-2000s, however, it was transformed into an *exclusive* support measure – and thus a more explicit means to accelerate consolidation of agricultural production (146–50). In 2002, the government required that municipalities develop agricultural "revitalization plans," which entailed identification and certification of local "bearer farms" and strategies to concentrate farmland in their hands (160). Requirements for certification were further specified in the 2005 "New Bearers' Management Stabilization Law," which provided the ground for linking the status of "certification" to eligibility for state support (Honma 2010, 155–6). In 2007, subsidies for rice and the major diversion crops were reorganized again with the "Across-Commodity Management Stabilization Countermeasure." Only formally certified "bearer farms" (household farms and agricultural production corporations) cultivating more than four hectares (ten hectares in Hokkaidō) or hamlet-based collective farms cultivating more than twenty hectares were eligible for the new form of direct support payments. This meant that for the first time in postwar history, the vast majority of Japanese farm households faced exclusion from paddy field subsidies. Moreover, participation in the rice production control scheme was "decoupled" from subsidization, which reduced incentives for farmers to participate in the scheme, and thus undermined rice price stability.[14] Under fierce resistance from the farm lobby (especially JA), the exclusive character of the new support scheme could not be maintained. Local governments retained the right to adjust the criteria for "certification" to local conditions, which made it possible to circumvent the acreage threshold (Gōdo 2010). Still, part-time rice farmers faced unprecedented pressure to professionalize their agricultural activities or leave commercial farming altogether.

In this context, hamlet-based collective farming became a loophole for small household farms to remain eligible for the full array of state support. Hamlet-based collective farming had been included in the "certified farmer" scheme since the early 1990s. When the restrictions on paddy-field subsidization were tightened in the mid-2000s, JA pressured the government to keep hamlet-based collective farms in the target group for the support scheme, as long as they were formally certified as "special agricultural groups" or met the requirements for this status, and cultivated more than 20 ha (Honma 2010, 159). Between 2006 and 2010 alone, the number of hamlet farms increased sharply from about 10,500 to more than 14,000 (MAFF 2017). Many preexisting hamlet farms formalized cooperation to comply with the requirements for certification under the 2005 New Bearer's Management Stabilization Law.

Even for hamlet farms that do not meet these requirements, pooling land and machinery could become an advantage in light of the growing significance of paddy field diversion subsidies, because it allows smaller farm households to engage in subsidy-productive crop rotation. In 2017, hamlet farms made up more than 11 per cent of the arable land in Japan (MAFF 2017), thus representing an important aspect of structural change that will be discussed in more detail in chapter 10.

The neoliberal turn in agricultural policies under Koizumi strained the relationship between farmers and the LDP. After losing the upper house elections in 2007, the LDP issued new support payments to encourage "full utilization" of paddy fields and intervened to stabilize the plummeting rice price (Gōdo 2010, 132–6). Despite these attempts to calm the waters, the DPJ further exploited farmers' frustration with the LDP. In the campaign for the lower house in 2009 – orchestrated by the former LDP politician and electoral strategist Ozawa Ichirō – the party promised a direct income support scheme for all commercial rice farmers (Gōdo 2010; Rosenbluth and Thies 2010). Reflecting the continued potential of the farm vote, the strategy contributed to the DPJ's triumph. The support scheme was installed in 2010,[15] followed by new direct payments for the major diversion crops. Subsidization was "recoupled" to participation in rice production control (Tashiro 2014b). Support policies have also continued to provide direct and indirect incentives for hamlet-based farming.[16] Yet this did not amount to complete reversion to the all-inclusive postwar approach to subsidization. The second Abe administration picked up the neoliberal path of the mid-2000s (Tashiro 2014b). The DPJ's inclusive direct income scheme for rice farmers was halved in 2014 and terminated in 2018. Simultaneously, participation in the rice production control scheme became voluntary again, thus replicating the shift of responsibilities to maintain the rice price to farmers and local cooperatives in the mid-2000s (see above). The Abe administration counterbalanced reduced state intervention by expanding subsidies for rice for animal feed and other diversion crops to enhance food self-sufficiency and stabilize the rice price indirectly (Honma and George Mulgan 2018) – again, however, aging part-time farmers who produce only rice are less likely to access the full array of these measures.

Farmland Deregulation and the End of the Owner-Cultivator Principle

The policy shift toward scale-enlargement and professionalization has applied strong pressure to the core principles governing farmland use in postwar Japan, i.e., the owner-cultivator principle and the exclusion of corporations. The former was undermined over the course of the 2000s by an increasing transfer of land use rights from aging farm households toward expanding "bearer farms" (Tashiro 2009). Between 2000 and 2010, the share of land used by certified farms and "bearer farms" equivalent to the level of certification grew from 27.8 to 49.1 per cent (Statistics Bureau of Japan 2012). As the result of legal restrictions and incentives for farmers to hold onto their land, this increase has been based primarily on the exchange of (formal or informal) land use rights (Hashizume 2013). This mode of farmland transfers has highly fragmented the holdings of expanding farms and has proven increasingly insufficient to prevent farmland abandonment (see chapter 8 for details). Thus, efforts to facilitate the "flow of land" to push structural change were included on the political reform agenda. During the 2000s, these efforts became increasingly intertwined with deregulation of corporate access to farmland, officially to increase the pool of future land users. This crucial turn is reflected in a statement by Ishiba Shigeru (LDP) at his inaugural press conference as minister for agriculture: "We need a mechanism in which farmland becomes concentrated in the hands of those who are ready and willing to farm it, regardless of whether they are individuals or corporations."[17] Eventually, in essence, a major revision of the Agricultural Land Law in 2009 replaced the postwar owner-cultivator principle with the principle of "separating ownership from use" and granted "general" corporations the right to lease farmland – thus signaling the end of the postwar farmland regime.[18]

Public Promotion of Farmland Consolidation

Public promotion of farmland consolidation has been an element of "bearer farm" policies since the outset. The 1993 "Law for the Promotion of a Stable Agricultural Management Base" stipulated that municipalities must carry out "farmland rationalization projects" to facilitate the flow of land toward the newly established category of "certified farmers." Overall, however, the impact of these projects remained very limited (Yamashita 2008) – not least because they failed to acknowledge leases as the dominant mode of farmland transfer and instead focused on arbitrating sales (Takahashi 2013; Tashiro 2014a, 6).[19] In 2009 the government introduced "farmland harmonization groups" to facilitate the exchange of land use rights. The reform reflected the new principle of "separating ownership and use" of farmland, an element of the revised Agricultural Land Law (Shōgenji 2012; Takahashi 2013). As public agencies located at the municipal level, farmland harmonization groups were to mediate the transfer of land use rights between landowners and expanding "bearer farms," thus officially recognizing leases as the dominant mode of land exchange. Since 2012, the use of public farmland allocation has been encouraged with incentive payments.[20] In order to be eligible, landowners were required to offer their land under "unconditional authority," i.e. without being able to decide who will rent their land (Shōgenji 2012). At least theoretically, this allows for a more rational (public) allocation of farmland into connected and thus less cost-intensive blocks. Importantly, the 2009 reforms reinforced the notion that the responsibility to organize farmland consolidation is a local issue. According to data provided by the MAFF, in practice the majority of harmonization groups were run by local JA, and many others were operated through cooperation between JA, local governments, and/or local agricultural committees (MAFF 2011b; Shōgenji 2012).

Corporatization from Within and the Entry of General Corporations into the Farm Sector

Corporate farming gained momentum over the 2000s with two policy developments: "corporatization from within" by promoting agricultural production corporations (APCs), and deregulation of farmland use by "general" (non-agricultural) corporations. Formally, farmers have had the right to form agricultural production corporations since 1962. Yet, as the result of strict legal restrictions, APCs have played only a minor role in the postwar Japanese agricultural sector. This has changed since APCs were included in the target group for farmland consolidation with the 1993 "certified farmers" scheme. In 2000, individual farmers were also allowed to create joint-stock corporations (George Mulgan 2006b, 141–5). Incorporated farms have become a preferential target for state support, including subsidized regular labor and trainee positions.[21] Between 2005 and 2015, the number of incorporated farms rose from 8,700 to 18,857 (MAFF 2016b, 19).

Although the right to *own* farmland has remained restricted to farm households and APCs, farmland access for "general" corporations has also been relaxed. Since 2003, general corporations have been able to lease farmland, first in special deregulation zones, and later in areas with a large share of abandoned land (George Mulgan 2006b, 157–9). For the first time in the postwar era, the 2009 revision of the Agricultural Land Law granted general corporations the right to lease farmland throughout all of Japan. By mid-2015, almost 2,000 general corporations had rented farmland (MAFF 2016b, 20), including food processors and retail giants venturing into the production of rice and other crops.[22] They remain an exception. In 2015, general corporations occupied less than 1 per cent of the total farmland, and the majority of corporations held only small plots between half a hectare and one hectare (MAFF 2015b, see also Jentzsch 2017a, 35–6).

While direct corporate farmland use is still limited, *indirect* access for "general" corporations to the farm sector was also deregulated substantially. Since their inclusion in the "certified farmers" scheme, the restrictions on corporate investments into APCs have been gradually relaxed. Investments in APCs were originally restricted to 25 per cent of the total capital of the latter, and less than 10 per cent per member – only municipal governments could invest in APCs without restriction. In 2000, ordinary (i.e., non-farm) joint-stock corporations were allowed to invest in APCs (George Mulgan 2006b, 141–5). With the revision of the Agricultural Land Law in 2009, restrictions for general corporations to invest in APCs were abolished. Since a further revision of the ALL in late 2013, only one executive *or* main employee of an APC must be a full-time farmer (MAFF 2015c), thus further blurring the line between APCs and "general" corporations (Jentzsch 2017a, 35–6).

Closely related, the government has heavily promoted diversification in the agricultural sector since the late 2000s, which has become known by the buzzword "6th industry."[23] Enterprises that link agricultural production with processing, marketing, and/or tourism are eligible for subsidy schemes (Muroya 2016). The second Abe administration strongly emphasized the role of such joint ventures between farmers and corporations as a crucial element of its approach to the economic revitalization of rural areas (MAFF 2015a). Against the background of deregulation of corporate access to farmland, the political emphasis on cross-sectoral agricultural entrepreneurship has thus become another important vehicle for the (direct and indirect) corporatization of the farm sector.

Farmland Deregulation and Local Responsibilities

Farmland deregulation remained highly contested after 2009. Critics have long argued that corporate land use "would not harmonize with family farm management and would throw regional water control and land utilization into confusion" (George Mulgan 2006b, 142). Indeed, corporate investments have been found to be unsustainable in several cases (Sekine and Bonanno 2016; see chapter 8 for details). Taking up these concerns, the revised Agricultural Land Law stipulates corporations must use farmland "appropriately," i.e. for agricultural purposes only and in "harmony" with local farmers (Takahashi 2013,

99). Corporations also have to take responsibility for farmland-related collective works (maintenance of irrigation systems, etc.) in the respective communities (Takahashi 2013; Gōdo 2014b). Thus, in line with other agricultural policy developments, farmland deregulation was accompanied with a shift of responsibilities from the central state to local agricultural committees, which were charged with overseeing these stipulations (Jentzsch 2017a). Since the 1990s, the competences of agricultural committees in farmland conversion have been expanded (Gōdo 2010, 88). On the one hand, it has become highly questionable whether the agricultural committees can (still) oversee corporate farmland use and farmland conversion adequately and in the interest of local communities (Takahashi 2013; Gōdo 2014a). On the other hand, however, the extended responsibilities have granted local stakeholders – including JA, local governments, and farm households themselves – some discretion over farmland deregulation and corporatization. The agricultural committee system – and the postwar principle of local control over farmland in general – has thus been targeted as a holdout of the "anti-business" agricultural support and protection regime (Tashiro 2014a). This viewpoint is reflected in a reform package brought forward by the second Abe administration.

Farmland Banks and Further Deregulation under the Second Abe Administration

In late 2013 the government introduced farmland intermediary management organizations – so-called farmland banks, as a new means to promote consolidation. Like the preceding farmland harmonization groups, farmland banks acquire and arbitrate land use rights. Land givers are also required to rent their land under unconditional authority and are rewarded with incentive payments. Farmland banks can also manage abandoned plots until a new user is found, if necessary outsourcing maintenance and land improvement to private companies and public (municipal) corporations (Kobari 2015). Accompanying the farmland bank reform, a 2013 revision of the Agricultural Land Law stipulated that local farmland registers had to be made public. Agricultural committees had kept these registers without a proper legal foundation, following different local standards and with varying accuracy (see chapter 4). At least in principle, the 2013 reform made every plot of abandoned land accessible for nationwide purchase. Furthermore, agricultural committees were de-democratized: all members are now appointed by the mayor and then approved by the municipal assembly. Their major field of activity moved to gathering information on farmland use, and away from overseeing transfers.[24] The reform package constitutes a further shift toward turning farmland from a resource governed by farmers and hamlets into "a commercial good" (Tashiro 2014a, 8). In practice, however, local stakeholders are still not entirely excluded from farmland consolidation, since the actual administrative tasks under the farmland bank system are consigned to municipal actors, again including local JA (Jentzsch 2017a, 2017c).

Interim Conclusion

Even without a wholesale breakdown of the agricultural support and protection regime, the postwar "anti-corporate" agricultural sector under uniform state support and protection is a thing of the past. Farms in Japan are now principally free to expand their holdings and become independent entrepreneurs, to engage in direct marketing and marketing arrangements with corporations, and to turn into corporations themselves. Reform – in combination with the aging labor force and the lack of successors – has already affected the agricultural production structure profoundly. Thousands of farm households have expanded their holdings and professionalized cultivation and marketing since the mid-2000s. The number of (mostly corporate) farms cultivating more than fifty hectares – albeit still relatively small – has grown particularly quickly (MAFF 2016b, 19).

Policy emphasis on entrepreneurship has challenged the all-encompassing welfare character of the postwar agricultural support and protection regime. The main profiteers of the postwar regime – part-time, small-scale, rice-farming households – now face less comprehensive access to state support. While small, part-time farms are still vastly in the majority, 65 per cent of the farming population was older than sixty-five in 2016, and the 2015 agricultural census suggested a rapid decline of farm household members below the age of forty-nine (Hashizume 2018). For aging part-time farm households, picking up on more profitable and more subsidy-productive forms of agricultural production is rarely a viable option, especially for rice farmers, who are even older on average, and less commercialized (Yamashita 2015a). As a result, more and more farmers give up their land. The share of "self-consumption" farm households that neither market their products nor receive state support has grown steadily (Gōdo 2014c). Increasing differentiation in the agricultural sector is depicted in figure 5.3. It is even more pronounced where the comeback of more inclusive subsidization after 2007 did not apply – for many non–paddy field farming households. In horticulture, for example, farms that are not formally

Figure 5.3. Categories of Farms (*left*) and Access to State Support (*right*)

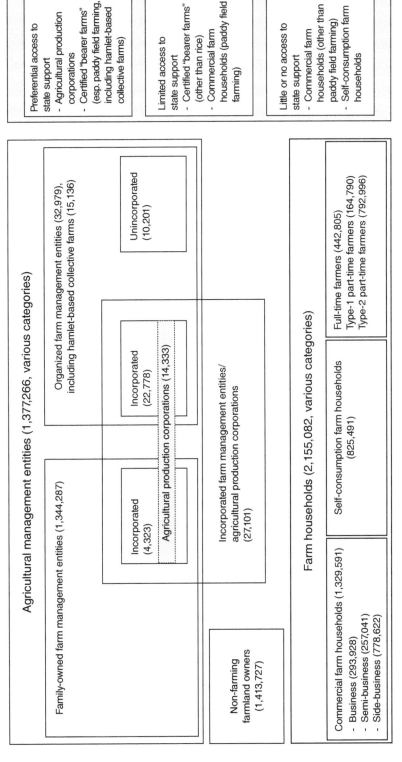

Source: Adapted from Hisano, Akitsu, and McGreevy (2018, 292). The numbers refer to the Agricultural Census 2015, except the number of hamlet-based collective farms, which are taken from MAFF (2017). See appendix for definitions of farm categories.

certified as "bearer farms" have become almost entirely disconnected from state support and are less sheltered against national and international competition. While rice imports outside the minimum quota remained subject to prohibitive tariffs, most fruit and vegetable products are protected by little or even no import tariffs (*Japan Times* 2014; Yamashita 2015b; OECD 2020).[25] To a far greater extent than in paddy field farming, generating income depends on entrepreneurial initiatives to link agricultural with new marketing channels, processing, and tourism (Kimura and Martini 2009, 94; Kingsbury 2012).

Reform has put the cooperative organization under growing pressure. Since the end of direct state control over commodity prices, business-oriented, entrepreneurial farms that have become the focus of state support have more opportunities and incentives to leave the cooperative corset to develop their own marketing strategies (Ōizumi 2018). The "dropout" of small farms from commodity markets and the state support system is similarly troubling for the future of the cooperative organization, whose power has been based on catering to its vast membership. Beyond the realm of agricultural politics, financial liberalization since the late 1980s has exposed cooperatives to competition with other banking and insurance providers. As local co-ops came under financial pressure (Gōdo 2001), the MAFF pushed JA to rationalize its organizational structure, such as by incentivizing the merger of local co-ops. Since the 1990s, the number of local JA has decreased sharply.[26] The remaining local co-ops have to struggle to retain their influence over their larger, less homogenous constituencies (Maclachlan and Shimizu 2016a). Signaling further erosion of the organization's political power, the Abe government pushed through a revision of the Nōkyō Law in 2016 (George Mulgan 2016). The impact of this reform on the organizational structure is potentially far-reaching, including less control over the local cooperatives on behalf of JA Zenchū. Moreover, reflecting decreasing agricultural incomes and the growing political emphasis on fostering "agri-business," the cooperative organization now formally has the objective to "raise the agricultural income" of its members (Tashiro 2017).

Shifting the Focus to the "Local"

These changes notwithstanding, the chapter has also shown that they have been unfolding alongside and in interaction with old and new forms of intervention and support. The increasing ambiguity of the agricultural support and protection regime underlines the insufficiency of unidirectional and ultimately oversimplifying concepts such as "liberalization" to capture institutional change.[27] Moreover, it reveals the limitations of macro accounts to assess the renegotiation underneath and beyond ambiguous state policies and the gradual change of the production structure.

As a result of the ambiguity of the "bearer farm" concept, this change can take very different forms – including large-scale consolidation on behalf of corporate entrepreneurs, but also consolidation of land in hamlet-based collective farms, which provides a relatively large number of part-time farm households with access to continued subsidization, and potentially enables local JA to retain some control over farmers and farmland as the most likely local ordering force behind such efforts.[28] Thus, I argue that it makes a fundamental qualitative difference *what type* of "bearer farms" emerge, and how these farms relate to – socially as well as economically – their hamlets, other farms, and the respective local co-op and administration. As state policies have shifted responsibilities to organize farmland consolidation to local JA, administrations, and farmers themselves, the same local actors that struggle to secure continued support and/or influence have potential discretion over the local manifestation of agricultural reform. Against this background, the remainder of this book shifts the focus to the "local" to analyze how agricultural support and protection is renegotiated by the actors inhabiting this regime.

PART THREE

Local Agricultural Regimes and Village Institutions

Throughout Japan, farmers, local co-ops, and local governments have been translating agricultural reform into local practice since the mid-1990s. There are substantial local differences in how these local actors have implemented and interpreted national reform. Chapter 6 introduces several localities to illustrate different local manifestations of this process. In order to analyze these differences more systematically, this book captures the "local" in the Japanese agricultural support and protection regime as a juxtaposition of local agricultural regimes, which are roughly bounded by the (often overlapping) jurisdictions of municipalities and the local branches of the cooperative organization JA. Within these boundaries, the changing macro-level rules intersect with informal village institutions – local social network ties, and norms and practices surrounding, for example, the use and exchange of farmland. Each of these local agricultural regimes produces a variant of national reform, ranging from less organized to more organized approaches to farmland consolidation. Local agricultural regimes differ in many other respects as well, including their size, socioeconomic structure, topography, or dominant crops. Despite these differences, however, local agricultural regimes are made up of the same institutional elements and are "inhabited" by the same groups of actors – they are thus local institutional arenas that vary in quality, but not in principle. To support this argument, chapter 7 takes a historical perspective to illustrate the postwar formation of local agricultural regimes and discusses the emerging of village institutions as their contested and ambiguous social and normative underpinning.

Chapter Six

Different Local Manifestations of Macro-Level Change

To reiterate the argument laid out in the introduction, consolidation of the agricultural production structure – the core objective in agricultural reform since the mid-1990s – is a contested political process, in which farm households, emerging agri-businesses, local cooperatives, and local agricultural administrations are entangled in a web of risks, opportunities, and potentially conflicting interests.

With the local agricultural regime in Hikawa as the main reference point, this chapter provides a small glimpse into the broad variety of ways in which these local actors have translated national policies into local practice. These different local manifestations have a functional dimension (the extent to which farmland has been consolidated in the hands of designated "bearer farms") and a political dimension (what types of "bearer farms" have emerged, and how they relate to incumbent actors such as the cooperative organization and small-scale family farms), which can be expressed on a spectrum between "organization" and "disorganization" (Höpner 2007). In organized local agricultural regimes, substantial farmland consolidation in the hands of designated "bearer farms" goes hand-in-hand with relatively tight control over farmland use and farmers' economic decisions on behalf of the local agricultural administration and/or the local branch of the cooperative organization JA. Less organized local agricultural regimes lack public-cooperative control over farmland consolidation, which means that expanding (corporate) farms face a more complicated access to favorable land, but also more opportunities (and more pressure) to become independent entrepreneurs, while aging part-time farms are more likely to abandon commercial agriculture.

Disparate Neighbors: Agriculture in Hikawa and Izumo City

Hikawa is a town of roughly 28,000 inhabitants, located between Matsue City, the capital of Shimane Prefecture, and Izumo City, the prefecture's second-largest city and the site of the famous Izumo Taisha. In 2011, Hikawa was merged into Izumo City. Driving through the former town is hardly a memorable experience. The national road No. 9 cuts through Hikawa from Lake Shinji in the east to Izumo in the west. It is lined with shopping centers, restaurants, pachinko parlors, apartments, and office buildings, together constituting the common scenery alongside the main traffic arteries in non-metropolitan Japan. Every once in awhile, one can catch a glimpse of the hilly, forested, and less inhabited southern part of Hikawa, and the large plain in the north, all covered with paddy fields and sprinkled with small agricultural settlements. Astute observers might notice that the land on the plain is well-kept, and some plots are comparatively large. But far more likely, visitors will cross the bridge over the Hii River that marks Hikawa's western border and enter the older parts of Izumo City without noticing that they have been to Hikawa at all. Upon closer examination, however, the Hii River also separates the organized local agricultural regime in Hikawa from the less organized local agricultural regime in the rest of Izumo City.

On the functional dimension, the local regime in Hikawa is marked by a relatively high share of land in the hands of designated "bearer farms," and a relatively efficient use of farmland. In 2017, 79.2 per cent of the active farmland in Hikawa was concentrated in the hands of certified "bearer farms" and hamlet-based collective farms (Izumo City 2017). As of 2019, Hikawa's farmland consolidation rate was in the top 10 per cent of municipalities in Japan (see figure 6.2). The remarkable consolidation of the agricultural production structure in Hikawa did not happen automatically, nor was it achieved through the entrepreneurial aspirations of local "bearer farms" alone. Rather, it occurred primarily as a result of the intervention of the Hikawa Nōgyō Kōsha, a public corporation founded by the local agricultural administration and the co-op JA Hikawa in 1994. Since the early 2000s, the Kōsha has acquired land use rights from retiring part-time farmers and allocated them to designated "bearer farms." As the key feature of the system, the Kōsha has been allocating land use rights under unconditional authority, i.e., without the interference of landowners or users. This has allowed a more rational allocation of land to expanding farms over the 2000s, which receive connected plots whenever possible to decrease production costs (see chapter 8 for details).

The cohort of large-scale "bearer farms" in Hikawa includes ten incorporated farms, the largest of which cultivates more than fifty hectares, and as such falls within the top 1 per cent of large-scale farms in Japan. Yet a major contribution to farmland consolidation comes from hamlet-based collective farms, which cover around 40 per cent of the total acreage in town (Hikawa Town Agriculture and Forestry Office 2017, 18), again an extraordinarily high share in national comparison (MAFF 2017). Figure 6.1 shows the distribution of farmland in Hikawa as of 2017. There are very few white spots of paddy land that are used by neither a hamlet-based collective farm (light grey) nor certified (incorporated and non-incorporated) household farms cultivating more than five hectares (dark grey). With the relatively efficient redistribution of farmland, the Kōsha system has also prevented farmland loss and abandonment. Between 1995 and 2012, the number of farm households in town declined from 2447 to 1637 – but since almost all of their land was allocated to "bearer farms," the overall amount of arable land decreased by only 32 hectares over the same time (Hikawa Town 1997; Hikawa Town Agriculture and Forestry Office 2013), and virtually no land has fallen idle (0.3 per cent in 2015; see Izumo City 2017).

The political dimension of the organized local agricultural regime extends beyond the objective to raise land use efficiency. The Kōsha system has allowed for the consolidation of the local farm sector on behalf of – and under control of – the local administration and the local co-op JA Hikawa. The emerging large-scale (corporate) farms in town have thus remained constrained in their economic freedom, not least because they cannot expand on their own behalf. As one pillar of the Kōsha system and a key actor within the local agricultural regime as a whole, the local JA Hikawa has retained a strong position socially, organizationally, and economically. In 2013, more than twenty years after deregulation of the domestic rice market gained momentum, all farms in Hikawa – including the largest corporate farms – still marketed virtually all their paddy field products via the local co-op (H-IF1; H-GS1). Meanwhile, the interests of smaller household farms are represented as well, as reflected in the proliferation of subsidy-productive hamlet-based collective farms. Moreover, farm households that want to reduce their acreage or give up farming can rely on a trusted system to pass on their land use rights.

Beyond farmland redistribution and proliferation of hamlet-based collective farming, the local agricultural regime in Hikawa has allowed local actors to accommodate changes in national subsidy policies to continue to harvest state support. For example, the Kōsha has administered a local scheme to organize rice production control, under which some or all tasks related to crop rotation are allocated from smaller farms to the cohort of large-scale "bearer farms." The incoming subsidies are then distributed between landowners and cultivators.

Figure 6.1. Farmland Distribution in Hikawa Town

Source: Hikawa Town Agriculture and Forestry Office (2017, 18).

As a result, even the plots of smaller holdings can often yield three crops in two years. In 2012, the paddy field utilization rate in Hikawa had reached 116 per cent, which is far above the prefectural and the national level (78 and 92 per cent respectively; see Izumo City 2013). Again, however, these efficiency gains are not the only aspect of this local rice production control scheme. It has also provided smaller farms, which cannot grow anything but rice, with access to paddy field subsidies they would otherwise be unable to receive, and thus stabilized the inflow of state support to the local agricultural sector as a whole, even during more exclusive subsidization and the aging of the farming population. Moreover, it has reinforced the role of large-scale farms as the extended arms of the agricultural administration – or "quasi-public infrastructures" (Höpner 2007) which fulfill a role that extends beyond maximizing their profits. In sum, while the organized local agricultural regime in Hikawa embraced the notion of raising efficiency, it has also muted the more liberal aspects of national agricultural reform since the

1990s – thus displaying a successful implementation and a remarkably selective local interpretation of this process.

Izumo City

Even though Hikawa became a part of Izumo City in 2011, the Kōsha system still ends at the banks of the Hii River as of writing this book. Despite numerous initiatives, neither the local cooperative JA Izumo (since 2015 a branch of the prefecture-wide JA Shimane) nor the local agricultural administration have been exerting a similar level of control over farmland use in the older parts of Izumo City. Consolidation of the agricultural production structure is far less advanced. As of 2017, 42.5 per cent of farmland under cultivation in Izumo (excluding Hikawa) was concentrated in the hands of "bearer farms," i.e., only little more than half of the consolidation rate in Hikawa, and below the national average of 52 per cent (MAFF 2016b). Many farmers have retreated from commercial farming or gave up as the result of aging and less generous agricultural support policies. Between 1995 and 2005 alone, the share of self-consumption farm households doubled from 17 to 33 per cent (JA Izumo 2010, 11). In sharp contrast to Hikawa, this development went hand-in-hand with farmland abandonment and farmland loss. In 2010, JA Izumo (16) reported that the acreage of abandoned land increased from 214 hectares in 1995 to 1072 hectares in 2005, i.e., almost 20 per cent of the arable land in Izumo at that time (excluding Hikawa, calculation based on JA Izumo 2010). Between 2000 and 2015, farmland under cultivation by commercial farms in Izumo (excluding Hikawa) decreased by 25 per cent, from 5,175 hectares to 3,902 hectares (JA Izumo 2010, Izumo City 2017). For 2015, the agricultural administration in Izumo City reported a share of abandoned land of 4 per cent (excluding Hikawa, see Izumo City 2017). Yet, especially compared to Hikawa, the information on land use and land abandonment in Izumo City is insufficient and often inconsistent, as a representative of JA Izumo admitted in late 2013 (I-JA1). It is thus safe to assume that more land was de facto not in use or is about to fall idle when the large number of aging self-consumption farm households give up agriculture without a designated successor to take over their tiny, scattered plots.

While "bearer farmers" in Izumo have a less organized access to connected plots of arable land and state support than in Hikawa, they are also subject to fewer institutional constraints on their entrepreneurial freedom. Recently, a small number of business-minded livestock and horticulture/vegetable farms have emerged in Izumo, signaling an approach to agriculture different from the longstanding over-reliance on (subsidized) paddy field cultivation (H-O1).[1] As of June 2019, among the ten "bearer farms" with the highest annual sales volume in Izumo (excluding Hikawa), seven were incorporated farms, and not one of them cultivated rice. Two of the largest farms run their own marketing or processing enterprises and do not rely on JA at all. In general, while the number of certified "bearer farms" has been decreasing, corporatization of large farms in Izumo is steadily progressing, thus indicating a consolidation by fewer, more professional holdings.[2] This does not mean that "bearer farmers" in general have turned their backs on JA. JA still handles the major portion of rice and grapes in Izumo, which make a relatively large share of the agricultural output in the older parts of the city (Izumo City 2017). Izumo has also seen emergence of subsidy-productive hamlet-based collective farms (Tashiro 2010), and the local branch of JA has remained involved in issues of local agricultural governance beyond marketing, including the promotion of "bearer farms" and land use (I-JA1). Yet neither the local administration nor JA holds coherent control over consolidation of the local agricultural production structure. This lower level of organization leaves space for – and requires – entrepreneurial responses to changing national policies on behalf of (corporate) farms, while offering fewer instruments to govern a more rational use of land or to prevent farmland abandonment.

Introducing Local Variety

Located right next to each other – and since 2011 even within the same municipality – Hikawa and Izumo represent potential differences between local manifestations of agricultural reform particularly well. To place these differences in context, figure 6.2 shows the share of farmland consolidation in the hands of "bearer farms" for selected municipalities (box) and the distribution of farmland consolidation ratios across all Japanese municipalities (bars and trendline). Farmland consolidation in Izumo (excluding Hikawa) is above the median value of 33.4 per cent – that is, the majority of municipalities have even lower farmland consolidation rates. Yet the data also include municipalities in which a high level of farmland consolidation cannot be expected for different reasons, such as unfavorable topographical conditions, depopulation, or a high degree of urbanization (see below). Thus farmland consolidation in Izumo City (excluding Hikawa) can be considered relatively normal. It is therefore also safe to assume that limited farmland consolidation, an increasing differentiation between a few professional agri-businesses and a growing number of aging (non-commercial) farm households, and (impeding) land loss reflect the dominant direction of structural change in Japan's agricultural sector, while organized local responses

Figure 6.2. Distribution of Share of Land in Hands of "Bearer Farms" across Municipalities, March 2019

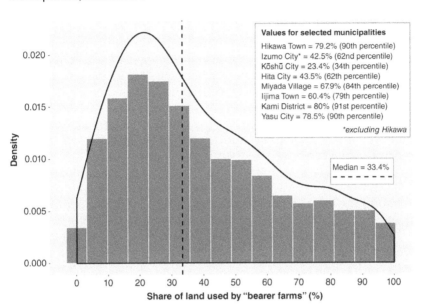

Source: Author's calculation based on data obtained directly from the MAFF in November 2019. Values for Izumo (excluding Hikawa) and Hikawa are taken from Izumo City (2017).
Note: The bars and the trendline indicate how many municipalities lie within a certain ratio of farmland consolidation, relative to the median value of all municipalities. The box gives the exact consolidation rates of selected municipalities discussed in this volume. Municipalities with a total amount of arable land < 30 ha and municipalities with consolidation rates of 0 per cent / > 100 per cent / no data were excluded.

to national reform are relatively unusual. On the other hand, however, Hikawa is also not the only local agricultural regime to display high levels of farmland consolidation (> 60 per cent) and/or elements of organization, including comprehensive public-cooperative control over the use and exchange of farmland. Further examples illustrate the broad variety of the local manifestations of national reform.

Variants of Collective Farmland Use in Miyada, Iijima, and Kami

Miyada Village and Iijima Town in the Kami-Ina Valley in Nagano Prefecture are prominent examples of localities that have built comprehensive institutions to organize farmland use and agricultural production with strong emphasis on collective farmland use (Tashiro 2009; Hoshi and Yamazaki 2015). Like in the Izumo region, agriculture in the Kami-Ina Valley is dominated by wet-paddy farming and has thus been confronted with the rapid aging of the mostly part-time agricultural labor force and the pressure to expand farm sizes. Yet local administrations and local chapters of the agricultural cooperative JA Kami-Ina have transformed the agricultural production structure in line with national policy, with strong emphasis on collective land use. In Miyada, farmland in the village has been practically "socialized" since 1980. The use and exchange of farmland is governed by a local farmland use committee, which includes local agricultural administration and the local branch of JA Kami-Ina. The system extends down to the hamlet level. In 2005, all paddy land in the village was formally consolidated in one collective farm, which secures continued access to the full array of state support for wet paddy farming. In 2015, the farm became a corporation (Jentzsch 2017c).

In Iijima Town, the "farm management center" coordinates the use and exchange of farmland on the basis of institutionalized cooperation between the local branch of JA Kami-Ina, the agricultural administration, and farmers themselves. Here, too, a large portion of the paddy land is cultivated by forms of collective farming that fall into the politically sponsored "bearer farm" category, creating a relatively high farmland consolidation rate of more than 60 per cent in 2019 (see figure 6.2). Despite their similarities and their spatial and organizational proximity (both localities belong to the same amalgamated local cooperative, JA Kami-Ina), the local agricultural regimes also display differences in their institutional setup and character. For example, the farm sector in Iijima Town has recently seen intensification of (corporate) agricultural entrepreneurship, diversification, and professionalization (Hoshi and Yamazaki 2015), while the local agricultural regime in Miyada Village remains predominantly geared toward sustaining highly subsidized part-time rice farming under the umbrella of the influential local cooperative branch, and with a strong normative orientation toward community preservation (M-O; see chapter 10 for details). Both local regimes, however, have prevented farmland abandonment with some success (JA-IT Kenkyūkai 2014).

In a similarly comprehensive local turn to collective farming, all hamlets in Kami District (including Shikama Town and Kami Town) in Miyagi Prefecture concentrated their paddy land in sixty-nine hamlet-based collective farms in response to the more exclusive paddy-field subsidization scheme that came into effect in 2007. This sudden and comprehensive turn to hamlet-based collective farming resulted in substantial farmland consolidation (80 per cent in 2019, see figure 6.2). It was organized by the local JA Kami Yotsuba, which has served both towns in the district since a cooperative merger in 1999 (K-JA1). More examples with similar characteristics can be found throughout Japan.[3]

Disorganization and Bifurcation in Kōshū City

Kōshū City is located in the eastern part of the Kōfu Basin (Yamanashi Prefecture). Surrounded by high mountains, the basin is densely populated and agriculturally active. In contrast to the Izumo area, the agricultural production structure is dominated by small-scale horticulture (mainly grapes and peaches), while rice plays virtually no role.[4] Illustrating growing differentiation within the agricultural support and protection regime, horticulture farmers in the basin have no access to the income support measures that apply to rice farmers and have long been far less protected from global market forces. In general, production of crops such as fruit, vegetables, and livestock is more commercialized than rice (Yamashita 2015a), not least because it is less land-intensive. This is also true for the Kōfu Basin, where even small farm households with less than one hectare of land continue to produce commercially.[5] Farm households tend to have direct marketing ties with longstanding customers in the Tōkyō area or the local wine industry. Yet most farms are also organized in shipping cooperatives at the hamlet level, which are typically (but not necessarily) associated with JA. JA also supplies the local wine industry, especially the larger enterprises (Kingsbury 2012).

Kōfu Basin contains several municipalities and cooperative districts, the boundaries of which were massively redrawn through cooperative and municipal mergers in the 2000s. The result is a patchwork of local agricultural (sub-)regimes governing the relation between types of farms, (former) local cooperative branches, and the local wine industry. In the eastern part of the basin, the agricultural cooperative JA Fruits Yamanashi covers the area of the amalgamated cities Kōshū and Yamanashi, and a small part of Fuefuki City. Within the cooperative district, the former town of Katsunuma – now part of Kōshū City and the historical center of the local wine industry – has retained a local agricultural sub-regime with elements of organization. The local administration, the Katsunuma chapter of JA Fruits Yamanashi, and the Katsunuma Winery Association have, inter alia, been regulating the price for wine grapes.

Despite such local elements of organization, however, transformation of the agricultural production structure in the basin has been far less organized than in Hikawa. Neither Kōshū City nor any other municipality in the basin displays comprehensive institutions to govern farmland use and exchange. In March 2019, the share of land in the hands of "bearer farms" in Kōshū City was only 23.4 per cent (see figure 6.2). Farmland under cultivation by commercial farms decreased by around 25 per cent between 1995 and 2015, from 2,065 to 1,541 hectares. The rapidly aging workforce and lack of successors cause a growing share of plots to remain unused. In 2015, 11 per cent of the arable land in Kōshū City was classified as abandoned (Zenkoku Nōgyō Kaigijo 2016; data on 1995 obtained from KB-Op1). Remaining land is still mostly cultivated by small household farms, which are unwilling or unable to respond to the policy incentives to expand and professionalize their businesses. Meanwhile, a small but growing cohort of (corporate) entrepreneurial farms has fully embraced subsidy-productive national policies to promote professionalization, corporatization, and diversification. These emerging agri-businesses tend to employ (subsidized) regular labor and engage in processing, direct marketing, and/or professional contract farming, and act with increasing independence from JA (e.g., KB-F1; KB-F2; KB-F6). In the absence of organized control over the process of consolidating the production structure, these farms exemplify the bifurcation between traditional small-scale, rapidly aging, and typically cooperatively organized farm households, and a small group of expanding entrepreneurial farms with diversified business models and preferential access to state support – a development that bears some similarities with the disorganized local agricultural regime in Izumo City (excluding Hikawa).

Sub-local Heterogeneity in Hita City

Hita City in Ōita Prefecture is marked by a heterogeneous local agricultural production structure with limited progress in farmland consolidation. The main agricultural products in Hita are rice in the plain areas, and horticulture products in mountainous areas. The Hita chapter of the amalgamated JA Ōita has been promoting the branding and the export of "Hita melons." Like in Izumo and the Kōfu Basin, there is no comprehensive public-cooperative control over farmland use in Hita. Between 1995 and 2015, the share of self-consumption farm households rose from 37 to 51 per cent, while farmland under cultivation by commercial farms decreased from 2,310 to 1,847 hectares. Seven per cent of the total farmland was classified as abandoned by the local agricultural committee in 2015 (Hita City 2017, 9–10). As of 2019, 43 per cent of farmland in Hita is consolidated by "bearer farms," i.e., close to Izumo City (excluding Hikawa). Farmland consolidation is partly due to hamlet-based collective farming, including a large incorporated collective farm that spans seventeen hamlets in a rice farming area that covers a former town south of the city center (Ht-CF). Yet, especially in the more remote parts of the municipality, there is a lack of "bearer farms" and acute or impeding farmland loss (Ht-O).

Within the boundaries of Hita City, however, the mountainous former town of Ōyama has retained a distinct, highly organized local agricultural sub-regime. Agriculture in Ōyama is dominated by the small-scale production of chestnuts, plums, and vegetables. Local farm households have successfully diversified, processed, and marketed their products under the leadership of the local Ōyama Agricultural Cooperative, which has refused to join the amalgamated JA Ōita. The local co-op enforces an organized, community-oriented approach to agriculture, which reinforces small-scale household farming as a source of additional household income, while explicitly refuting the national policy goals of professionalization and scale-enlargement (O-JA).

Agriculture in Yasu between Organization and Disorganization

The agricultural sector in Yasu City (Shiga Prefecture) displays characteristics that differ from organized regimes such as Hikawa, Miyada, or Ōyama, but also from less organized regimes such as Izumo and Kōshū. Yasu is a densely populated municipality on the southern shore of Lake Biwa. Within commuting distance of the Kansai metropolitan region, the city has a growing and relatively young population. More than 95 per cent of arable land in the city is used for wet-paddy rice cultivation, and the land has been subject to an unusually high degree of land improvement (98 per cent of paddy land). Under these favorable conditions, the local agricultural production structure has changed in line with major policy trends since the early 2000s to an exceptional degree. By 2015, the share of land used by "bearer farms" in Yasu had increased to 70.3 per cent, and the average farm size had reached 2.46 hectares, about twice as much as in 1995 (Yasu City 2017). In March 2019, farmland consolidation in Yasu – like Hikawa – fell in the top 10 per cent of all municipalities (see figure 6.2). Moreover, despite a sharp decrease in the number of farm households, the share of abandoned land even declined since 2005, against the national and prefectural trend. Only about 1.7 per cent of the total arable land in Yasu was classified as abandoned in 2015 (compared to 5.1 per cent in the prefecture; see JA Ōmifuji 2017). Agricultural production in Yasu is also shaped by forms of hamlet-based collective farming. All farm hamlets in town have long engaged in block rotation in the context of the rice production control policy. Other than in Hikawa, Miyada, or Kami, however, they are not certified "bearer farms" but remain informal associations, mainly to co-ordinate rice production control (Y-O2).

The most important difference from Hikawa is that consolidation of the production structure in Yasu is not the result of comprehensive control over farmland transfers on behalf of the administration or the local JA Ōmifuji (which also serves the neighboring Moriyama City). As one consequence, large farms in Yasu have more fragmented holdings than in Hikawa. Moreover, there is intense competition for land in plain areas, but farmland loss (or impeding farmland loss) in less preferential areas. The agricultural administration does not (and is not able to) intervene in the prices for farmland leases and has very limited capacities to govern farmland redistribution (Y-O2). Still, agriculture in Yasu also displays some elements of organization. Transformation of the local agricultural production structure has been spearheaded by one of the earliest and largest agricultural production corporations in Japan, which has expanded its holdings to more than two hundred hectares by 2017. This pioneer farm has remained closely associated with the local agricultural administration and the local co-op, and to some extent acts as a private ordering force in the local agricultural regime. This includes, for example, taking on less favorable plots of land and supporting hamlet-based farms, both of which meet the objective of the local agricultural administration to balance the interests of expanding "bearer farms" and small-scale farm households (Yasu City 2017).

Making Sense of Local Variety

The localities introduced above offer a glimpse of the broad variety of local manifestations of national agricultural reform. How can we make sense of these differences? There is no simple answer, because consolidation of the agricultural production structure depends on many factors, including topographical features and the local socioeconomic situation. Mountainous and remote areas with higher aging rates and fewer opportunities for large-scale wet-paddy farming are structurally disadvantaged in farmland consolidation. Yet, especially in western Japan, such disadvantaged areas also display high shares of hamlet-based collective farming, which emerged as a means to adapt to the double pressure of agricultural reform and demographic aging (Kitagawa 2008; Yamamoto 2011). The dominance of crops other than rice also affects consolidation. Land use rights for horticulture land are harder to exchange than wet-paddy land, since the land-taker will have to either use the existing fruit trees or remove them to plant a new crop, which is both costly and time-consuming (KB-JA1). Thus, the mountainous Kōshū City is more prone to land loss than Yasu or Hikawa, where well-developed plain paddy-land makes for a large part of the respective localities. On the other hand, horticulture is less land-intensive, and the products are easier to process and/or to market directly than staple foods such as rice or soy. This means that even a small acreage can be the basis for a viable, independent agricultural business. Horticulture products are also less politicized. In general, we can thus expect rice farming areas to have higher consolidation rates, and potentially also a stronger and more influential local cooperative than horticulture areas.

To assess the impact of socioeconomic factors, figures 6.3–6.5 show the demographic characteristics (population density, proportion of elderly residents), industrial structure, and fiscal strength[6] of the localities introduced in this chapter in relation to all municipalities in Japan in 2000 and 2015.

Protracted Local Institution-Building

Most strikingly, the data show that Yasu City (and here especially the former Yasu Town) stands out as a fiscally and demographically stable municipality, with a high population density and a low share of employment in the primary sector. These characteristics have supported the relatively successful farmland consolidation in Yasu. The urban industrial structure and the proximity to the Kansai metropolitan area make for good local off-farm employment opportunities, which means that fewer young residents leave the city, and increases the pool of potential successors to take over farmland. According to local officials, a relatively high share of landowners still resides in the city, thus facilitating the exchange of land use rights (Y-O2). In contrast, a large share of absent landowners obstructs farmland consolidation (see chapter 8). Moreover, a positive demographic development and the presence of large companies also stabilizes the local fiscal situation, which in turn can have positive effects on the agricultural infrastructure, as illustrated by the high share of well-developed paddy land in Yasu (Yasu City 2017). Well-developed land facilitates farmland consolidation, because the use rights for standardized plots of paddy land can be exchanged relatively easily, and the land is accessible for large-scale machinery, which makes it attractive for professional, more capital-intensive farms.

Albeit to a lesser extent, Hikawa also displays relative socioeconomic stability, including employment opportunities in the secondary sector and a positive demographic development, which some respondents

Figure 6.3. Demographic Characteristics of Selected Localities Relative to Median Value of All Municipalities in Japan, 2000 and 2015

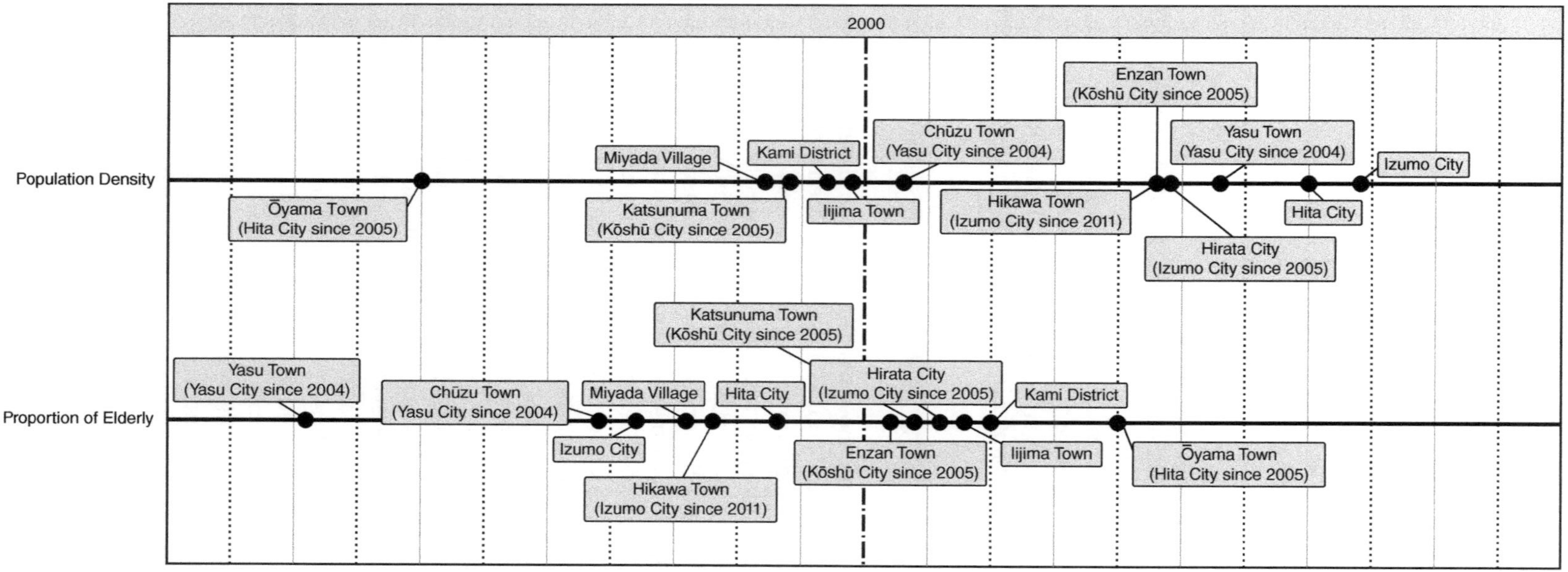

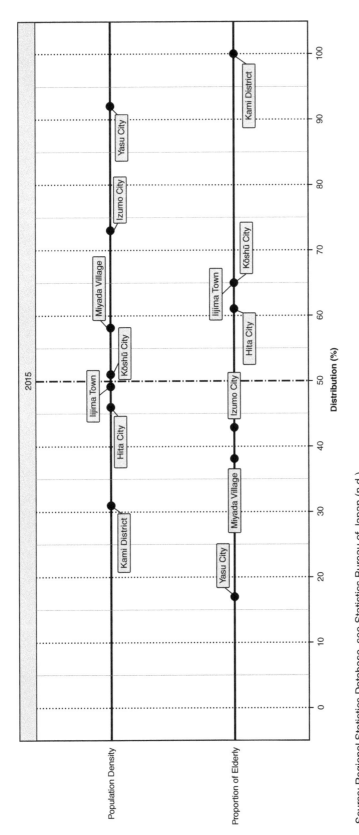

Source: Regional Statistics Database, see Statistics Bureau of Japan (n.d.).

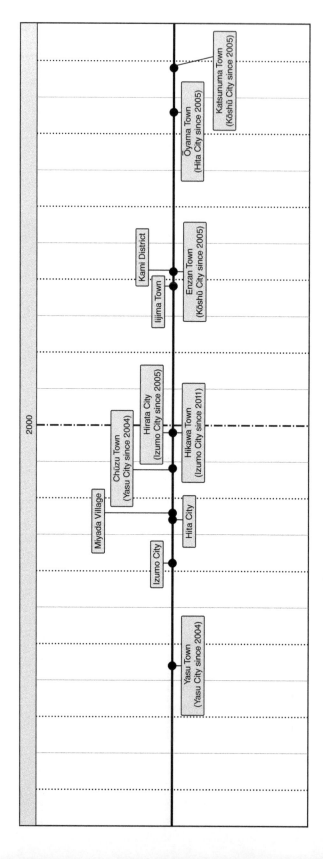

Figure 6.4. Share of Employment in the Primary Sector in Selected Localities Relative to Median Value of All Municipalities in Japan, 2000 and 2015

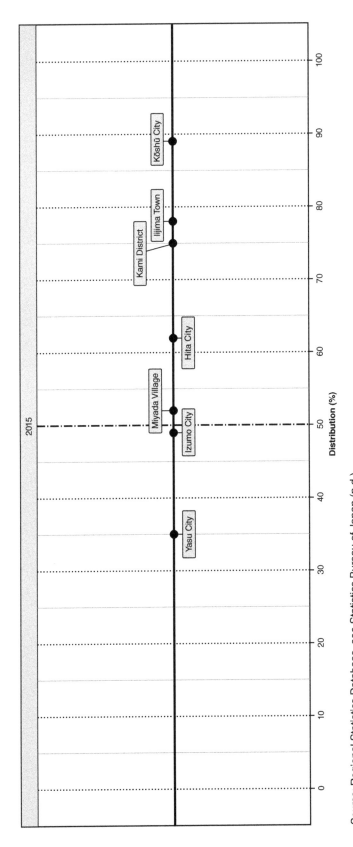

2015

Distribution (%)

Kōshū City

Iijima Town

Kami District

Hita City

Miyada Village

Izumo City

Yasu City

Source: Regional Statistics Database, see Statistics Bureau of Japan (n.d.).

Figure 6.5. Fiscal Strength Index of Selected Localities Relative to Median Value of All Municipalities in Japan, 2000 and 2015

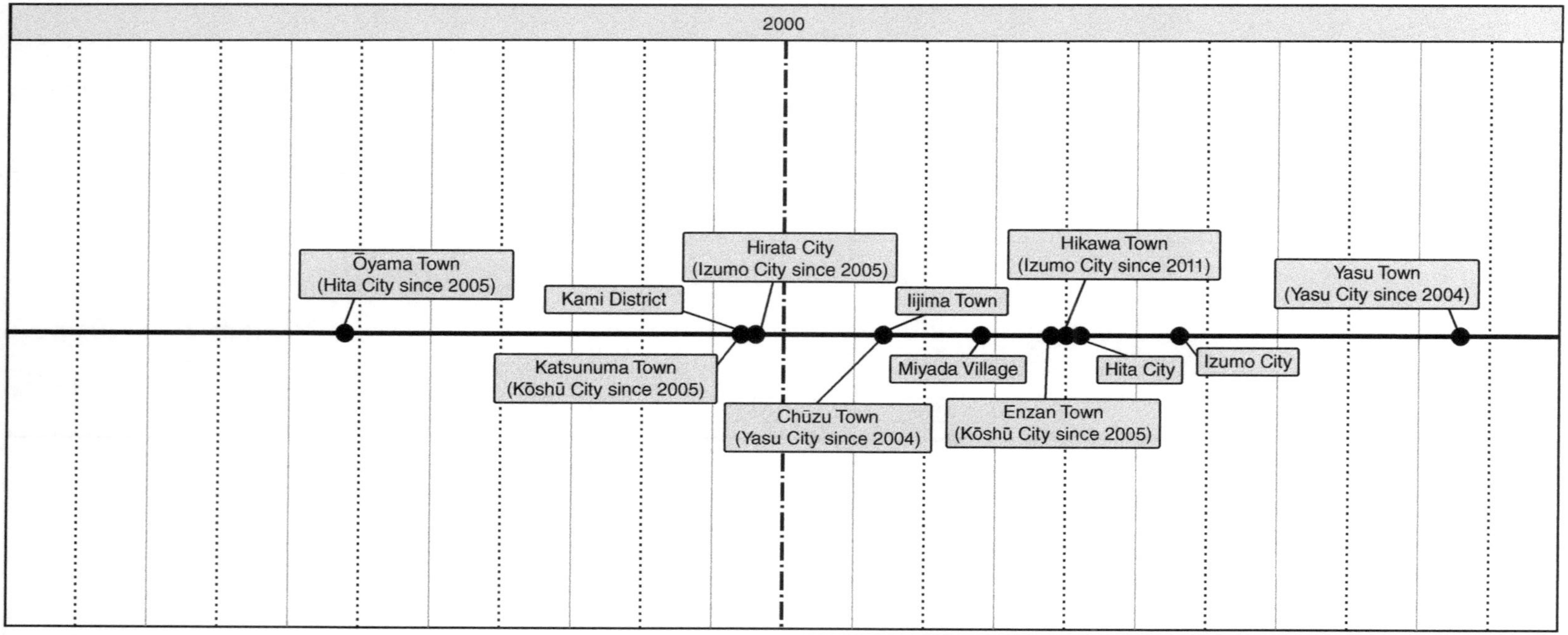

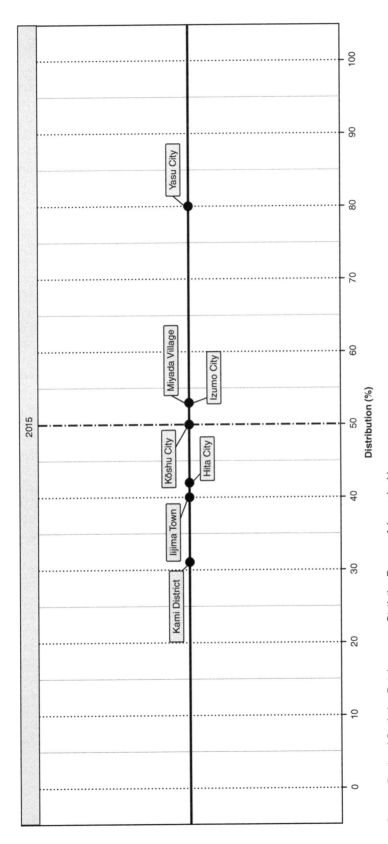

2015

Distribution (%)

Yasu City

Miyada Village

Izumo City

Kōshu City

Hita City

Iijima Town

Kami District

Source: Regional Statistics Database, see Statistics Bureau of Japan (n.d.).

have linked to the success of the Kōsha system (H-F4b). Iijima Town and Kami District are weaker in demographic terms, but (like Miyada) have a relatively high share of employment in the secondary sector. The availability of off-farm employment might have sustained (part-time) rice farming and – closely related – supported the strong proliferation of hamlet-based collective farms in these localities. In contrast, the former town of Katsunuma (now Kōshū City) is not only marked by horticulture farming and a mountainous topography, but also faces a relatively critical socioeconomic situation, the combination of which helps to explain the particularly high share of abandoned land in Kōshū City.

Beyond such obvious differences, however, the picture is rather inconsistent. In the remote and mountainous former town of Ōyama (now Hita City) – a very rural locality in its socioeconomic profile – farmland has mostly remained in use. Here, the rural characteristics seem to have *supported* development of commercially successful agricultural diversification organized by the local co-op (O-JA). Small-scale horticulture farming thus does not necessarily lead to land abandonment, weak cooperative structures, and individual entrepreneurship.

Moreover, it is important to note that neither the availability of plain and well-developed land nor the proximity to urban centers necessarily leads to higher levels of farmland consolidation. Much to the contrary, developed land in or around larger settlements is also most suitable for urban development – and even more so in the outskirts of the metropolitan centers along the Pacific Coast, where land prices skyrocketed before the burst of the economic bubble. In many localities, urban development has led to a patchwork of agricultural, residential, and commercial land use, which now obscures farmland consolidation (Gōdo 2007). While a stable socioeconomic situation and favorable topographic features certainly facilitate a high share of farmland consolidation, the explanatory power of this constellation thus remains limited. When farmland consolidation in Hikawa gained momentum around the year 2000, the town's socioeconomic profile did not display striking differences relative to Japanese municipalities in general. In fact, it was similar to neighboring Izumo City, which also had a relatively urban industrial structure and a stable fiscal situation. Still, farmland consolidation subsequently took very different paths in these neighboring localities. These differences are somewhat related to the fact that the urban core of Izumo and the remote mountainous areas are structurally disadvantaged for farmland consolidation. Yet, even in the former city of Hirata – a plain and relatively rural part of Izumo City north of Hikawa – the acreage of abandoned land increased rapidly from 41 to 205 hectares between 1995 and 2005 (JA Izumo 2010). Such differences suggest that local governance of farmland affects farmland consolidation in specific ways that cannot fully be explained by the socioeconomic and topographical situation.

The intent of this brief discussion is not to downplay the relevance of topographic and socioeconomic factors. Thorough quantitative analysis would produce a more systematic understanding of how these factors relate to each other, and to local differences in consolidation of the agricultural production structure. Yet this is not the analytical focus of this book, which aims to investigate local differences in the *quality* of farmland consolidation – that is, to what extent, how, and by whom access to farmland and state support is organized, or in other words the actual process of renegotiating the local agricultural support and protection regime.[7]

In-depth analysis of the Hikawa case reveals that the organized local agricultural regime is the result of protracted local institution-building, which rests not least on integration of local social ties and (hamlet-level) norms and practices, or village institutions. Within the overlapping social, spatial, and political boundaries of the local agricultural cooperative JA Hikawa (1961–2015) and the town (1955–2011), these village institutions have provided the social and normative foundation for the Kōsha system. Similarly, the organized approach to collective farmland use in Miyada Village also rests upon longstanding cooperation between the local cooperative branch and the local administration, and integration of hamlet-level social ties and norms surrounding farmland use into local agricultural governance. More generally, I argue that the specific ways in which village institutions have been integrated into local agricultural regimes in Japan have shaped the different local responses to agricultural reform since the mid-1990s. Before this argument is developed in more detail in part 4, the following chapter directs attention to the principal *similarities* of local agricultural regimes and discusses the postwar emergence of village institutions as the social and normative foundations of these local regimes.

Chapter Seven

Postwar Formation of Local Agricultural Regimes and Village Institutions

This chapter takes a broader historical perspective on the postwar formation of local agricultural regimes. From this vantage point, the local agricultural regime in Hikawa does not represent an outlier – rather, it emerged as a variant of a process that has patterned the "local" in the agricultural support and protection regime throughout postwar Japan. All local agricultural regimes share a basic set of actors and a formal framework. In each municipality – the lowest level of administration in the postwar Japanese state – the main actors involved in local agricultural governance are the responsible branch(es) or office(s) of the local government, the local agricultural cooperative, and farmers. Further important actors are local agricultural committees, which oversee the use, exchange, and transformation of farmland at the municipal level, and land improvement districts, which are farmers' associations to solicit land improvement projects and maintain irrigation facilities. As a result of their history as territorial institutions and their close association with the state, local agricultural cooperatives have typically mirrored local administrative boundaries. Together, municipal and cooperative jurisdictions have thus constituted the spatial and political boundaries of local agricultural regimes. Within these boundaries, the formal framework intersects with informal village institutions, which make up the social and normative underpinning of local agricultural regimes.

The Emerging Boundaries of Postwar Local Agricultural Regimes

Hikawa Village was founded in 1955, from the merger of an area historically referred to as the "Six Villages of Naoe-bu." As a result of its demographic development, the village became a town in the early 1960s, but this change did not affect its administrative boundaries

(Ikeda 1972). In 1961, Hikawa Nōkyō (called JA Hikawa since 1992) was established through the merger of six local cooperatives that had each served one of the "Villages of Naoe-bu." Thus, both the postwar town of Hikawa and the cooperative continued to operate within longstanding spatial, social, and political boundaries. In this respect, Hikawa represents a development that was typical for postwar Japan. Hikawa was founded in the context of the Shōwa amalgamation (1953–7), a wave of municipal mergers that fundamentally shaped the administrative landscape of postwar Japan. The number of municipalities dropped from more than 10,500 at the end of the Pacific War to about 3,800 in 1957 (Fukutake 1980, 166; Kramer 2015). Like in Hikawa, many local cooperatives – which had already mirrored the administrative landscape – soon followed the redrawn municipal boundaries after the Shōwa amalgamation. Consequently, the number of local cooperatives dropped sharply in the 1960s. Larger municipalities often had more than one local cooperative operating within their jurisdictions, which typically echoed the boundaries of pre-amalgamation towns and villages. Over the following decades, however, many of these smaller co-ops merged as well, partly for economic reasons, but also in response to political pressure on the co-ops to mirror municipal boundaries (Tashiro 2018, 12–17). As a result, the number of local cooperatives eventually drew near the number of municipalities (see figure 7.1). Meanwhile, exceptions notwithstanding, municipal boundaries remained mostly stable, until the "Heisei mergers" between 2002 and 2006 brought a new wave of drastic municipal restructuring, the disruptive effects of which will be discussed separately in chapter 11.

In Hikawa, the local agricultural administration, the agricultural committee, the local branch of the prefectural agricultural administration, and the land improvement district have all been integrated in the "Hikawa Agriculture and Forestry Office" since the early postwar years. JA Hikawa (then still called Hikawa Nōkyō) became a statutory member of this administrative body in 1963. The newly amalgamated co-op erected its massive new headquarters right next to the local government building in 1965. Again, this alignment is typical for many localities throughout Japan. It physically demonstrates the proximity between the cooperative and public administrations. Given their quasi-public tasks in local agricultural governance, local cooperative branches came to be known as "second local administrations" in the emerging postwar state (George Mulgan 2000, 209). The close association between local co-ops and local governments was reinforced through national regulations. For example, local cooperatives were granted influence over local farmland governance through statutory membership of cooperative

Figure 7.1. Development in Number of Local Cooperatives and Municipalities in Postwar Era

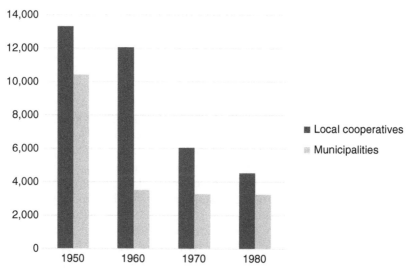

Source: Ishida (2002).

representatives in the respective local agricultural committees – the public bodies overseeing farmland issues on the municipal level (see chapter 4). Thus, while formal integration of public administration and cooperative organization has been particularly strong in Hikawa, it also exemplifies a pattern of local agricultural governance that is taken for granted by farmers, officials, and co-op staff throughout Japan, even in less organized local agricultural regimes such as in Izumo City or the Kōfu Basin.[1]

Land improvement districts (LID) are another crucial element of local agricultural governance. LIDs are set up on farmers' initiative to manage issues that range from raising funds for land improvement projects to taking responsibility for maintenance of dams or irrigation canals. As such, they are formally independent from both the local administration and the cooperative. Yet close cooperation among the three – such as in Hikawa – has not been uncommon, not least since farmers' membership in land improvement district and local cooperatives was very likely to overlap, and local governments had an interest in coordinating the inflow of prefectural and national funds for land improvement projects (George Mulgan 2000, 80–2; Latz 1989).

Together, local cooperative districts and post-amalgamation towns and villages came to form the spatial, political, and social boundaries of postwar local agricultural regimes, the local arenas in which the emerging agricultural support and protection regime was enacted. Closely associated with each other, local cooperatives and local governments executed national policies and programs such as the rice acreage reduction policy (*gentan*) and – together with land improvement districts – acted as "the key units through which many of the postwar agricultural programs have been channeled" to the local level (Kelly 1990b, 216). Beyond agricultural support in the narrow sense, this also included allocation of public works projects as a particularly prolific means for politicians to "pay back" their local electorates (George Mulgan 2001, 2006c; Matanle, Rausch, and the Shrinking Regions Research Group 2011; Gōdo 2007). Against the background of these historically grown relations, local co-ops, local agricultural administrations, and farmers have also taken on responsibility to draft local plans for farmland consolidation in the hands of "bearer farms" since the mid-1990s.

Village Institutions: Changing Social and Normative Foundations
of Local Agricultural Regimes

Beyond their formal framework, local agricultural regimes rest on informal *village institutions*. The term is intentionally vague, in that it encapsulates local social ties, as well as traditional norms and practices that surround agricultural production, cooperation, or the use and exchange of farmland. Historically, village institutions have revolved around the farm hamlet as the most important element of rural social organization in Japan. Rapid socioeconomic changes in the early postwar decades have deeply affected the traditional patterns of rural social organization. Yet these patterns have not simply faded away. On the one hand, hamlets were integrated into postwar administrative and political structures, and on the other hand, the emerging agricultural support and protection regime allowed many farm households to continue farming as a side-business (and a lifestyle), which has weakened the effects of de-agriculturalization that can be observed in other industrialized countries, and preserved the farm hamlet as a crucial social unit, despite its decreasing agricultural character (Hisano, Akitsu, and McGreevy 2018). At the same time, however, farmers and other rural dwellers also gained new opportunities for social, political, and economic interaction beyond and across hamlet boundaries, but often within the borders of the respective local agricultural cooperatives and/or towns and villages. As a result, the social and normative underpinning of local agricultural regimes came to be constituted by multifaceted, ambiguous, and potentially contradictive sets of what I call village institutions. This process deserves more attention.

Farm Hamlet

Over centuries, farm hamlets – clusters of usually fewer than 100 house-holds – have been the "bedrock of rural society" (Jussaume 1991, 53) in Japan. Historically, these natural settlements are best characterized as mutually dependent "agricultural production units" (Fukutake 1980). Hamlets have a long history of creating and enforcing rules about how, when, and by whom the land in the hamlet could be used (Dore 1984, 354). These rules rest upon the notion that the farmland within the hamlet boundaries is a *collective resource*. It went hand-in-hand with the "basic, and enduring, principle ... that 'the land in the mura should be used for the benefit of those who live in the mura'" (Iwamoto 2003, 222). Deeply rooted in Japan's institutional history, this notion has also sur-vived the onset of private ownership rights in the nineteenth century, and postwar de-agriculturalization (Iwamoto 2003). This is not least because land use in Japan has been inseparably connected to water use and irrigation, the coordination of which was essential for wet-paddy rice cultivation. Hamlets have created and maintained complex irriga-tion systems (Haley 2010, 318), which have further reinforced a territo-rial logic of social organization within clearly demarcated boundaries. Upon the foundation of farmland and irrigation control, hamlets came to be bound together by "a lasting quality of mutual assistance in social rituals and ceremonies, marriages, funerals, or festivals, as well as of cooperation among neighbors in the construction and repair of homes and farm buildings" (Fukutake 1980, 75).[2] At least until the end of the Pacific War – and even longer in more remote areas – these hamlet rela-tions fundamentally shaped the lives of the majority of Japanese (Jus-saume 1991).

The contemporary definition by the MAFF stresses the character of hamlets – or "agricultural settlements" (*nōgyō shūraku*), as they are officially referred to – as natural settlements, i.e., private institutions (MAFF 2011a, 157). Historically, however, the relation between the hamlet as a natural settlement and an administrative unit is hard to disentangle (Fukutake 1980; Haley 2010). The social, territorial, and political boundaries of the administrative village of the Tokugawa pe-riod (*gyōsei mura*) and natural settlements have mostly coincided. The subdivisions (typically referred to as *buraku*) of Meiji-era villages were again mostly identical with the administrative village of the Tokugawa period – all while the *buraku* also "continued in its status as a self-governing entity" (Fukutake 1980, 78). During the Pacific War, social organization patterns in the hamlet were adapted to be exploited as instruments of total state control. It was against this background that the Occupation authorities ordered abolition of hamlet-level associations, and their urban counterparts – neighborhood associations – after the Pacific War (89–93).[3] Yet neither of them disappeared in postwar Japan. Much to the contrary, hamlets still display a striking level of continuity. The massive socioeconomic changes in the postwar era notwithstanding, more than 95 per cent of the hamlets the MAFF counted in 1970 had existed before 1880, and most of them were much older (Fukutake 1980, 77; Jussaume 1991, 50).[4] The Ministry of Agriculture has continued to recognize "agricultural settlements" as elemental forms of rural social organization below the municipal level (MAFF 2011a, 157). Despite ongoing de-agriculturalization, the 2015 agricultural census still counted more than 138,000 of these settlements (MAFF 2016a, 130). While not all hamlets have such a long history, some farmers interviewed in Hikawa in 2013 could trace the family history in the same hamlet over ten generations and more. Interviewees in the Kōfu Basin reported similarly long hamlet histories.

Integration of Hamlets into Local Administrative and Cooperative Structures

This continued relevance of the hamlet is not least due to the fact that despite their abolition by the Occupation authorities, postwar municipalities in Japan have never ceased to rely on hamlets as convenient and well-tested informal "channels of administrative communication," an "inexpensive tool for the collection of taxes," garbage collection, and many other administrative tasks (Fukutake 1980, 164–74).[5] Hamlets were integrated directly as a more rural form of the ubiquitous neighborhood associations, or indirectly, as subdivisions of other sub-municipal administrative districts.[6] Thus, like neighborhood associations, hamlets became "straddlers of the state-society boundary," a form of private, collective ordering that continued to function as a de facto unit of local administration (Pekkanen 2006). In Hikawa, the integration of hamlets into local agricultural governance took a particularly institutionalized form under the so-called *shinkōku* system, which was introduced in 1960. *Shinkōku* are local administrative units between the hamlet and the municipal levels.[7] Other than hamlets themselves, *shinkōku* are stipulated by municipal law. Two to three hamlets form one *shinkōku*. In total, there are sixty-one *shinkōku*, each of which appoints one chair. The chairs constitute the Hikawa Shinkōku Assembly, which functions as an intermediate between the hamlet level and the agricultural administration. *Shinkōku* have been responsible for implementing agricultural policies at the hamlet level, such as rice production control.

Simultaneously, hamlets were integrated into the postwar cooperative organization. As briefly mentioned in chapter 4, Nōkyō's local branches incorporated preexisting hamlet-level forms of organization, including the agricultural practice unions (*jikkō kumiai*). Like hamlets and neighborhood associations, these practice unions have a history as both historically grown private institutions and elements of compulsory formal structures. After the Occupation authorities disbanded the compulsory wartime agricultural cooperatives, hamlet-level practice unions continued as self-governing, voluntary organizations (Saitō 2005). As such, they came to constitute the root system of the postwar cooperative organization, or the "bottom of the JA pyramid," as the head of a practice union in the Kōfu Basin described it (KB-F8). Instead of fading away, the cooperative systems of the hamlet flourished under the Nōkyō umbrella. By 1960, 86 per cent of all hamlets had adopted cooperative shipping, and many hamlets had established joint-use facilities for storage rooms or rice peeling (Fukutake 1980, 82–3). The entanglement between hamlets and co-ops also extended beyond purely practical matters. For example, decisions on cooperative activities were not made without consulting the respective hamlet heads, and local cooperatives engaged in interest regulation between hamlet members in disagreement over investing in a joint facility or land improvement (Gōdo 2010, 66; X. Gao 2013). According to the agricultural census, the majority of agricultural settlements still maintained a practice union in 2015, despite ongoing de-agriculturalization and socioeconomic differentiation (MAFF 2016a, 130), although some act independently from JA.[8]

Hamlets and Hamlet Norms in Postwar Local Agricultural Governance

The emerging legal framework of the postwar agricultural sector also continued to rely on – and left space for – hamlet-level self-organization. For example, postwar land improvement legislation reinforced the hamlet as the "basic unit responsible for control and allocation of water" (Fukutake 1980, 79–82). The 1949 Land Improvement Law based the allocation of land improvement on the consensus and the initiative of the participating farmers and their respective hamlets (Latz 1989). Via the administrative framework of local land improvement districts, hamlets thus became further integrated into local agricultural regimes throughout Japan. Apart from lobbying for funding for land improvement projects, the key function of land improvement districts is to oversee irrigation management and maintain dams and irrigation channels after the projects are completed. Within this formal framework, hamlets continued to be "substantially free to devise their own institutions unchallenged by the government" to organize these tasks (Sarker and Itō 2001, 91).[9]

The normative underpinning for the postwar principle of local self-governance of farmland matters (see chapter 4) also reflects the institutional history of hamlet-level social organization. The planning and execution of the postwar land reform rested partially on the normative and social infrastructure of the hamlet. Land reform committees that were engaged in assessing ownership and use of farmland routinely involved hamlet-level assistants, often the hamlet heads themselves. Arguably, this enhanced the acceptance of the land reform among the rural population, because "the interests of the community and its long-established values" were represented (Iwamoto 2003, 224–5). The agricultural committees set up subsequently in every municipality to oversee provisions of the Agricultural Land Law are the "institutional heirs" of the earlier land reform committees (McDonald 1997, 58). In this sense, the notion of local self-governance of farmland reinforced hamlet-level norms and practices as an element of postwar local agricultural regimes – the consequences of which will be discussed below.

Hamlet-level social organization also became the micro-foundation for carrying out the rice acreage reduction program (*gentan*). Since the *gentan* was run without solid legal underpinning until the mid-1990s (see chapter 4), allocating and monitoring target rates for rice acreage reduction required substantial local coordination and control by the local cooperative branches – which were able to carry out this task because hamlet-level organizational patterns were integrated (Gōdo 2010, 2013). Even in more recent agricultural reform, the farm hamlet is still assumed to be the basic social unit for local social organization, as exemplified, for example, by the fact that national policies have stipulated local governments and local co-ops to base the consolidation of farmland in the hands of "bearer farms" on hamlet-level discussion rounds, and the policies to promote hamlet-based collective farming as a means for farmland consolidation (see chapters 8 and 10 for details).

Changing Postwar Hamlet

The principal continuity of the hamlet as a social unit should not be confused with the mere persistence of traditional rural social organization in Japan.[10] Hamlets and hamlet patterns of social organization underwent significant change in the postwar era. With the onset of rapid economic growth, social and spatial boundaries between rural and urban areas grew increasingly vague. By the late 1970s, the once predominantly agrarian character of the Japanese countryside had made way for a heterogeneous socioeconomic structure that became typical for "regional Japan" (Kelly 1990b).[11] The millions of private landowners who emerged from land reform soon faced pressure and opportunities to seek new sources of (off-farm) income (Dore 1978; Kelly 1990b). Hamlets all across Japan turned from relatively isolated, mutually dependent "agricultural production units" into occupationally, socially, and economically diverse entities (Tokuno, Tsutsumi, and Yamamoto 2008). While agriculture lost its role as the predominant source for livelihood, the emerging agricultural support and protection regime rendered part-time farming a widespread and lucrative household strategy (see figure 7.2). Again, the local agricultural regime in Hikawa is typical for this development. In 1960, 1,525 farm households in town counted as full-time. By 1975, only 170 were left. Meanwhile, the total number of farm households had decreased only marginally from 3,253 to 3,054 (Hikawa Town 1997). From the 1980s onwards, the share of farmers per hamlet declined more sharply throughout Japan. Many "agricultural settlements" in and around urbanizing areas increasingly became inhabited by households with little or no connection to agriculture. In more rural settlements, agriculture remained more salient, but the socioeconomic constitution of hamlets was marked by seasonal and/or permanent labor migration (Fukutake 1980, 86–8).

Growing socioeconomic heterogeneity and the parallel integration into Nōkyō's cooperative structure had significant impact on hamlet-level organization patterns. For example, while prewar agricultural practice unions were an "inseparable part of hamlet life" that included non-farming hamlet members as well, postwar *jikkō kumiai* became increasingly associated with Nōkyō and the farming hamlet members alone, rather than being an integral element of the hamlet as a whole – thus diluting the "unity" between the *jikkō kumiai* and the non-farming hamlet members (Fukutake 1980, 82–9). Other patterns of traditional hamlet-level cooperation became obsolete as land improvement and mechanization under the Agricultural Basic Law progressed. Improved land is typically connected both to inflow and outflow of water directly through open channels, later via pipelines (Latz 1989, 43). Land improvement enabled most farmers throughout Japan to grow rice mechanically, and alone (Dore 1978, 99–111). In Hikawa, the plain areas were subject to a series of land improvement projects from the 1960s onward, which rendered traditional irrigation patterns obsolete (see figure 7.3). By 2013, only some of the most remote hamlets in town had retained traditional plot-to-plot irrigation (H-GS1).

Figure 7.2. Share of Farm Household per Hamlet, 1970–90

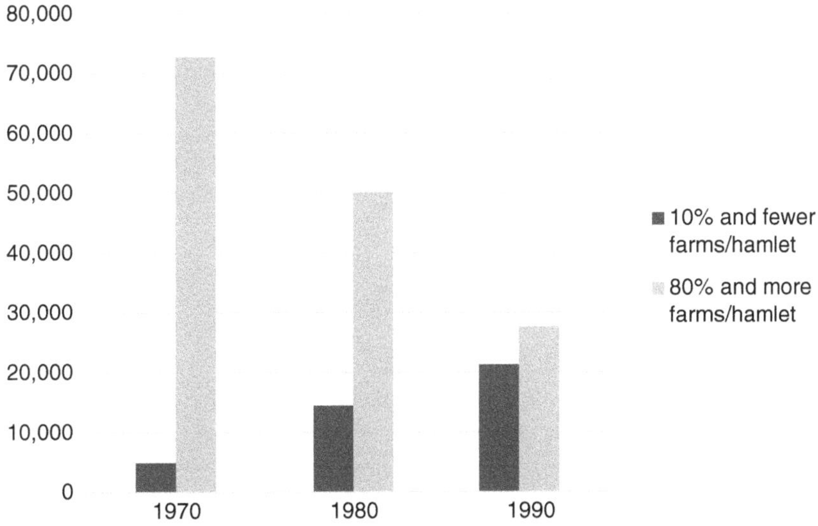

Source: Tokuno, Tsutsumi, and Yamamoto (2008, 167).

Along with modernization and socioeconomic differentiation, other patterns of communal labor – such as joint harvesting – also faded away during the 1960s, as an older respondent from Hikawa recalls (H-JA3). This development is not restricted to rice-farming areas. In the Kōfu Basin, horticulture farmers in their late sixties also reported that more extensive forms of communal labor started to lose significance when they were still young.

Hamlets as Flexible Institutions

Instead of disappearing altogether, however, hamlets have adapted to changes in the political and socioeconomic structure – and should therefore be understood as flexible institutions rather than relics of an agrarian past. Contemporary hamlets have multiple functions that reflect the postwar shift from agriculture to other issues of mutual concern. By 2010, the share of farmers per hamlet had decreased to 9.7 per cent. Yet more than 90 per cent of all hamlets still held regular meetings. While the capacities of hamlet-level self-organization are threatened by aging and outmigration, 82 per cent of all hamlets helped to plan and promote events such as local festivals, and more than 77 per cent in

Figure 7.3. Farmland Rationalization – Reduced Complex Coordination Necessary in Plot-to-Plot Irrigation (*above*) by Connecting Rationalized Plots to Underground Irrigation (*below*)

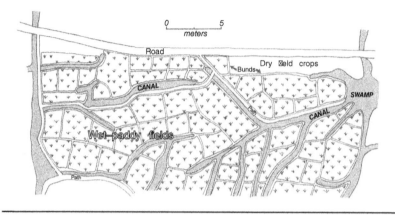

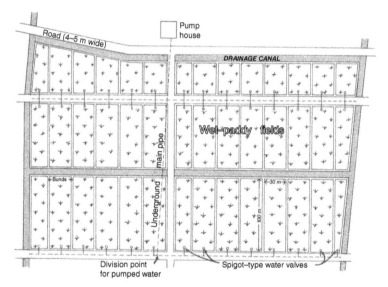

Source: Adapted from Latz (1989, 43).

hamlet "beautification." Almost half of all hamlets carried out tasks related to community health and welfare. Meanwhile, agriculture-related work such as communal maintenance of irrigation channels was still common in the majority of hamlets in 2010 (Statistics Bureau of Japan 2012).[12] While traditional irrigation patterns often became obsolete, hamlet-level cooperation shifted toward "updated" tasks such as joint cleaning of drainage and irrigation ditches or maintaining irrigation ponds in the context of land improvement districts (Sarker and Itō 2001). Enforcement of hamlet functions and responsibilities has also been flexible. Instead of relying on communal labor alone, some aspects of communal labor were commodified, i.e., hamlets paid designated members to carry out the tasks, or hired external labor (Fukutake 1980, 124–6; X. Gao 2013). Other hamlets enforce monetary sanctions for members who fail to (or are unable to) contribute to communal labor such as joint cleaning of irrigation channels (fieldwork, Y-F1; H-JA1). Recently, rural sociologists have pointed out that hamlets and hamlet functions can survive even in the face of depopulation – such as when younger generations return temporarily to help with tasks such as weeding and cleaning irrigation channels (Odagiri 2014; Okubo, Mohammed, and Inoue 2016).

Local Social Ties beyond Hamlet Boundaries

While hamlet members grew less dependent on each other, the postwar integration of hamlets into local co-ops and municipalities facilitated formation of dense local social ties *beyond and across* hamlet boundaries – but often within the overlapping social, spatial, and political boundaries of municipalities and cooperative districts. Governance tasks like rice production control, allocation of land improvement projects, or management of large-scale modern irrigation facilities all require a certain degree of coordination across hamlets, but within the overlapping constituencies of local co-ops and municipalities. Beyond the realm of agriculture, the local political-administrative environment after the Shōwa amalgamation made for an increasing need for inter-hamlet cooperation and political bargaining, which led to new opportunities and pressures for development of diverse, cross-hamlet local social network ties (Dore 1984, 352–3). Throughout Japan, networks of several hamlets – often within the boundaries of historical towns and villages from the pre-Shōwa amalgamation period – cooperate in organization of tasks that include large-scale collective farms or sub-municipal initiatives for "revitalization" of the respective areas.[13] Again, the *shinkōku* system in Hikawa is a particularly formalized example of this development, in that all hamlet clusters are also firmly integrated into a municipal framework.

   As a linchpin between hamlets and the local administration, local co-ops provided a particularly productive platform for social interaction and cooperation beyond and across hamlet boundaries. Nōkyō (often together with local governments) rendered joint investments possible that hamlets were not able to handle alone, such as large-scale facilities (Fukutake

1980). For example, since the 1960s virtually every rice-growing locality in Japan has built a country elevator to dry and ship rice. Importantly, these mutual investments reflect the territorial confinements of the respective local agricultural regimes in that only members of the respective coopera- tive can use them, while neighboring farmers are excluded.[14] This echoes the crucial institutional feature of Japanese agricultural cooperatives as *territorial* organizations: they are "based on enduring personal relation- ships built up through frequent face-to-face encounters and kinship ties within restricted geographic areas" (George Mulgan 2000, 212) – an or- ganizational logic that resonates with the institutional history of hamlets as clearly demarcated socio-spatial units (Marshall 1984).

During the postwar decades, the number of non-farmers who joined the cooperatives as associated members rose steadily. While this change arguably diluted the social coherence and the agrarian character of the co-ops (Gōdo 2010), it also meant that the social network ties under the cooperative umbrella came to entail a dense and overlapping web of groups, clubs, and organizations – many of which are not directly related to farming (George Mulgan 2000, 219–21). They all provide countless op- portunities for long-term social ties between farmers, part-time farmers, and non-farmers alike. In Hikawa, such local groups include a commit- tee that discusses hamlet-based collective farming, study groups, the Young Farmers' Association, or the "Agri-Ladies Network," all of which are directly or indirectly associated with the local JA. Beyond formal or- ganizational ties, farm households, the co-op, and the local agricultural administration in Hikawa became tied to each other by friendship, neigh- borhood, or kinship. More generally, while Nōkyō's *initial* rise to compre- hensive membership has often been associated with traditional forms of social pressure in the hamlet to join the organization (such as ostracism),[15] its *continuous* local social embedding is better understood as a result of integration of hamlets and local co-ops into broader local agricultural re- gimes. Being a member in the local co-op also became a vital element of local social connectedness, a matter of access to information (e.g., on sub- sidy schemes), as well as the everyday needs, from gasoline via financial services to groceries – all of which meant that leaving the co-op would have been "grossly inconvenient," especially for part-time farm house- holds (George Mulgan 2000, 215).

From Traditional Rural Social Organization to Village Institutions

Macro accounts of the postwar trajectory of the Japanese agricultural support and protection regime have long perpetuated a rather static no- tion of traditional social cohesion in rural communities, which has often been raised as an informal institutional complement to electoral rules and the political and economic power of the cooperative organization (George Mulgan 2006c; Horiuchi and Saito 2010). Other accounts have emphasized the erosion of traditional agrarian norms, values, and practices (Fukutake 1980), not least as an explanation for the farm sector's path into crisis (Gōdo 2010). Yet the discussion above shows that binary notions of continuity or erosion of traditional rural social organization can hardly convey the complex dynamics that underlay the emerging social and normative foundations of postwar local agricultural regimes. On the one hand, the hamlet has remained viable, not least for local (agricultural) governance, and agricultural legislation has resonated with traditional agrarian norms and practices on farmland use and agricultural cooperation in the hamlet. On the other hand, increasing socioeconomic differentiation has rendered these hamlet norms and practices increasingly hard to enforce, as many residents turned to new "opportunities of exchange and production … outside the hamlet membership" (Marshall 1984, 68) and beyond the realm of agrarian production.[16] Against this background, the social and normative underpinning of postwar local agricultural regimes is multifaceted and ambiguous, is governed by potentially contradictive sets of norms and practices, and is composed of diverse social network ties between farmers, hamlets, co-ops, and administrations.[17] These *village institutions* became valuable resources for local actors to access a broad variety of public goods, albeit not necessarily in the best interest of the remaining farmers, or the trajectory of Japan's agricultural sector as a whole.

Institutional "Drift" in the Agricultural Committee System

The example of postwar farmland governance illustrates this argument well. Over the postwar decades, farmland in Japan became fragmented through seemingly uncontrolled urban development. Large parts of regional Japan today display a chaotic juxtaposition of (often empty) apartment blocks, pachinko halls with oversized parking grounds, shopping malls, or newly constructed roads next to and often surrounding plots of farmland. I argue that a substantial part of the explanation for farmland fragmentation can be found in the changing normative and social underpinning of postwar local agricultural regimes, which caused local control over farmland matters to "drift" (Mahoney and Thelen 2010b) from an institution to protect farmland into an institution that allowed local actors to achieve capital gains through farmland conversion.

Formally, the rules to prevent farmland abuse and to control the conversion and the exchange of arable land have been relatively strict throughout the postwar era, with local agricultural committees as the key actors overseeing these rules in every local agricultural regime. Agricultural committees consist of delegates from the local cooperative, the municipality, and the land improvement district, as well as members elected from and by farm households in the constituency. The committees were, inter alia, legally obliged to ratify farmland deals after scrutinizing the "abilities and sociability" of the recipients' side or even to enforce the liquidation of farmland use rights in case of "inappropriate" use (Gōdo 2007). Regulations on conversion of farmland to non-agricultural use have been particularly strict. Municipalities were obliged to create designated zones in which farmland conversion would be ruled out (Gōdo 2007; McDonald 1997). However, these regulations have been stricter on paper than they were enforced in local practice, where the conversion of farmland to non-agricultural purposes became subject to widespread manipulation.

As land prices rose with the onset of high economic growth, for many farm households the major benefit from owning farmland shifted from cultivating it toward selling (Iwamoto 2003; Gōdo 2007, 2010). Consequently, the agrarian norm of maintaining and preserving farmland as a common resource became increasingly challenged by the notion of regarding farmland as a private asset (Gōdo 2010, 117–19), thus undermining the role of the former as the foundation for local farmland governance (70). At the same time, emerging local social network ties between farmers, local politicians, co-ops, and construction companies became a valuable resource to circumvent farmland regulations. In order to make profitable gains from farmland conversion, agricultural committees and the municipal governments have often stretched "their interpretation" of the rules to protect farmland "to suit themselves" (Gōdo 2007, 15), i.e., to realize a project even if it disrupted surrounding arable land. The reciprocal logic of local social network ties fueled this pattern: with opportunities for conversion frequently available, land-owning agricultural committee members tended to support conversion for their peers, hoping for similar support when they themselves got the chance to convert their land (17). Even public works projects to *improve* the agricultural infrastructure became subject to this dynamic. Gōdo (2007, 2010) argues that improved farmland – flat, square, and connected to roads and irrigation – also provides ideal conditions for non-agrarian use, such as apartment blocks, so that agricultural land improvement was often followed by conversion to other purposes. Especially before the burst of the bubble economy in the late 1980s, many small-scale part-time farm households continued rice farming while waiting for an opportunity to sell their land profitably for non-agricultural use – the opportunities for which occurred frequently, given rapid urban development and extensive public infrastructural investments. Thus, substantial parts of arable land came to be used inefficiently by part-time cultivators with little or no interest in commercial agricultural production, while farmers with an interest in scale-enlargement and professionalization found it hard to obtain a larger acreage. Both the fragmentation of farmland and the blocking of arable land for large-scale cultivation by "alibi" rice farming have massively contributed to the present crisis in the agricultural sector of Japan (Gōdo 2007, 2010; K. Yamashita 2008). Ironically, the cooperative organization itself also contributed to this development. Across Japan, the cooperative bank invested heavily in real estate during the growth of the economic bubble (Bullock 1997).

LDP policy-makers had little interest in reregulating farmland prices or in rescinding authority over farmland matters from the local level. Much to the contrary, under the SNTV electoral system, "catering to the property owning instincts of farmers, especially in urban areas, proved a very effective vote-winning strategy" (Iwamoto 2003, 235). The shift from (agrarian) hamlet ties to village institutions supported the effectiveness of this strategy. In the early 1950s, the major arena for organizing rural voting behavior was the (still mostly agrarian) hamlet. Hamlet leaders issued a recommendation to vote for a certain candidate, and the hamlet usually followed their advice (George Mulgan 2000, 382; Dore 1984, 325–43). Yet, with the integration of hamlets into municipalities and local co-ops, new local leaders emerged as the major players mobilizing rural votes for campaigning politicians, including the heads of local cooperatives and land improvement districts, municipal politicians, or leaders of other local groups such as the chamber of commerce or the fire fighters' association (Dore 1984; George Mulgan 2000, 383). Campaigning politicians in rural and semi-urban areas continued to organize and activate their local support bases along the lines of hamlets and historical villages.[18] Yet the currency for electoral support corresponded to increasingly heterogeneous local support bases, in which agrarian and non-agrarian interests became inseparably intertwined, both socially and economically (Kelly 1990b) – as physically manifested in the patchwork of urban development and agrarian land use throughout Japan.

Village Institutions and Rice Production Control

While "drifting" local farmland governance illustrates the eroding enforceability of traditional agrarian norms in postwar local agricultural regimes, the trajectory of another pillar of the postwar support and protection regime – the rice production control program – illustrates the *adaptability* of traditional norms and practices as a means to access public goods. As mentioned above, hamlet-level organizational patterns and the social embedding of the local co-ops in local agricultural regimes have facilitated the introduction of the rice acreage reduction program (*gentan*) since 1970. The fact that the complex and unpopular *gentan* displayed almost perfect participation rates over several decades without a solid legal foundation (Gōdo 2013) points to the salience of village institutions as organizational resources for (part-time) rice farmers and the cooperative organization, who both benefitted from the ever-increasing rice price. Under the *gentan*, many hamlets revived the historical notion of treating farmland as a collective resource that had become essentially obsolete with the onset of mechanization and modern irrigation (Toyama 2012). To enhance productivity and soil fertility, but also for a more comprehensive access to the subsidies connected with the *gentan*, hamlets throughout Japan developed models of group farming to engage in subsidy-productive "block rotation" of rice and certain diversion crops like soy or wheat.[19] Hamlet members also formed machinery co-ops to jointly purchase and use the special machinery for growing these crops. Reviving or reinterpreting such cooperation patterns typically occurred under the guidance of the local branch of Nōkyō (e.g., Shōji 2009; H-GS1; H-CF2; H-CF5; M-O). From the late 1970s onwards, the government allocated subsidies for pooling farmland for crop diversion (Toyama 2012, 139), thus formally reinforcing the adaptation of hamlet-level cooperation to extract state support, and the role of Nōkyō in organizing such efforts. The subsidy-productive potential of hamlet-level cooperation remains salient, as the policies supporting hamlet-based farming in the 2000s show particularly well. Some local agricultural regimes have also developed broader local cooperation schemes to govern rice production control and extract the related state support more efficiently – the comprehensive rice production control scheme in Hikawa being a particularly sophisticated example, but not the only one (see chapters 8–10 for details).

Together, the examples of farmland fragmentation and hamlet-level cooperation under the *gentan* illustrate the ambiguity of village institutions as resources to access public goods. To some extent, the adaptation and transformation of local social organization has contributed to the increasing structural problems of the agricultural sector in postwar Japan. From the perspective of local administrations, local co-ops, and farmers themselves, however, devising (informal) strategies to sustain part-time farming as a lucrative household strategy and – closely related – to channel public investments to the respective localities has been a productive means to achieve social security in Japan's structurally weaker peripheries.

Interim Conclusion

The two chapters in this part have moved from introducing the contemporary differences between local agricultural regimes to discussing their common institutional origins. From a broader historical perspective, all local agricultural regimes throughout postwar Japan were shaped by the emergence of multifaceted, ambiguous village institutions within the often-overlapping boundaries of local co-ops and municipalities. Returning to the local perspective, however, this process has not occurred uniformly. Hikawa, where the integration of all hamlets in town into the local agricultural regime was formalized with the *shinkōku* system, highlights the fact that beyond broader drivers of socioeconomic and political change, the trajectory of each local agricultural regime is also the result of a distinct local historical process. These local processes are highly relevant in the context of this book. I argue that how, by whom, to what extent, and which aspects of village institutions have been integrated into the respective local agricultural regime throughout the postwar period also affects how the more recent agricultural reform has been implemented and interpreted locally. This argument will be developed in more detail in the following part of this volume.

PART FOUR

Village Institutions as Dynamic Resources: Local Renegotiation of Agricultural Support and Protection

The four chapters in part 4 analyze the role of village institutions in local responses to agricultural reform since the mid-1990s. Together, the chapters show that and how norms and practices in land use and exchange, agricultural cooperation patterns, and local social network ties between farmers, local co-ops, and local governments continue to shape farmland consolidation and access to state support. I further argue that differences in how village institutions have been integrated into local agricultural regimes shape local interpretations of agricultural reform. The analysis of the trajectory of the local agricultural regime in Hikawa in contrast to and in comparison with evidence from other localities shows that the comprehensive integration of village institutions can serve as the social and normative foundation for an organized approach to farmland consolidation, in which farmers' entrepreneurial decisions and aspirations remain subjected to objectives associated with the interests of the local cooperative and small rice-farming households – despite the formal expansion of economic freedom through national reform.

This two-tiered argument will be developed with a closer look at the process of exchanging and accumulating farmland, and – closely related – how control over farmland redistribution directly relates to control over what type of "bearer farms" emerge (chapter 8). Against this background, chapters 9 and 10 analyze the role of expanding (corporate) farms and hamlet-based collective farms respectively. Finally, chapter 11 puts the local findings in a broader context by focusing on macro-institutional change that has disrupted the boundaries of most local agricultural regimes over the course of the 2000s. This has arguably reduced the prospects for building comprehensive local institutions for an organized approach to farmland consolidation, thus amplifying the (neo)liberal potential of the ambiguous national reform.

Chapter Eight

Farmland Consolidation as a Social Process

Against the background of farmland fragmentation, a shrinking agricultural workforce, and a growing share of abandoned land, promoting the accumulation of land (use rights) in the hands of designated "bearer farms" has been a proclaimed goal of national policy-makers over the 2000s, and a growing concern for local governments, local co-ops, and farmers throughout Japan (N. Taniguchi and Lee 2013). Beyond functional implications, if, to what extent, and how business-oriented (corporate) farms accumulate land are crucial factors determining the pace and direction of institutional change in the agricultural support and protection regime as a whole.[1]

Upon closer examination, the exchange of farmland (use rights) in Japan is a social process that extends far beyond the realm of economic transactions (Tōjō 1992; K. Yoshida 2012, 2015; Isaka 2015). Village institutions continue to play an important role in it. Farmland use rights are exchanged along local social ties, and according to norms on the appropriate use and maintenance of farmland. As a result, expanding "bearer farms" have to juggle large numbers of formal and informal land use deals, often charged with unwritten rules and social obligations – all of which add up to complicated and thus costly access to land, in both social and economic terms. Furthermore, over the 2000s this social mode of farmland transfers has proven an insufficient means to prevent farmland from falling idle – either for lack of "bearer farms" willing or able to take on land, or because the available land is unattractive for expanding agri-businesses, or because the established channels for land exchange are disrupted as owners pass away or move elsewhere. On the other hand, analysis of successful farmland consolidation in Hikawa and supporting evidence from Kami-Ina District show how the protracted integration of village institutions into local agricultural regimes can *support* farmland redistribution and a more rational (public) allocation of land toward certain expanding farms. National policy-makers have taken up the approaches in Hikawa and Kami-Ina as models for policies to publicly govern farmland exchange. Yet, as will be argued below, the lack of local (informal) control over farmland matters limits the prospects for local intervention, and thus amplifies the effects of gradual deregulation of corporate access to farmland.

The Social and Normative Dimensions of Exchanging Farmland

Landowners in Japan have long been reluctant to sell their land to other farmers, in order to maintain the family property, or in expectation of a lucrative opportunity to convert it to other purposes, or both. Over the 2000s, however, land prices and the prospects of selling farmland profitably to non-agricultural use have greatly decreased, especially in more remote areas, so that farmers are often unable to sell their land, even if they (or their heirs) would like to. Leasing has thus remained the dominant mode of farmland transfers in Japan. As a pronounced effect of structural change in the Japanese agricultural sector, the share of land that is exchanged under leases has greatly increased since the mid-2000s (Hashizume 2013, 118–19).

In the absence of successors within the family and lucrative opportunities to sell their land, many farmers keep cultivating until old age. When they must give up some or all of their land, farmland norms serve as a catalyst for the transfer of land use rights. Given the mosaic pattern of land use in Japan, abandoned plots harm surrounding farmers, because they allow the spread of pests or disrupt the flow of irrigation water. Moreover, abandoned land is a visible sign of socioeconomic decline, community disorder, or even moral disintegration (N. Taniguchi and Lee 2013, 6–7).[2] Thus, landowners face the social obligation to prevent their arable land from falling idle. At the same time, they also need to find a user who can be trusted to maintain the land according to local rules and practices, eventually including participation in communal labor. This is particularly salient in rice growing areas, where the maintenance of irrigation channels and field boundaries has been a historical element of hamlet duties, remains vital for agricultural production, and is sometimes woven into practices of communal labor. Yet, even in the horticulture-dominated Kōfu Basin, the mosaic pattern of farmland ownership and use requires farmers to follow a variety of implicit and explicit rules for weeding, pest control, or irrigation (KB-F1; KB-F7). Given the normative dimension of farmland ownership and use, farmland is typically transferred within local social networks – often entirely informally. With the increase of farmland transfers and de-agriculturalization, the socio-spatial boundaries within which such transfers occur have long surpassed the hamlet (Isaka 2015). Expanding farmers accumulate farmland via social ties within the broader family, from peers from high school days, joint membership in the local co-op and/or various other clubs, or introductions from the local agricultural committee and other administrative bodies involved in facilitating land exchanges (K. Yoshida 2015) – that is, within the locally confined social networks underlying their respective local agricultural regimes.

Plots are small (typically thirty ares for developed paddy land), so full-time paddy field farmers must handle dozens or even hundreds of individual land use agreements. For example, as of 2017 the largest corporate farm in Yasu City operated about 220 hectares of paddy land, making it one of the largest farms in Japan (Y-F1). The farm started as an agricultural production corporation in 1991 with twenty hectares scattered across ten hamlets. By spring 2017, the farm has rented more than a thousand plots from more than five hundred owners in forty-three hamlets, most of them in the founder's hometown Chūzu, since 2005 a part of the amalgamated Yasu City (Y-F1). Large rice farmers in other areas have similarly fragmented holdings (T-F). Albeit on a smaller scale, less land-intensive forms of cultivation rely on the same mode of accessing land. An expanding grape farmer in Kōshū City handles several dozen individual land use deals (KB-F1), most of them within the confines of his hometown Enzan (since 2005 part of Kōshū City). These fragmented land use patterns can be seen as spatial expressions of the local social network ties of the expanding farmers. Prominent positions in the local co-op and/or administrative bodies like the agricultural committee or the municipal assembly and the reputation of their farm households provide the social "starting capital" for farmland accumulation among expanding farmers (e.g., H-F1; KB-F1; KB-F2; Y-F1; T-F). Upon expanding their acreage, such farms can also build a local reputation as trustworthy land user, so that they can accumulate farmland via indirect social ties or upon being approached by owners looking for somebody to take over their land (H-F4a). As a particularly sophisticated example in this respect, the founder of a large corporate farm in Yasu City has employed his longstanding reputation as a trusted land user as the basis for turning the absorption of unwanted land into a business model, which is advertised on large billboards in his hometown (Y-F1). As will be discussed in more detail in chapter 9, this business model has a normative dimension, in that the farm also absorbs the land as a service to the aging landowners in the community.

Economic and Social Costs of Farmland Fragmentation

A direct consequence of the social mode of farmland transfers is that large farms have typically been unable to consolidate their holdings. KB-F1 spends much of his working hours behind the wheel, as some of his plots are a twenty-minute drive apart from each other. Grape farming in the Kōfu Basin is mostly manual labor – yet the tasks that require machinery (e.g., spraying pesticides) or allocation of building materials become a logistical and time-consuming challenge, because the equipment has to be transported from plot to plot. Farmland fragmentation is an even bigger problem for land-intensive, mechanized paddy field farming. The sheer size of full-time rice farming operations requires the use of large-scale machinery. Yet professional rice farmers have to use trucks to move harvesters and tractors between their tiny, scattered plots, which are often several kilometers apart. In the case of the large corporate farm in Yasu City, some plots are located 8.5 kilometers away from the company's headquarters, where most machinery is stored (Y-F1a). Thus, even comparatively large holdings are hardly able to produce economies of scale (H-GS1; T-F; Y-F1; Y-F1a). This is an important finding when assessing the actual effects of scale-enlargement in Japan, which the Japanese government promotes as a means to reduce labor input and production costs. While the share of larger holdings has indeed increased significantly since the 2000s, the extent to which this increase makes agricultural production more efficient remains highly questionable. Moreover, farmland fragmentation also raises environmental costs, since all large farmers encountered in the field are highly dependent on fossil fuels to get around.

Apart from the economic and environmental costs of farmland fragmentation,[3] farmland fragmentation is accompanied by social costs. Acquiring land within several hamlets requires highly localized, non-codified knowledge of the complicated relation between ownership, use, and individual and communal responsibilities in each hamlet. Moreover, especially where demand for land is still high (e.g., in flat, well-irrigated paddy field areas), negotiating leases can strain personal ties and is thus particularly stressful for large farmers (H-F2; H-F4a; KB-F1). In less developed areas, many land use deals involve no lease, since it has become so hard for landowners to find a trustworthy tenant that they can no longer demand compensation (KB-F1; T-F). Yet such deals still entail social costs, such as the occasional exchange of labor and materials or other favors to be returned at any time and in any form (KB-F1).[4] While lease-free land use deals can also be formalized (e.g., through a contract issued by the local agricultural committee), other land use deals remain completely informal. Such deals pose an economic risk for the user, who might lose access to the land if there is conflict.[5] Even formal land use contracts entail a variety of (implicit) informal aspects. For example, while the formal lease contract typically specifies which party is responsible for maintaining the piece of farmland in question, the actual meaning of farmland maintenance is also determined by norms and rules in each hamlet – and even neighboring hamlets may differ in the details of these rules and their enforcement. For example, some hamlets still enforce land maintenance duties such as weeding and cleaning irrigation channels traditionally (i.e., as a social obligation), while others also allow users to pay a fee to relieve them of these tasks (Y-F1; H-CF1). Moreover, formal land use deals can involve implicit agreements like the exchange of material or information. A farmer in Kōshū City referred to such agreements as the "secret part" of land exchange. In one of his land use deals, the only aspect specified in the formal contract – the user had to take care of the (unspecified) farmland maintenance tasks – was meaningless in practice. Instead, the owner weeded the plot himself in order to avoid conveying the impression to his neighbors that his land was not looked after appropriately (KB-F3). Yet the benefits of the implicit agreements surrounding the land use deal and the fact that it was embedded in a long-term personal relationship seemed to outweigh this contract violation – as of 2018, the land use deal was still active.

In general, business-oriented farmers preferred formal deals to avoid social conflict and for more stable access to arable land (Y-F1; T-F; H-F1; H-F2). In order to reduce the social costs of farmland exchange, the large-scale corporate farm in Yasu City mentioned above even enforces a point-based system assessing the quality (and thus the leases) of the plots in question. Despite this rather unusual level of formalization and standardization, however, mutual trust remains the basis for his land use deals. In order to maintain his reputation as a trustworthy land user, the farmer implicitly commits to modify or dissolve lease contracts according to the requests of owners or the respective hamlets (Y-F1), thus granting land users and hamlets a certain level of control over their land. Such flexibility based on mutual trust gives the farm an important advantage vis-à-vis less personal forms of farmland exchange via public agencies such as farmland harmonization groups and – more recently – farmland banks. Accordingly, a lack of trust between landowners, (corporate) land takers, and public agencies has been obstructing the national policies to promote public allocation of farmland, let alone to "outsiders" (Kobari 2015). This will be taken up in more detail below.

Limitations of Social Farmland Transfers

Beyond hindering consolidation, the established social mode of farmland transfers has also become decreasingly able to prevent farmland loss in general. Around the year 2000, when the "first Shōwa generation" reached retirement age, a sudden supply of unwanted land overstretched the capacities of the established channels of farmland exchange in many localities (N. Taniguchi and Lee 2013). Especially semi-urban and remote areas tend to have a surplus of unwanted or unusable farmland – albeit for slightly different reasons. In semi-urban areas, the peculiar pattern of agrarian, residential, and commercial use prohibits efficient cultivation. Residents in semi-urban neighborhoods often complain about dirty roads and the use of heavy machinery or fertilizers, thus rendering surplus farmland in such areas unattractive for professional farmers (KB-F2; H-CF6). In remote and mountainous areas, land supply increases as the result of depopulation. Entrepreneurial farms that rely on mechanized and cost-efficient cultivation are less inclined to rent the surplus land in less accessible areas (fieldwork; H-GS1).

Thus, increasing the number of competitors in the farmland market – for example, through further farmland deregulation – does not necessarily resolve the problem of farmland loss. In Yasu City, for example, local authorities reported intense competition for the well-developed land in the plain on the shore of Lake Biwa, while the plots in more remote areas of the city were at risk of falling idle (Yasu City 2017). More recently, the transfer of spare farmland via the established channels has become complicated even in areas with relatively favorable farmland conditions. One reason is the growing number of "absentee landowners," i.e. heirs who moved to another city long ago (Hashizume 2013; Gōdo 2014c). Their land becomes harder to access for local farmers, or even falls out of the established local social channels of transfer entirely (H-GS1; H-JA4) – thus, even if there are business-oriented farms willing to take on more land, they might be unable to obtain the land use rights, or even contact the owner.[6] In contrast, a relatively low number of absentee landowners in Yasu City has significantly supported the exchange of farmland, according to local officials (Y-O2).

Village Institutions and Public Control over Farmland in Hikawa

As much as the established social mode of farmland transfers has been complicating farmland consolidation, the comprehensive, protracted integration of village institutions into local agricultural regimes can be the social and normative foundation for alleviating some of these problems. A closer look at the local governance of farmland exchange in Hikawa illustrates this argument well.

Within the local agricultural regime in Hikawa, the personal and thus fragmented farmland exchange was overcome by allocating farmland use rights to expanding farms through the public corporation Hikawa Nōgyō Kōsha. The Kōsha system has been crucial for the exceptionally high share of farmland consolidation in town and is arguably the most outstanding feature of the organized local agricultural regime (see figure 8.1). The Kōsha system made farmland accessible beyond the confines of personal social network ties and allowed for a more coordinated allocation. The most important characteristic of the system is that owners yield their land use rights to the Kōsha without being able to specify a certain land user, i.e., under "unconditional authority." The Kōsha then allocates the land to expanding farms. This system has rationalized consolidation of farmland and reduced production costs for larger farms.

The local system of public farmland allocation was established from 2000 onward. At that time, the agricultural sector in Hikawa was confronted with the local manifestation of the "first Shōwa generation" retirement wave. Several large cultivators in town had to give up their holdings in response to illness or old age. Many smaller farm households saw their abilities to keep farming waning as well. Meanwhile, the onset of more exclusive subsidization for certified "bearer farms" was already on the political horizon, thus further undermining incentives for smaller farms to continue farming. Contrary to many localities confronted with the same problem (including neighboring Izumo City), the local agricultural administration in Hikawa seized this opportunity to *expand* its control over the local farmland market and thus the redistribution of arable land to certified "bearer farms."

It is important to note in this context that farmland exchange in Hikawa had displayed characteristics that were remarkably similar to those of other localities before the system of public allocation gained momentum. One large-scale local farmer remembers, "Previously, I only had individual contracts. Therefore the farmland was scattered all over Hikawa" (H-F4).

A crucial step toward comprehensive public control over farmland allocation was the introduction of a town-wide standard for lease contracts in 2005. As in other localities, leases in Hikawa had depended on the personal relations between owner and user. Since 2005, the Kōsha evaluates farmland according to its infrastructural features (pipelines, road access), soil quality, shape, and size. Depending on how high a

Figure 8.1. Consolidation of Farmland Use Rights under the Kōsha System

Source: Documents provided by the Hikawa Town Agriculture and Forestry Office.

paddy field scores, the Kōsha rents it out for a fixed lease. Moreover, the Kōsha harmonized and codified the locally accepted tasks and responsibilities that come with renting land and enforces them. If land users leave maintenance tasks to the owner, they have to pay an additional fee;[7] if they carry out maintenance themselves, they pay only the standard lease. This has further reduced the social costs associated with land use transfers. A large farmer in Hikawa explains the effects of the standardization of farmland exchange: "With individual contracts, many problems can occur ... If the deal is done via the Kōsha, there is a third party involved, and direct talks with the owner are not necessary anymore ... That unpleasant feeling to fight about money now completely disappeared" (H-F2).

"One Town, One Field": Social and Normative Foundations of the Kōsha System

At first glance, public allocation of farmland under unconditional authority seems to clash with the established practice to transfer land on the basis of social network ties, mutual trust, and shared norms, as well as the interests of owners to retain control over their land as a private asset. Still, by 2013 the Kōsha procured 83 per cent of all land use deals in Hikawa (Hikawa Town Agriculture and Forestry Office 2017).[8] This extraordinary high level of compliance suggests that the Kōsha system is not merely an administrative technique, but an institution that is deeply embedded in the local agricultural regime. Within the local institutional context, public allocation through the Kōsha does not contradict the social and normative aspects of farmland exchange – much to the contrary, it reflects the comprehensive integration of village institutions into the local agricultural regime. Upon this foundation, the Kōsha system itself has become the norm for farmland exchange in town.

The institutional roots of the Kōsha system reach back to the postwar integration of hamlets into the local agricultural regime via the *shinkōku* system. The *shinkōku* system has been formally reinforcing the social ties between the local agricultural administration (including JA Hikawa) and all hamlets in town since its introduction in 1963. This has, inter alia, provided the former with comprehensive access to hamlet-level information. For example, a town-wide survey on farmland use and ownership in 2002 yielded a response rate of 94.3 per cent. To put this result into perspective, we can look at neighboring Izumo City, where access to hamlet-level information is far less institutionalized. A similar survey on the situation of "bearer farms" in Izumo in 2012 produced a response rate of merely 59 per cent (I-JA2) – a remarkable difference that a respondent from Hikawa explicitly pointed out to me as indicating the strength of the ties between hamlets and the local agricultural administration in Hikawa (H-GS1). The latter used its informational edge to create a comprehensive local "bearer farms plan" and to produce a map of farmland ownership and use of every plot in town. This map provided an indispensable resource for the task of redistributing land to "bearer farms" (H-GS1; H-JA1), and a significant advantage vis-à-vis other localities. Even in local agricultural regimes with a relatively high share of farmland consolidation and reliable information on farmland ownership – such as in Yasu City – detailed information on farmland *use* is not available (although highly desirable, according to local officials, Y-O2). In Kōshū City and Izumo, similar resources were not available at all (KB-JA1; I-JA2).

The Hikawa Nōgyō Kōsha itself – jointly founded by the local administration and JA Hikawa in 1994 – was born out of the highly integrated local agricultural regime. As such, the Kōsha is generally trusted with handling land transfers appropriately. In formal interviews and ad hoc conversations with respondents in Hikawa, trust in the local agricultural administration and JA Hikawa was a common answer to why the Kōsha system works. Not only the Kōsha itself, but also the land users are deeply embedded in the social fabric of the town. Four large farm-ers benefitted mostly from the onset of farmland redistribution in the early 2000s. With one exception, these farmers were sons and relatives of well-established figures in the local agricultural regime. At least two of the farms represent families of pre-war landlords (H-F1; H-F3). That is, the land recipients were trusted members of the community and already experienced in handling numerous land use deals before the onset of public allocation under unconditional authority. As the Kōsha system gained momentum over the 2000s, the previous logic of farm-land exchange was thus upheld in the sense that the Kōsha distributes land only among local peers within a dense, spatially bounded social network. No land was transferred to farmers from outside the town's borders – not even after Hikawa was merged into Izumo City in 2011.[9]

Beyond their allocation, the Kōsha also has the legitimacy to set and enforce the rules that surround the exchange of land use rights. The normative foundation of this position arguably also goes back to the in-tegration of hamlets into the local agricultural regime. Public farmland allocation rests upon the notion that all farmland in town should be treated as a collective resource. This normative foundation is expressed explicitly in the slogan One Town, One Field – a phrase that had be-come the leitmotif of the local approach to agricultural governance since the early 2000s (Hikawa Town Agriculture and Forestry Office 2013). The notion of an ordering force that governs farmland as a collec-tive resource bears striking resemblance to the institutional history of the farm hamlet. I argue that hamlet-level norms provided the institu-tional "raw material" for the Kōsha system. Long before public alloca-tion of farmland was introduced in the 2000s, the notion of using land as a collective resource had (re)gained significance on the hamlet level in Hikawa.[10] In 1991, the first shinkōku in Hikawa formally collectivized paddy field cultivation under the motto One District, One Farm (Jin-dai 2008, 92). The striking resemblance to the later town-wide motto is hardly coincidental: the collective farm was set up under direction and guidance from the local administration and JA Hikawa (Jindai 2008), who subsequently promoted the farm as a model for other hamlets and shinkōku in town (H-GS1). Carried by the close social and organizational ties between hamlets, local JA, and administration, the normative foun-dation for traditional hamlet-level aspects of farmland governance was thus shifted to the level of the whole town. As I will point out in more detail in chapter 10, the proliferation of the notion of using land as a collective resource on behalf of the local agricultural administration is also reflected in the strong role of hamlet-based collective farming in Hikawa today. A similar argument can be made for the comprehensive local system to govern rice production control. Under this system, the local agricultural administration allocates the tasks in diverting paddy land from rice to other crops from smaller farms to the large cultivators, and then distributes the related subsidies between both parties. Coordinating rice production control has been among the core functions of the Kōsha since it was founded in 1994. The system is closely related to public farmland allocation, in that it is also an expression of the notion to exploit land and state support collectively, and thus projects (and substitutes) hamlet-based cooperation on the level of the local agricultural regime. Thus, the strong proliferation of hamlet-based farming, coordinated crop rotation, and subsequent emergence of public farmland allocation are all elements of a protracted local institution-building process, in the course of which the use of farmland in Hikawa became both astonishingly mobile, and at the same time subjected to comprehensive public and cooperative control.

Local Bargaining Power

Throughout Japan, de-agriculturalization, socioeconomic differentiation, and a growing number of land use deals beyond hamlet boundaries have rendered enforcing farmland norms (such as proper maintenance) increasingly difficult (see chapter 7). Hikawa has not been spared from de-agriculturalization and the accompanying effects on hamlet-level self-organization (H-GS1). Yet, as the Kōsha system has embodied and standardized hamlet-level norms and practices, it has partially supplemented the fading capacities of hamlets to govern farmland matters. As such, the Kōsha system has emerged through institutional agency rather than the persistence of traditional norms and practices. While hamlet-level norms have provided the "raw material" for the Kōsha system, modifying and transposing these norms has been a matter of the "superior bargaining power" (Knight and Ensminger 1998, 106) of the local administration and the local co-op within the local agricultural regime. To build consensus for the new mode of public farmland allocation, the administration, the co-op, and local figures of "respect and creditability"[11] promoted the system in prolonged hamlet-level discussion rounds between 2000 and 2002 (H-GS1). Further, public farmland allocation was reinforced by subjecting other elements of local agricultural administration to the Kōsha system. Introduction of the standardized leases in 2005 illustrates this process well. To seize comprehensive control over the local farmland market, all farmland transfers in town had to be subjected to the Kōsha's standard lease system. To this end, the local agricultural committee – the formal body in charge of local farmland control in Japan – had to accept standard leases as well. The social and organizational ties within the local agricultural regime facilitated this task. A main architect of the Kōsha system is a former local JA official, who was already involved in creation of the pioneer hamlet farm in 1991. He also represents a longstanding local farm household that is involved in one of the oldest hamlet-based collective farms in town. The year before the standard leases were introduced, he became director of the agricultural production corporation Green Support, which plays a crucial role in the Kōsha system (see chapter 9). Under his influence, the agricultural committee offered no resistance to the standardized leases. He recalls, "At that time, I was a member of the agricultural committee myself … My experience was that landowners would tell me that they have good farmland, while upon a closer look it turned out to be not so good … So I said 'Let us create a points-based system …' I explained it to the agricultural committee, and they agreed" (H-GS1).

Standardized leases became an important instrument of farmland control. Because the local agricultural committee accepted the system as well, landowners could not bargain for higher leases, even if they refused to use the Kōsha service. In addition, the local agricultural administration promoted public allocation by offering an incentive payment for giving land to the Kōsha – years before such incentive payments became national policy in 2011. Consequently, between 2005 and 2006 alone, the acreage handled by the Kōsha almost doubled (Izumo City 2013, 30). Operating within clearly demarcated and overlapping social, territorial, and political boundaries, the Kōsha system subsequently reinforced itself: the more land it distributed, the stronger its position as a local ordering force of farmland matters grew – eventually turning into the pillar of the organized local interpretation of national agricultural reform in Hikawa.

Village Institutions and Farmland Governance in the Kami-Ina District

Evidence on land use governance in the local agricultural regimes in Miyada Village and Iijima Town in the Kami-Ina District (Nagano Prefecture) supports the findings from Hikawa. Despite differences in organizational forms, comprehensive local control over farmland in the Kami-Ina District also rests upon the protracted and comprehensive integration of village institutions into the respective local agricultural regime.[12]

Like in Hikawa, the origins of village-wide control over farmland use and exchange in Miyada are to be found in a comprehensive approach to local governance of the rice acreage reduction policy (*gentan*). In 1980, the village founded a farmland use committee to coordinate the diversion of rice to other crops. The committee consisted of the local administration, the local co-op, and representatives of all hamlets in the village. Over time, joint deliberation to organize rice production control developed into a comprehensive local system to decide over the use and exchange of farmland. Under this system, any cultivation tasks that cannot be taken over by the owners themselves are distributed in the respective hamlets, or – if necessary – among the hamlets. Allocation of land use rights and cultivation tasks originally fell within the formal responsibility of the village administration, and later moved to the local cooperative branch as the result of changes in national policies. Despite several adjustments in the organizational setup of local agricultural governance during the 2000s, the hamlets themselves have remained the core social unit to decide upon farmland use (M-O). The protracted integration of all hamlets in the village thus provides the social and normative foundation for the organized approach to local farmland governance. The seven hamlets that have formed Miyada Village since the nineteenth century, the local cooperative branch, other local groups and the village administration are tied to each other by longstanding and durable socio-spatial relations (Kramer 2015). Like in Hikawa, these dense social and organizational ties seem to have carried the notion of treating farmland as a collective resource from the hamlet level to the level of the municipality – in the words of a local official, farmland use and exchange in Miyada are governed "as if the whole village was one hamlet" (M-O).

Another parallel to the trajectory of the Kōsha system in Hikawa is the interlinkage between farmland exchange and collective cultivation on the hamlet level. Every hamlet in Miyada maintains a cultivation cooperative, which since 2005 has been a sub-unit of a village-wide collective farm, to which all farm households in the village belong (see chapters 9 and 10). All machinery for the cultivation of rice and the major conversion crops (wheat, soy, and soba) is owned and used cooperatively under the umbrella of the Miyada branch of the local JA. Thus, like in Hikawa, farmland governance in Miyada is firmly embedded in protracted local institution-building that captures all aspects of local agricultural governance. The normative foundation of this approach is reflected in the slogan One Village, One Farm. The striking similarity with the leitmotif in Hikawa is hardly coincidental. Respondents from Hikawa have hinted that the "Miyada method" has been an inspiration for the Kōsha system.[13]

More directly, the Miyada method also had an impact on farmland governance in the local agricultural regime in Iijima Town, which belongs to the same cooperative district of JA Kami-Ina (Hoshi and Yamazaki 2015, 165). Despite organizational differences, the underlying notion of communal governance of farmland use and exchange is similar in Iijima (Hoshi and Yamazaki 2015). For example, integration of all farm households into the local agricultural regime via preexisting sub-municipal social units is a crucial feature of agricultural governance in Iijima Town as well. Here, historical administrative units located between the contemporary town and the hamlet have been employed as the socio-spatial and organizational basis for collective cultivation and land use deliberation (Tashiro 2009). Moreover, the local agricultural regime in Iijima has also incorporated elements of traditional hamlet rules and norms into specific formal rules governing farmland use. For example, although farmland ownership and use have come to be separated under the town-wide land use system, the "farmland management center" encourages landowners to engage in hamlet duties. For that purpose, the town-wide lease system sets financial incentives for owners to maintain their land (Ij-O).

In sum, while the local agricultural regimes in Iijima, Miyada, and Hikawa differ considerably from each other in their concrete organizational features, production structure, and character (see also chapter 10), local actors in each have translated preexisting (hamlet-level) norms and practices into municipal-level control over farmland (and over farmers, to some extent). In all three cases, these shifts were carried by dense, longstanding, and territorially contained social and organizational ties between hamlets, local co-op, and local administration.

The Local Origins of National Farmland Legislation

Despite their local characteristics, the local agricultural regimes discussed above were not built independent from or in outright opposition to national agricultural policies. Rather, the local trajectories reflect local interpretations of major shifts in the national agricultural support and protection regime, from the introduction of rice production control in 1970, to the onset of more exclusive state support for "bearer farms" in the early and mid-2000s, and the promotion of corporate farming since the late 2000s. Furthermore, local agricultural regimes in Hikawa and the Kami-Ina District have also influenced recent national farmland policies from below (Jentzsch 2017c). This influence is evident most directly in the case of the Hikawa Nōgyō Kōsha. By the mid-2000s, the Kōsha system had overtaken national policies on farmland consolidation in the hands of "bearer farms." Yet, with the nationwide introduction of "farmland harmonization groups" following revision of the

Agricultural Land Law in 2009 (see chapter 5), the core feature of the Hikawa Kōsha – allocation of farmland use rights through a local public body under "unconditional authority" – became national policy. Between 2010 and 2011, more than 1,600 farmland harmonization groups were founded throughout Japan (MAFF 2011b). In 2011, the government introduced incentive payments for owners and users relying on public allocation – a practice that the Kōsha had already adopted in 2005. In preparation for the 2009 revision of the Agricultural Land Law, the MAFF endorsed Hikawa as one of nine model localities to devise methods to consolidate farmland under the principle of "separating ownership and use" (MAFF 2007). According to Tashiro (2010, 173), the Hikawa Kōsha took the MAFF by surprise when it carried out the project on the basis of a well-established local farmland allocation system. Delegates from Hikawa took several trips to Tokyo to explain their model.[14] One main architect of the Kōsha system personally acknowledged the direct influence of the Hikawa Kōsha system (H-GS1), and the prefectural government of Shimane explicitly referred to Hikawa as "pioneering" national policies in separating ownership and use of farmland (Shimane Prefectural Government 2008). Local agricultural regimes in Miyada and Iijima have received attention from researchers and the Ministry of Agriculture as well (Hoshi and Yamazaki 2015; Tashiro 2009; Tsunoda 2012). Although their influence appears to be less direct than in Hikawa, the adoption of the principle of separating ownership and use in the 2009 revision of the ALL and the idea of public allocation of farmland use rights under unconditional authority is also connected to these local models (Tsunoda 2012).

Village Institutions and the Limitations of Publicly Sponsored Farmland Transfers

In practice, the national policies on farmland consolidation since 2009 – farmland harmonization groups as well as subsequent farmland banks – have not come near to establishing a rational public allocation of farmland under "unconditional authority" like in Hikawa or the Kami-Ina District. I argue that this is because the national policy was unable to transport the distinct social and normative underpinning of the local models to other localities (Jentzsch 2017c).

It is hard to assess the national impact of farmland harmonization on group policy. Yet its limitations are reflected partly in the fact that the overall share of land in the hands of "bearer farms" has increased very slowly since 2009 (MAFF 2016b), and there are low levels of consolidation in the majority of municipalities (see figure 6.2 in chapter 6). The local perspective helps to elucidate the problems of the national policies to publicly promote farmland exchange. In practice, the majority of local farmland harmonization groups were set up directly by the respective local JA. Other groups were run in cooperation between local JA and administrative bodies such as the agricultural committee.[15] In other words, the farmland harmonization groups were absorbed by the same local actors that have been involved in local farmland governance throughout the postwar era – and thus reproduced the established local practice of exchanging farmland in Japan. The harmonization group in Kōshū City in the Kōfu Basin illustrates this argument well. The local cooperative JA Fruits Yamanashi set up the farmland harmonization group in 2010. According to the cooperative official in charge, this was a natural decision – the cooperative was a well-established social platform for connecting tenants and owners before, not least because it provided a trust basis between both parties (KB-JA1). As a consequence, the newly founded harmonization group did not alter the mode of farmland transfers in the area and was unable to get farmland allocation under comprehensive control. By 2013, most land use deals were still be made through local social network ties, including completely informal arrangements (KB-JA1; KB-F1; KB-F6). This was not least the result of a lack of basic informational resources available to the officials in charge (KB-JA1). Formally exchanging land under "unconditional authority" via the harmonization group became the precondition for receiving accompanying incentive payments. In practice, however, farmers preferred to agree to a land use deal informally, and turned to the local administration only after they had reached an agreement to have it "publicly allocated" to them – thus informally overruling the formally required distribution mode while still securing access to the related subsidies. According to a local entrepreneurial farmer, policies to promote public farmland allocation have not substantially affected the way he obtains farmland, and the accompanying subsidies were mere "candy" in his eyes (KB-F1). Without the protracted integration of village institutions that underlies the Kōsha system in Hikawa, village institutions in Kōshū City thus undermined (rather than supported) the practice of public farmland allocation under "unconditional authority."

The principle of allocating land under "unconditional authority" could not replace the established mode of personal farmland transfers in other localities as well. Recall in this context the case of the large corporate farm in Yasu City, which has accumulated more than two hundred hectares of paddy land mostly independently from public allocation, and grants owners informal control over their land, despite the formal contract (Y-F1; Y-F1a). In general, lack of trust, combined with distaste for the duration of the contracts (typically ten years), has led owners to avoid public allocation agencies, or to find ways to circumvent the formal requirements informally – which are facilitated by local social network ties between owners, users, and local administrations/cooperative branches involved in farmland allocation.[16] In contrast, the protracted integration of village institutions into local agricultural governance within narrow socio-spatial boundaries allows the administrative technique of public farmland allocation to take effect as an accepted method to govern farmland use and allocation. An agricultural official from Miyada pointed out this crucial difference explicitly: "Land in Miyada is exchanged under 'unconditional authority.' But in reality, everybody knows each other, and everybody knows who uses whose land" (M-O).

Farmland Banks and Deregulation of Corporate Farmland Use in the Context of Declining Local Control

The farmland bank policy, which practically replaced the farmland harmonization groups in 2014, is similarly based upon the notion of public allocation of farmland use rights under "unconditional authority." Although farmland banks are located on the prefectural level, the actual tasks of organizing land use exchange are contracted to the municipal level, again often including local JA (Andō 2014). Consequently, the new policy has not resolved the lack of a social and normative underpinning for public farmland allocation. Yet the introduction of farmland banks was accompanied by more substantial incentive payments, so that landowners are keen to use them – albeit allegedly still informally circumventing the allocation under "unconditional authority."[17]

In Hikawa, while the financial burden of taking on land use rights has moved from the Kōsha to the prefecture, the principal mode of allocation has not changed since 2014. The Hikawa Kōsha – and not the distant prefectural farmland bank – still functions as the local agency to resolve conflicts between owners and users on maintenance or proper use. Upon the preexisting local institutional foundation, the agricultural administration in Hikawa utilized the new farmland banks far more quickly and more comprehensively than the rest of the prefecture – which meant better access to the related subsidies for local hamlet-based collective farms (H-O1; see chapter 10 for details). Officials from Miyada also report that the farmland bank policy has not affected the principal mode of deliberating local land use and exchange. Formal exchange of land use rights via farmland banks is perceived as more troublesome administratively, and farmers and landowners also dislike the lack of flexibility and control as the result of long formal contract duration. Still, the local agricultural administration extracted subsidies by strategically (re)exchanging formal land use titles within the local agricultural regime (M-O). Again, however, such organized control over farmland use cannot be assumed to be the norm. Overall, neither the harmonization group policy nor the introduction of farm-land banks has thus brought farmland consolidation in Japan under comprehensive public control. Socio-spatially embedded professional farms see no significant benefit in using the service, compared to infor-mal access to land (KB-F1; Y-F1; Y-F1a). Hamlet-based collective farms use the new system first and foremost in order to access the related sub-sidies by formally (re-)renting the land they have already been using collectively (Ht-CF; K-JA1; Shinagawa 2017; see chapter 10).

While the effects of a more rational use of land remain limited, the opening local farmland markets to nationwide bidding, which came with the introduction of farmland banks in 2014, raised concerns about "predatory" corporate farmland use.[18] Formally, corporations are re-quired to engage in agricultural production and act "in harmony" with local farming practices (Takahashi 2013). Yet, where the capacities for public and informal local control over farmland matters have been de-clining, this notion is increasingly challenged. In the organized local re-gime in Hikawa, redistribution of farmland among local "bearer farms" safeguards against the uncontrolled entry of external corporate inves-tors. In localities with surplus farmland and lack of local "bearer farms," however, external corporations have parachuted into local farm sectors even before formal legalization of corporate farmland use in 2009, at times with the enthusiastic support of local governments hoping for so-cioeconomic revitalization. As Sekine and Bonanno (2016) have pointed out in several case studies, these expectations have proven unrealistic sometimes. One obvious risk is that corporate franchise farms disap-pear quickly when the investor decides to terminate or relocate produc-tion, thus exposing the vulnerability of local farm sectors to "corporate hypermobility." In some cases, the resistance of landowners and other local actors caused corporations to shift production elsewhere (Sekine and Bonanno 2016, 107–32). Other analysts have also voiced concerns that weak local farm sectors can be exploited by large "downstream" re-tail companies seeking direct access to farmland and cheap (unskilled) labor.[19] Not surprisingly, publications associated with JA view the entry of corporations into the farm sector particularly critically, and even as a potential threat to the livelihood of rural communities (Muroya 2013, 2016; Keizai Hōrei Kenkyūkai 2011) – underscoring the potential threat of corporate farming to the future of the cooperative organization.

Insufficient local control over farmland use can also impair utilization of surrounding plots. This can be illustrated with the spread of solar panels, which have appeared in farming regions throughout Japan since the introduction of a feed-in tariff in 2012 (Feldhoff and Kremers 2020). Use of farmland to generate solar power was deregulated in 2013, provided that the land underneath is still used for agricultural production, such as roots or mushrooms (*Nikkei Asian Review* 2017). However, the capacities of local agricultural committees to oversee these and other legal requirements are increasingly limited, creating leeway for fraudulent farmland use (T-F).[20] In the Kōfu Basin, solar panels have spread over recent years. An uncontrolled spread of solar panels is problematic, given the patchwork pattern of farmland ownership and use. Often located amidst intact fields, the panels block farmland for further consolidation by neighboring land users. Fruit farmers have also complained that the panels affect surrounding plots by blocking sunlight and emanating heat.[21] Other concerns include soil erosion and disruption of water flows, increasing risks of wildfires or the appearance of the landscape in general (Feldhoff and Kremers 2020).

Similarly, critics have also warned about illegal conversion of farmland, such as by construction companies. In 2015, construction companies already made for 11 per cent of the general corporations renting farmland (MAFF 2015b). Against the background of the Abe administration's emphasis on public infrastructural projects (*Nikkei Asian Review* 2016), it remains at least questionable if the motives of these companies to obtain land use rights are purely agricultural. In any case, where local (informal) control over farmland erodes, farmland deregulation has graver consequences in practice than the gradual pace of national deregulation might suggest (Jentzsch 2017a).

Interim Conclusion

This chapter has shown that village institutions still shape farmland consolidation in Japan's agricultural sector. How they do it is also a matter of local institutional agency, that is, if and to what extent village institutions have been integrated into the local agricultural regime as the social and normative foundation for comprehensive public-cooperative control over farmland use and exchange. In the absence of such local institution-building, the established social mode of farmland transfers contributes to a more complicated access to farmland for expanding farmers, and eventually farmland loss. Against this background, scale-enlargement and further deregulation of the farmland market can have only limited effect on resolving the problems of abandoned land

and inefficient farmland use, which are deeply rooted in the social and normative underpinning of local farmland governance. In the absence of organized control over farmland transfers, even socially embedded large-scale corporate farms are hardly able to obtain large chunks of connected plots that are necessary to save time and labor. Moreover, those plots that are most likely to fall idle are also least attractive for either local expanding farms or external investors.

Evidence further shows that farmland exchange under "unconditional authority" is not an administrative technique that can be applied ad hoc anywhere in Japan. Without a historically cultivated social and normative foundation such as in Hikawa or Miyada, the national policies to promote public farmland allocation adopted from these local models have thus been less efficient and are more likely to benefit external corporate investors instead of local expanding "bearer farms."

Finally, the case of Hikawa illustrates that farmland consolidation is essentially a political process, not just a matter of enhancing the efficiency of agricultural production. This is because exchanging and consolidating land also shapes emergence of expanding farms, and the extent to which consolidation challenges small-scale part-time family farming and the role of the local cooperatives. Control over farmland consolidation also entails control over farms and/or the inflow and distribution of state support – and thus ultimately over institutional change in the agricultural sector. The following chapters will discuss this aspect in more detail.

Chapter Nine

Local Variations of Agricultural Entrepreneurship

Farmers in Japan now face few regulatory obstacles to expand their holdings, develop marketing channels outside the cooperative organization, and diversify their economic activities. Much to the contrary, business-oriented (corporate) farms have become the main targets of support policies and are often framed as forming the frontline against vested interests in agricultural support and protection in general, and the influence of JA in particular. National and international media feature young entrepreneurs who turn to the countryside with innovative ideas for agricultural cultivation and marketing (T. Yoshida 2016); or independent organic rice producers who regard international competition as a business opportunity rather than a threat (Tabuchi 2014). Some public intellectuals push similar narratives (Yamashita 2005, 2015b; Harada 2012). Playing a double role, the president of Wagoen Farm, a large, diversified agri-business in Chiba, is an outspoken critic of JA with a regular media presence (Asakawa 2009). Another prominent example of independent entrepreneurship hails from Ōgata, a model settlement created on reclaimed land in Akita Prefecture in the 1960s. Already in the 1980s, farmers from Ōgata had gained a national reputation for defying the rules of the rice production control scheme to maximize their profits from selling rice and have since pursued development of industrial rice farming. Today, the Ōgata Village Akita Komachi Rice Producer Association is among the largest commercial rice producers and marketers in Japan.[1]

Beyond such prominent cases, thousands of "bearer farms" throughout Japan have expanded and professionalized their businesses over the 2000s, including a growing number of incorporated farms. If and to what extent these emerging agri-businesses emancipate themselves from cooperative and administrative control also shapes the pace and the direction of institutional change in the agricultural support and protection regime. Upon closer examination, however, there are considerable local differences in how such expanding (corporate) "bearer farms" relate to the respective local co-op, administration, and other farms. The following chapter argues that these different roles are shaped by the respective local agricultural regime.

Large-Scale Farms in the Local Agricultural Regime in Hikawa

In the organized local agricultural regime in Hikawa, public-cooperative control over farmland is directly linked to control over farmers. Apart from hamlet-based collective farms, which occupy the largest part of the acreage in Hikawa (see chapter 10 for details), and several medium-sized farm households (five to twenty hectares), five large-scale farms have formed the top level of Hikawa's agricultural production structure since the Kōsha system emerged in the early 2000s. One of these – Green Support – is an agricultural production corporation co-founded by JA Hikawa and the Nōgyō Kōsha itself. Among the other four, two still operate as regular household farms, and two are corporations. Each of these farms has between forty and fifty hectares under cultivation (full use rights) and additionally carry out services for smaller farms, which puts them in the top 1 per cent of Japan's largest farms.[2] They have professionalized their farming operation by investing in large-scale machinery and (in the case of the corporate farms) employing regular labor, partly even from outside the town (H-F1). The Kōsha system provides these farms access to comparatively well-connected, highly developed farmland, allowing for more efficient agricultural production. Yet the large farms are hardly independent agri-businesses. Within the institutional context of the local agricultural regime, their entrepreneurial freedom is explicitly subdued to the interests of the farm sector as a whole. The agricultural administration – via the Kōsha system – guides farms administratively in several respects. For example, the Kōsha system prevents an "uncontrolled" accumulation of farmland on behalf of expanding farms. As one architect of the Kōsha system explained, "If Farmer A received two hectares last year and Farmer B received only one, we will give Farmer B two hectares in the following year. We have to keep the balance between all of them ... The Kōsha decides on land issues irrespective of personal matters. Our criteria are transparent. We can explain them to everybody" (H-GS1).

The Kōsha monitors farmers' performance in order to guide decisions on farmland allocation: "Farmer A operates his farm as a corporation, and his staff changes year after year. We have to monitor his business style (*kigyōsei*) properly. Let me give you an example. Farm A is larger than Farm B. If one employee quits at Farm A and changes to Farm B, Farm A needs to be asked how this could have happened. Employee volatility can be a hazard for the future performance of a company, right? So we have to consider the performance of the company before we assign farmland" (H-GS1).

Notably, when explaining the Kōsha system, the same respondent explicitly raised the renegade entrepreneurship in Ōgata Village as the polar opposite to the approach taken in Hikawa (H-GS1). Ultimately, the Kōsha system is a means of administratively containing private entrepreneurship and thus reflects the notion that private economic interests are subordinate to the overall well-being of the local farm sector: "Say this field belongs to Farmer A and that field belongs to Farmer B. Between both fields, we have another plot – who will you give it to? Both want to expand. What do you do? If you give it to the person who pays the highest price, the principle of capitalism (*shihon shugi no genri*) will come into play. The richest persons will become the largest farmers. This would create winners and losers among the Hikawa farmers. But we do not do it this way" (H-GS1).

This aspect of the Kōsha system speaks directly to the non-liberal (i.e., organized) character of the local agricultural regime, which the son of a large farm household in town described jokingly: "From an economic viewpoint, the system is like communism" (H-F4b).

Large-Scale Farms as Quasi-Public Service Providers

Beyond their dependence on public farmland allocation, the large farms are entrenched in the local agricultural regime in other ways. For example, the large farms (including Green Support) are the executive agents of the Kōsha in the coordinated crop diversion system – that is, they employ the labor force and the large-scale machinery at their disposal to carry out some or all of the tasks related to paddy-field diversion from smaller farms. As pointed out before, this system has enhanced land-use efficiency, but also has made the land held by small-scale "rice-only" farmers available for subsidy-productive conversion crops, which not least helps the smallholders themselves to continue farming under the umbrella of state support. Moreover, the integration of the large-scale farms in the crop diversion system further illustrates how control over farmland is intertwined with control over farmers in Hikawa. While their involvement provides the large farms with a stable source of income and access to subsidies, it also ties them further to the Kōsha system. Additionally, large farms also engage in other agricultural services for smaller farms. For example, they operate modern rice drying facilities that smaller farms usually do not have. Some smaller farms – including hamlet-based collective farms – have their rice harvest dried, peeled, and packed for them at large farms. Farmers tend to prefer this drying service to the huge JA-run country elevator, because they can receive a share of their homegrown rice for self-consumption, which is not possible at the country elevator (H-CF3). In other localities, such services are commercialized on behalf of the owners of the respective facilities, who might also act as commercial wholesalers (e.g., T-F). In Hikawa, however, the service is organized by the Nōgyō Kōsha, which assigns customers according to their location and sets the prices (H-F1). JA Hikawa then collects the rice that is not set aside for household consumption at the farm gate. In this sense, the drying service is a publicly administered community service to mediate the interests of small-scale farmers, professional farm households, and the local co-op.

As another element of indirect control, the agricultural administration provides all farms in town with comprehensive information on the ever-changing state of agricultural policies and subsidy schemes, as well as on how to apply for what type of support. While the service provides large farms with excellent access to the full array of state support, it also reinforces their dependency on the agricultural administration. The head of the largest corporate farm in Hikawa reported that state support made for about half of his income and that he completely relies on information from the Agriculture and Forestry Office before deciding what crops to grow in the next season in order to extract these subsidies (H-F1).

As a result of their entrenchment in the local agricultural regime, even the largest corporate farms have mostly continued to rely on the cooperative organization, and have not registered as wholesalers themselves.[3] As of 2013, JA Hikawa still marketed virtually all rice and diversion crops produced in town (H-GS1). Thus, while the local agricultural production structure in Hikawa was rationalized and professionalized, the deregulation of the rice market hardly affected JA Hikawa's local monopoly. With farmland use in the hands of selected large farms and hamlet-based collective farms, and farmland exchange firmly under public control, both the entry of external corporate investors and the rise of entrepreneurial contenders from within were contained. Consolidation of the agricultural production structure under the Kōsha system is a local reinterpretation of national agricultural policies that reflects the conservative interests of the established local actors, including JA Hikawa. In the organized local agricultural regime, corporate farms remain constrained in their economic decisions by "institutionally sanctioned collective interests" and act as "quasi-public infrastructures" (Höpner 2007), fulfilling tasks that extend beyond the narrow goal of profit maximization.

Green Support: Corporate Farming for the "Public Good"

This notion is epitomized in Green Support, which has a special role among the large-scale corporate farms in Hikawa. Before the company was founded in 2003, the Kōsha itself had taken over some cultivation tasks in the crop diversion system. Yet, within the emerging public farmland allocation system, Green Support was established as the agricultural "muzzle" of the Kōsha, which has since concentrated on administrative tasks. Although it has legal status as an agricultural production corporation, Green Support is far from being a purely commercially oriented farm. Socially, organizationally, and normatively the company is firmly tied to the Kōsha system.[4] As such, Green Support explicitly serves the "public interest" rather than striving for profits (H-GS1). Like other large farms that have emerged in Hikawa since 2004, Green Support takes over cultivation tasks under the local rice production control system. Moreover, Green Support functions as an element of comprehensive public control over land in Hikawa. Some of the available land in town exceeds the capacities of large farmers or is unattractive for them as a result of its remote location, condition, or soil quality. Green Support takes over cultivation of such inferior and cost-intensive farmland. The company thus acts as a last resort against farmland abandonment in the less developed, mountainous parts of the town, and at the same time creates leeway for a more rational farmland use for the other large farms (H-GS1).

The company also provides job opportunities for part-time farmers, who work at Green Support off the rice season (H-F5). Moreover, the company steps in if farmers have temporary problems in cultivating their plots, such as when they are ill. Green Support can cultivate their fields for up to one year (H-JA4). In this context, the integration of village institutions into the local agricultural regime becomes particularly explicit: "When someone has a problem, Green Support takes over the part of mutual support. This is like the village functions (*mura no kinō*) from former times. The person does not have to pay much money for our help. He has his own machines. I only arrange the manpower. It is a matter of charity" (H-GS1).

Deeply embedded in the local agricultural regime, Green Support carries and thus reinforces traditional hamlet-level norms and functions of mutual support, which have become increasingly hard to enforce within hamlets alone. National support policies are employed to support this function locally: because it has formal status as an agricultural production corporation, Green Support receives the full range of agricultural subsidies for "bearer farms." Within the local agricultural regime, Green Support thus represents an interpretation of corporate farming that highlights communal self-help in the interest of small farmers and the agricultural administration, instead of the onset of profit-oriented agricultural entrepreneurship.

Other JA-Related Corporations

In this context, it is worth noting that Green Support's business model is not unique. Local co-ops throughout Japan have either invested in or directly formed agricultural corporations. These corporations typically act as trustees for abandoned land, revitalize plots, manage land redistribution, or cultivate surplus land (N. Taniguchi and Lee 2013). The legal basis for such JA-related corporate farms is the deregulation of corporate access to farmland, introduced in 2009. Yet they function as a safeguard against the perceived threats posed by corporate farming. Their involvement aims to prevent free land from being absorbed by other corporations, whose striving for "private gains" may cause "trouble with the local community," as a JA official from Yamagata put it (cited from N. Taniguchi and Lee 2013, 2). In contrast, revitalization of abandoned land by local JA or JA-related corporations is framed as a public service. Not least, like in the case of Green Support, the activities of the JA-related farms are subject to state support, and JA-related corporations provide subsidized employment opportunities for JA staff and local farmers (N. Taniguchi and Lee 2013). For example, the JA-funded corporation Aguri Kaihatsu in Izumo City provided regular employment for six people in 2013, while cultivating only thirty hectares – supported by national subsidies for revitalization of abandoned land (I-JA2). The rationale for Aguri Kaihatsu's activities was providing non-profit-oriented support for a troubled local farm sector (JA Izumo 2010, 68).

What distinguishes Aguri Kaihatsu in Izumo and similar enterprises in other localities from Green Support in Hikawa is less a defensive stance on corporate farming; rather it is the extent to which Green Support is embedded in the local agricultural regime. In other localities, impact and economic viability of JA-related corporations have been limited, as both local JA and administrations lack financial, personal, and organizational resources to revitalize large chunks of abandoned arable. Further, some farmers have exploited the services provided through the JA-related corporations, e.g., by demanding revitalized land back for personal use (N. Taniguchi and Lee 2013). In contrast, Green Support's social and normative embedding in the local agricultural regime in Hikawa makes for a stable business environment – for example, in the form of access to high-quality farmland to counterbalance the burden of cultivating less favorable plots (H-JA4) – and prevents free-riding.

Agricultural Entrepreneurship in the Kōfu Basin

To analyze the variations of agricultural entrepreneurship across different local agricultural regimes, we will first turn to the Kōfu Basin in Yamanashi Prefecture, where horticulture is prevalent. In the absence of organized control over farmland consolidation, expanding "bearer farmers" in the area face more complicated access to land or subsidies, but more freedom to exploit new forms of state support as entrepreneurs, thereby not least emancipating themselves from local cooperative structures.

Contrasting Local Agricultural Histories

It is important to reiterate that the differences between the Kōfu Basin and Hikawa are rooted in different agricultural histories. Fruit farming is less land-intensive and less dependent on storage and joint shipping, more commercialized, and more exposed to (international) market pressure than paddy field farming. Fruit farmers in the Kōfu Basin developed direct marketing channels throughout the postwar era, facilitated not least by the relative proximity of the Tokyo metropolis (fieldwork; see also Kingsbury 2012). Direct marketing has contributed to less dependence on the agricultural co-op. This is not to say that JA is without influence. It played a vital role in collecting, processing, and marketing horticulture products throughout the postwar era, and is routinely involved in local agricultural administration. Still, independent agricultural entrepreneurship is more prevalent in the Kōfu Basin, at least in comparison to Hikawa.

Closely related, agriculture in the basin has been intertwined with the local history of alcohol production. Throughout the postwar era, farmers, local cooperatives, and wineries – including large-scale corporations – have been tied to each other in a dense web of local social relations and cooperation. A main factor underlying these relations was postwar farmland legislation, which excluded wineries from direct access to arable land. Wine makers had to rely on grapes obtained from local farmers directly and/or the cooperative organization, or use imported raw materials (Kingsbury 2012, 2014). Yet local actors also found numerous informal ways to circumvent the provisions of the Agricultural Land Law. Many family-owned wineries gained access to farmland through relatives or other local social ties (Kingsbury 2012, 168–9). In this sense, local social ties between farmers, local co-ops, local governments, and (corporate) wineries have long been employed to create informal leeway for entrepreneurship within the regulatory corset of postwar agricultural support and protection – and even helped pave the way for national regulatory change. Yamanashi was among prefectures that lobbied for deregulation of corporate farmland access in the early 2000s and became the site for local "special deregulation zones," which prepared the ground for the 2009 revision of the Agricultural Land Law (173–6).

Importantly, there are considerable differences across the basin in the degree to which JA has been involved in organizing relations between farmers and the wine industry. Katsunuma, a former town within Kōshū City, has the largest number of wineries in the basin, some of them owned by multinational corporations. Within the boundaries of the former town a distinct set of rules still governs relations between farmers, wineries, and the Katsunuma chapter of JA Fruits Yamanashi. For example, the co-op, local government, and Katsunuma Winery Association fix the annual price for Kōshū grapes for wine production. This scheme not only stabilizes the supply of grapes to wineries, it also reinforces the role of the co-op in the collection and marketing of grapes, and local agricultural governance. In contrast, the connections of wineries with JA in neighboring Enzan have grown weaker over recent decades.[5] While attempts to establish a similar scheme in the prefecture were canceled in the mid-1990s, the local scheme in Katsunuma survived absorption of the local co-op by the larger JA Fruits Yamanashi in 2001, and the subsequent merger of the town into Kōshū City in 2005. In recent years, however, its coverage has eroded (KB-F16; see also Kingsbury 2012; and chapter 11 on the impact of municipal and cooperative mergers).

Against this background, there have been two main directions of agricultural structural change in the basin. First, corporate wineries are increasingly venturing into agricultural production. Especially the larger wineries in Katsunuma produce only a small share of their grape supply themselves (Kingsbury 2014, 37). Yet, as grape farmers are aging and Japanese wine grows in popularity, wine producers are under pressure to expand grape production in order to secure supply. In the spring of 2019, four large beverage companies announced plans to double their vineyards throughout Japan by 2027 (*Nikkei Asian Review*

2019). Second, local household farms incorporate their agricultural business, develop independent marketing strategies for fresh and processed products, or engage in highly professionalized contract farming for (corporate) wineries, thus picking up on national "bearer farmer" policies and the policy focus on the "6th industry," i.e., linking agricultural production, processing, and marketing/tourism. While both developments challenge the small-scale, household-based production structure in the Kōfu Basin and the position of JA, the role of these local "bearer farms" deserves particular attention.

From Family Farms to Agricultural Entrepreneurs

Traditional family farms and expanding (corporate) "bearer farms" in the Kōfu Basin are embedded in their local institutional environment. Local social network ties and farmland norms still govern the exchange and use of land within a highly fragmented pattern of land use. Long-standing local social ties between wineries and farmers remain an important factor for securing the supply of high-quality grapes.[6] Moreover, farmers gain access to state support and other resources through personal ties with the local administration and the local JA. Social structures of the hamlet are still the root-work of the cooperative organization, especially in joint shipping of the harvest (KB-F8; KB-F4; KB-F5). While rooted in these local social structures, entrepreneurial "bearer farms" create alternatives to accepted farming practices, and expand and professionalize their social networks, thus becoming agents of institutional change in their local agricultural (sub-)regimes. Some concrete examples will help to illustrate this argument.

  KB-F6 runs a successful diversified agri-business in an area of Yamanashi City that spans nine hamlets. The hamlets had constituted a local cooperative district throughout the postwar era, which eventually was absorbed by the amalgamated JA Fruits Yamanashi in 2001. Yet the area has retained its socio-spatial sense of belonging, and the hamlets have been substituting some functions of the former co-op branch (KB-F8) – thus forming a local agricultural sub-regime within the boundaries of Yamanashi City and JA Fruits Yamanashi.[7] Each hamlet runs a shipping union, which still cooperates on the level of the old cooperative district. Despite a decline of traditional forms of communal labor, mutual assistance between households during funerals or illness is still a part of hamlet life. Other hamlet functions (sewer cleaning, garbage collection) were also still intact in 2013 (KB-F8a). Inter-hamlet cooperation within the boundaries of the former cooperative district has a long history. In the 1950s, the hamlets and the co-op jointly invested in a winery to process grapes that could not be marketed as table grapes. Despite the merger into JA Fruits Yamanashi, the winery has continued to produce wine from surplus grapes grown exclusively by farmers in the nine hamlets (KB-JA2).

While most farm households in the area lack successors and struggle to maintain their land, KB-F6 has departed from the typical pattern of household-based production. Located right next to the old winery, KB-F6 has incorporated and diversified his business, and enjoys access to the full array of state support measures for "bearer farms" – including national and prefectural subsidy schemes to employ regular labor and trainees. The farm runs a modern café that sells homemade products. As the result of an active social media presence, the café attracts customers from all over Japan. On the one hand, the expanding agri-business remains embedded in the social structure of the former cooperative district. The father of the current household head was among the farmers investing in the cooperative winery. His son is still a member of JA Fruits Yamanashi. He regards membership in the local co-op and in the village community as more or less equivalent, and other farmers in the area explicitly expect him to keep his membership (KB-F8). On the other hand, his entrepreneurial ambitions have caused him to "stick out" within the local community, putting stress on his local social ties, and also caused him to grow out of the local agricultural (sub-)regime. The farm has stopped relying on JA for marketing, so it also does not take part in hamlet-based joint shipping. Instead, the harvest – mainly peaches and grapes – is processed on site or marketed directly to large retail companies. Initially, this arrangement caused conflicts with the local JA. Against the background of the decline of family farming in the area, however, JA eventually had to give up its resistance to the new business model. By 2019, some older farmers in the former cooperative district started to market their products through the large corporate farm instead of JA – thus rendering the farm a direct competitor to the cooperative organization (KB-F6).

A few kilometers to the east, but still within the boundaries of the amalgamated JA Fruits Yamanashi, KB-F1 steadily expanded his holdings to become one of the largest grape producers in the former city of Enzan (since 2005 a part of Kōshū City). In 2014 he opened his own winery, which relies almost exclusively on his own grape production. KB-F1 runs an incorporated agri-business with prime access to state support, including subsidies for hiring trainees and revitalizing abandoned land. Most importantly, the winery was realized with a major grant under the policy framework to support the "6th industry." KB-F1 also introduced innovative cultivation techniques to grow western grape varieties and employs regular, professional labor from outside the basin[8] – all of which sets him apart from the majority of farmers in his hometown Enzan, and the Kōfu Basin in general. KB-F1 is the son of a respected local grape grower and JA official, and continues to rely on a dense local social network for access to farmland, materials, and information. His network also includes local and prefectural officials, often based on longstanding personal ties, e.g., from joint high-school days in Enzan. KB-F1 also routinely cooperates with the other wineries in Enzan, for example in organizing PR events to promote local wines.[9] These wineries are typically longstanding family businesses that produce grapes and/or rely on supply from surrounding farmers, or were founded as cooperative enterprises to process unmarketable (inferior) table grapes. In contrast, KB-F1 built his winery from scratch, with the goal to process his own grapes and market his wine directly to exclusive restaurants and hotels in Tokyo and the Kansai region. This shift from an area-typical table-grape producer to an innovative winemaker has gone hand-in-hand with diversification of his social network. Beyond his highly localized social ties in the former city of Enzan, KB-F1 has built a professional, extra-local network that includes researchers, MAFF officials, and restaurants and sommeliers in several major cities. As one aspect of this development, KB-F1s business activities increasingly exclude the local JA.[10] As his business developed beyond the scope of small-scale household farming, the local cooperative also lost its appeal as a "gate-keeper" for information on cultivation techniques, business strategies, or state support. This function has been absorbed by municipal and prefectural agricultural administrations, with which the farmer is in frequent contact. Beyond consultations over land exchange or support schemes, he is regularly selected to take part in official hearings and committees as a certified "bearer" of local agriculture.[11]

One member of KB-F1s professional network is KB-F2, a fruit farmer who lives in the outskirts of the prefectural capital Kōfu City – that is, in a different municipality and local cooperative district. Like most other farm households in his semi-urban neighborhood, KB-F2 has sold a piece of land for urban development – a highly lucrative source of prosperity before the burst of the economic bubble (KB-F4; KB-F5). Yet, in sharp contrast to his local peers, KB-F2 has reinvested revenue of the land sale in his agricultural business. He has since incorporated his farm and employs regular (subsidized) labor. The prefecture has formally recognized KB-F2 as an agricultural advisor. Together with KB-F1, he holds seminars on grape cultivation. Apart from producing for direct sales and local wineries, KB-F2 carries out highly professionalized contract farming for large-scale corporate wine producers. In 2013, the farm relied on JA only for marketing surplus grapes and insurance. Upon expanding his business, the farmer severed his living space from his workplace by renting and buying farmland far beyond the narrow social and territorial confines of the local shipping cooperative in his neighborhood. As a result, he rarely takes part in the local cooperative activities of the remaining small-scale household farms in his neighborhood anymore. Interviewees on both sides indicated that the diverging business paths also went hand-in-hand with a growing social distance (KB-F1; KB-F4; KB-F5).

Bifurcated Structural Change in the Kōfu Basin

The three examples introduced above highlight a sharp contrast to organized structural change in the local agricultural regime in Hikawa. In the absence of an ordering force such as the Hikawa Nōgyō Kōsha, agricultural entrepreneurs in the Kōfu Basin have used the changing focus of national agricultural policies to emancipate themselves from the cooperative organization, and to some extent also from the underlying local social and normative environment. The farmers introduced above are outspoken about their entrepreneurial ambitions, and regard independent entrepreneurship as the only way forward for agriculture in the Kōfu Basin, if not Japan as a whole. This attitude can go hand-in-hand with a certain disregard for traditional forms of small-scale, household-based farming and the cooperative organization. KB-F1 is particularly outspoken about his emancipation from JA.[12] In his eyes, farmers who sell their grapes to JA lack ambition and a sense for quality, which he sees in sharp contrast to his own business model. KB-F2 also regards his approach to agriculture as superior to the aging, small-scale farm households in his neighborhood. While he expects small-scale household farming to fade away for lack of successors, he takes pride in the fact that he could convince his son to take over his business. Similarly, KB-F6 stated that surrounding small-scale farmers lack his courage to seek new business models, and values economic entrepreneurship and "freedom" more than cooperative forms of production and marketing.

Such views are a local manifestation of a national development in agricultural diversification. Throughout the postwar period, the cooperative organization has been strongly involved in processing and direct sales of agricultural products – such as in the cooperative winery introduced above. Since the mid-2000s, however, as new policies to promote the "6th industry" coincided with gradual deregulation of the Agricultural Land Law, this approach has been increasingly challenged by retail and processing corporations seeking direct access to farmland, and entrepreneurial farmers expanding their own processing and marketing abilities (Muroya 2016). Meanwhile, small-scale part-time farms tend to lack the capabilities to make use of the new subsidy schemes on their own (Konno and Kudō 2014).

More generally, the examples suggest that the lack of organized control over consolidation of the agricultural production structure in the local agricultural (sub-)regimes in the Kōfu Basin results in bifurcation, in that a small number of expanding (corporate) farms are subject to subsidies and support schemes that are out of reach for the majority of smaller household farms, obtain prominent positions in local and prefectural agricultural administrations, and at the same time grow apart from the local cooperative and aging small-scale household farms. In this process, the entrepreneurial farmers are drivers of institutional change, while the cooperative organization is reduced to the passive role of catering to its rapidly aging clientele of small-scale farms.

Large-Scale Corporate Farming in Yasu City

To put the contrasting manifestations of agricultural entrepreneurship in Hikawa and the Kōfu Basin into perspective, we turn to the local agricultural regime in Yasu City (Shiga Prefecture), where rice farming is prevalent. As mentioned in chapter 6, the trajectory of the local agricultural regime over the 2000s has been marked by a relatively successful consolidation of farmland in the hands of designated "bearer farms." Among these farms is one of the earliest and largest corporate rice farms in Japan. As the result of steady expansion since the onset of "bearer farm" policies in the early 1990s, this farm alone occupies more than 200 hectares of paddy land, which is almost 10 per cent of the total arable land in Yasu. The farm expanded in the absence of comprehensive public/cooperative control over farmland transfers. But a closer look at the role of this corporate farm also reflects its social and normative embedding in the local agricultural regime, which feeds into the conservative interests of the established local stakeholders, including small-scale farm households and the local JA.

Y-F1 founded the farm in 1991 with the political and financial support of the local co-op, which provided 25 per cent of the firm's capital. Despite its legal status as a corporation, and its massive scale-enlargement and professionalization, the farm has remained closely attached to the local co-op socially, economically, and organizationally (Y-F1). Its expansion has been embedded in longstanding social and professional relations with the local co-op and the administration. The founder of the farm had served earlier on the executive board of the local co-op, as a member in the local agricultural committee, and held a seat in the city assembly. Against this background, the farm's role within the local agricultural regime extends beyond maximizing corporate profits. Similar to the large (corporate) farms in Hikawa, it takes over cultivation tasks associated with the rice production control scheme from smaller farms, including hamlet-based collective farms. These tasks are a paid service and as such a pillar of the farm's business model. On the other hand, however, involvement of the large farm helps smaller farms (again including hamlet-based collective farms) to carry on rice farming as well. The farm also supports the formation of *new* hamlet-based collective farms, which is explicitly in line with the local administrative and cooperative agenda. A business pamphlet of the farm lists supporting the foundation of new hamlet-based farms under the item "relations with the administration."[13] According to data provided by the agricultural administration, Y-F1's farm has taken over the paddy field diversion tasks of two hamlet-based collective farms entirely (Yasu City 2017).[14] Thus, although the local agricultural regime in Yasu does not display the level of organization seen in Hikawa, the expansion of the large-scale corporate farm was not purely an expression of individual entrepreneurship, nor did it happen at the expense of JA and small-scale part-time farmers. On the contrary, Y-F1 acts as a potent partner for the local administration and the co-op in governing structural change in the local farm sector, and enhances the inflow of state support to the local agricultural regime as a whole.

Large-Scale Corporate Farming as an Element of Local Farmland Governance

The social and normative underpinning of Y-F1's role in the local agricultural regime is most prominently reflected in his approach to farmland accumulation. As mentioned in chapter 8, the farm gains access to land via social network ties of Y-F1 and his reputation as a trustworthy land user. Accordingly, about 75 per cent of the farm's more than 1,000 land use deals are concentrated in his hometown of Chūzu, which was an independent municipality until it became a part of Yasu City in 2004. Only a small number of plots are located in neighboring Moriyama City. Yet even these deals are not "extra-local" in the strict sense, in that they are still confined within the boundaries of the same local co-op, i.e., within the same local agricultural (sub-)regime.[15] In order to reduce transaction costs associated with maintaining a large number of small-scale land use deals, Y-F1 has privately defined formal rules for farmland accumulation, such as a standardized points-based system to determine leases. Other than in Hikawa, where a similar system was created and enforced for the whole town through the intervention of the Hikawa Nōgyō Kōsha, the local agricultural committee in Yasu or the administration itself are not involved in making and enforcing these rules (Y-O1). But despite a lack of comprehensive public control over farmland exchange, the farmland system applied by Y-F1 still reflects the integration of social ties and farmland norms. As mentioned in chapter 8, the farm is implicitly committed to modify or even terminate its formal land use deals upon request of the owner and/or hamlet, should any conflicts over the proper use and/or maintenance of the land arise (Y-F1). More importantly, beyond economic purposes, the massive accumulation of land by Y-F1's farm also stabilizes local farmland governance in times of eroding abilities of aging farmers and hamlets to use and maintain their land. Accordingly, Y-F1's approach to farmland accumulation has a strong normative connotation: the corporation explicitly takes on land to protect it from falling idle and/or to maintain it properly (Y-F1). Thus, the farm bears some similarity to the communal character of Green Support in Hikawa, in that it operates as a local ordering force for farmland use in times of an aging and shrinking agricultural workforce. This entails not least that the corporate farm also takes on land that is less favorable from a strictly economic point of view. In doing so, the farm partially counters the imbalance in the local farmland market, which is marked by strong competition for flat paddy land among expanding farms, but impeding farmland loss in less favorable, mountainous parts of the city. With this task, the farm addresses an explicit concern of the local agricultural administration (Yasu City 2017). Local officials themselves have highlighted the role of Y-F1's farm as a safeguard against farmland loss in the city (Y-O2). Reflecting the same objective, the farm also cooperates with an agricultural production corporation that was founded by the local JA to utilize less favorable land (Y-F1a).

In sum, the role of this large corporate farm is less defined by opportunistic profit-maximization, and more by close personal and economic ties to the local JA, responsibilities for local coordination of rice production control, and the social and normative underpinning of farmland use and transfers reaching down to the hamlet level. Deeply embedded in the local agricultural regime, the corporate farm thus partially serves as an executive agent to govern farmland consolidation on behalf of the local agricultural administration and the local JA in the absence of more comprehensive public instruments to intervene in the local farmland market.

Interim Conclusion

The contrasting roles of agricultural entrepreneurship show that neither scale-enlargement nor corporate farming is in itself an expression
of resistance against the local agricultural establishment, including the
local JA. Rather, the cases analyzed in this chapter reveal that the role of
expanding (corporate) "bearer farms" – and thus the liberal potential of
reforms promoting scale-enlargement and corporate farming – depends
on their embedding within the local institutional context. This context
shapes the extent to which emerging "bearer farms" emancipate themselves from their local cooperative, the relation between large-scale
(corporate) farms and small-scale part-time farming, and whether large
farms act as profit-oriented entrepreneurs or "quasi-public infrastructures" (Höpner 2007), i.e., service providers in local farmland land governance or rice production control. Furthermore, it shapes whether and
how successfully local agricultural cooperatives can employ corporate
farming to access state support and control farmland consolidation as
a whole.

Especially in rice-farming areas, these local variations of agricultural entrepreneurship hinge on if and to what extent local cooperatives and/or administrations can control farmland consolidation. In
Hikawa, the Kōsha system has supported a local interpretation of the
role of expanding (corporate) farms that is efficiency-oriented, but also
non-liberal in that large-scale corporate farms operate under strong
public and cooperative intervention. While the degree of organization
is particularly high in Hikawa, emerging agricultural entrepreneurs in
other locations are also embedded in the social and normative underpinning of local agricultural regimes – potentially with a similar impact
on their role, as the quasi-public character of the large corporate farm
in Yasu shows. In less organized local regimes, however, emerging entrepreneurs are more likely to resort to village institutions selectively
and strategically – which means they might also break away from the
narrow social structure of their hamlets and/or villages, commonly accepted farming practices, and the cooperative organization.

Chapter Ten

Hamlet-Based Collective Farming and Village Institutions

This chapter shifts the focus to another type of designated "bearer farms": hamlet-based collective farms. This form of agricultural production has (re-)gained salience in the mid-2000s in the context of the reform of paddy field subsidization (see chapter 5), which fueled a sudden increase of hamlet farms in the latter half of the 2000s. In 2017, 516,817 farm households in 30,737 hamlets were organized in 15,136 hamlet-based collective farms, which comprise more than 10 per cent of agricultural land use. Hamlet farms have different levels of formalization and vary in their internal organization. The majority still operate as voluntary associations, which qualify for the full array of state support as certified "bearer farms" only if they meet certain requirements. More recently, hamlet-based collective farming has also contributed substantially to the proliferation of corporate farming in Japan. The share of incorporated hamlet farms steadily increased to 31 per cent in 2017 (MAFF 2017).

Regardless of the level of formalization, hamlet-based collective farming – which is most common in paddy-field cultivation – has been a substantial factor in structural change in Japan's agricultural sector (Hashizume 2013, 2018). On average, hamlet farms have thirty-two hectares under cultivation (MAFF 2017). They often engage in "block rotation" to rationalize rice farming and cultivation of conversion crops under the rice production control scheme. At least potentially, hamlet-based collective farming thus enables more efficient use of farmland, machinery, and labor in times of an aging agricultural workforce (Tashiro 2006).

Beyond these functional aspects, hamlet farming also has important political and social implications. The hamlet-farming boom in the mid-2000s absorbed many aging and small-scale farm households that would otherwise have given up agriculture entirely (Shinagawa 2017). Hamlet farming is thus also a strategy to sustain post-retirement,

state-supported paddy field farming in times of a more exclusive subsidy regime and a declining labor force. Against this background, I argue that hamlet-based collective farming illustrates the role of village
institutions as dynamic resources in the changing agricultural support
and protection regime particularly well. Hamlet farming is not only
an expression of the continued salience of the hamlet as an institution, but also shows the adaptability of seemingly obsolete traditional
hamlet-level norms and practices to the challenges of an aging workforce and changing support policies. Moreover, I argue that the local
proliferation of hamlet farming depends on how hamlets – and village
institutions as a whole – are integrated into the local agricultural regime. A strong local proliferation of collective farming can secure a high
inflow of state support to the local agricultural regime as a whole, and –
especially for the local branches of JA – to establish a defensive, inclusive local interpretation of structural reform.[1]

The Social and Normative Foundations of Hamlet-Based Collective Farming

Hamlet-based farming resonates with the historical notion of the hamlet as an "agricultural production unit" (Fukutake 1980), as it evokes
images of an agrarian past in which (rice) cultivation was a communal, cooperative affair. But these days are long gone in most parts of
contemporary Japan (see chapter 7). Inclusion of hamlet-based farming in the changing subsidy regime has thus been criticized as a form
of cultural folklore to rectify concessions to the farm lobby. The increase of hamlet-based farming in the mid-2000s has been criticized as
"policy-reactive" (Toyama 2012) or superficial (Tashiro 2014b), and thus
at least implicitly inferior to "natural" forms of hamlet farming. Meanwhile, community-oriented hamlet-based farming has been framed
positively as a means to address rural social problems such as aging
and depopulation beyond the goal of securing state support (Kitagawa
2012; Yamamoto 2013).

Beyond such ideal-typical distinctions, I argue that the ability to adapt
to changes in the political and socioeconomic environment renders the
hamlet a viable institutional resource for local actors in the changing
agricultural support and protection regime. Although rice farming
lost its communal character decades ago in most parts of Japan, fieldwork has shown that hamlets can build on kinship, neighborhood and
non-agricultural social ties (e.g., sports teams, travel groups, H-CF5;
H-CF7), and hamlet norms and practices as the foundation to *revive
and reinterpret* communal agricultural cooperation. The hamlet-farming

boom in the 2000s shows that for policy-makers and farmers alike, the hamlet is still taken for granted as the social unit for agricultural cooperation – even if the motivation to found a hamlet-based farm is (also) access to state support. In more abstract terms, founding a hamlet-based farm can be captured as a form of productive exchange: "the exchange process through which two or more parties organize and combine their resources to produce some good or service not (as cheaply) available to any separately" (Marshall 1984, 17). According to Marshall (1984), productive exchange has been the foundation of the hamlet as an institution throughout the history of rural Japan. Although contemporary hamlets have little in common with the agrarian settlements of the past, founding a hamlet-based farm arguably follows the same logic: members organize and combine land, labor, and machinery to produce a good that became increasingly difficult to obtain for part-time farming households in the mid-2000s: state support.

Reviving and Adapting Hamlet Norms and Practices

Hamlet-based farms routinely incorporate hamlet practices into their organizational setup. Interestingly, these include elements of traditional agricultural cooperation that have largely become obsolete since the postwar period. In Hikawa, for example, hamlet farms revived practices such as forming female work groups, joint lunches in the fields, and skill-based labor division among hamlet members – all of which older respondents from the area have described as common practices that had disappeared with the onset of mechanization and part-time farming since the 1960s (see chapter 7). Apparently, however, these practices have remained in the institutional repertoire of hamlet life and could be reanimated in hamlet-based collective farming. Moreover, many hamlet-based collective farms founded in the mid-2000s rest on older (sub-hamlet-level) cooperation patterns such as shared machinery or block rotation in rice production control – patterns that could be reactivated, extended, and formalized with the onset of more exclusive state support for "bearer farms" in the 2000s (e.g., H-CF2; H-CF5; M-O; K-JA1). Once founded, hamlet farms tend to rely on organizational practices from other domains of hamlet self-organization. For example, hamlet farms in Hikawa have adopted the mode of decision-making and selecting leaders from the hamlet – that is, creating "study groups" to prepare for difficult decisions and a "screening board" to select leaders (H-GS1; H-JA4).[2] Further, hamlet farms also tend to reproduce the norm that the male household head represents the household in important decisions (e.g., H-CF5; H-AL).[3]

Hamlet-based collective farming does not necessarily include all farming households, let alone all members of the hamlet. In fact, only less than one-quarter of all collective farms are all-encompassing (MAFF 2017). The exclusion of one or several farm households from the hamlet farm *can* reflect conflict or even a lasting social division within the hamlet (H-CF2), but it does not have to. Marshall (1984) has shown that postwar hamlets can endure conflict over some issues without lasting effect on other hamlet affairs. Even if not all households join the hamlet-based collective farm, hamlet membership still provides the social foundation for the farming operation (H-CF1; H-CF2; H-CF5). On the other side of the spectrum, about 25 per cent of all collective farms involve more than one hamlet (MAFF 2017). Such cases can also be found in Hikawa, where many collective farms operate on the *shinkōku* level, involving members from two to three hamlets. According to the leader of H-CF5, longstanding ties and cooperation between the hamlets in the *shinkōku* "from childhood to old age" rendered founding a joint collective farm a "natural decision." Yet there are also *shinkōku* in Hikawa in which efforts to set up joint collective farms have failed as the result of lasting inter-hamlet conflicts (H-CF4; H-JA4). In Iijima Town, collective farms have formed within the boundaries of Meiji-era villages. Again, this shift rests upon historical inter-hamlet social ties within the confines of these historical villages, which form an intermediate socio-spatial unit between hamlets and the administrative structure of the contemporary town (Tashiro 2006, 190–1). Throughout Japan, the merger of hamlet farms into larger entities of historical villages has gained momentum in the light of the aging workforce.[4] In principle, however, the hamlet remains the core social unit for founding collective farms in Japan, while any expansion beyond hamlet boundaries is contingent.

Changing Land and Labor Relations

Across the different forms and types of collective farms, the most common normative foundation for hamlet-based farming is the motive to protect the hamlet land from falling idle, or against renting or selling it to "outsiders." This notion has been shared by respondents from all hamlet farms I have encountered in the field and is also commonly reported in the literature (Kitagawa 2008; Tashiro 2009; Shinagawa 2017). In the household, collective land use helps families retain control over their land as their ability to cultivate the land on their own declines. At the same time, pooling farmland is also a useful means to retain control over the land within the hamlet's boundaries. Reflecting this notion, the leader of a hamlet farm in Hikawa argued that forming the collective farm had helped to uphold hamlet norms (e.g., how to properly maintain farmland), whereas renting land to "outsiders" would lead to "disorder" (H-CF4). In this sense, collective farming resonates with the traditional notion that the land in the hamlet is not only private property, but also a collective resource to be governed by hamlet members.[5]

As mentioned above, most hamlet-based collective farms still operate as voluntary associations. In such associations, collective farming does not formally affect land use rights, as members simply pool their land for joint use. Only incorporated hamlet farms can formally obtain land use rights from members as well as non-members. In any case, farmland *ownership* typically stays intact. This also means that landowners in collective farms remain responsible for the maintenance of their land, at least in principle. However, not all members in collective farms stay equally active as farmers. Typically, some or all paddy-field cultivation tasks move to a limited number of "operators," often former part-time farmers who have retired from their main jobs. Other members help only occasionally, or even stop farming altogether (H-CF1; H-CF2; H-CF5; M-O; Ht-CF). Non-farming members might even be unable or unwilling to continue the basic maintenance of their farmland. Consequently, some hamlet-based farms have transformed the tasks of maintaining irrigation and drainage channels and field boundaries into a paid service for non-farming landowners – that is, they have formalized previously unwritten "hamlet duties" in the context of running the hamlet-based collective farm (e.g., H-CF1; H-CF5).[6]

This finding already suggests that hamlet-based collective farming not only incorporates, but also *alters* hamlet norms and practices. As part of this process, collective farming turns independent (part-time) farmers into wage laborers. While the details vary, in 2013 members in Hikawa typically received a fixed wage of around ¥1,000 per hour they work for the collective farm.[7] Additionally, hamlet farms typically distribute annual dividends according to the acreage each member provided to the collective farm. At least until the farm becomes a corporation (see below), even minimal participation in farming activities entitles members to claim this dividend (H-CF2; H-CF5). Distribution of the income of the collective farm operation among all members is a common pattern throughout Japan (see, e.g., Shinagawa 2017). On the one hand, it provides members with guaranteed returns, and secures them against the risks of household farming, such as illness or injuries, and increasing labor shortages (H-CF5; H-CF7). On the other hand, however, revenue distribution also creates weak incentives to invest labor – a "moral hazard" that collective farming operations are confronted with not only in Japan.[8]

Collective farming changes labor relations within households as well. As individual part-time (rice) farmers, most households cultivate their land in the evenings and on weekends. In busy times, every household member is obliged to take part. Hamlet farming tends to bring a new, gendered division of labor. Mechanized wet-paddy farming becomes purely male labor, while the cultivation, processing, and marketing of dry field crops such as vegetables and land maintenance tasks fall into the realm of the female members. Especially female respondents perceived this new division of labor as a relief, in that it leaves some time for hobbies like gardening or travel (e.g., H-CF5; H-CF7). On the other hand, respondents also consistently reported that younger household members no longer perceive farming as a family duty in hamlet farms, eventually adding to the projected shortage of young labor and successors.[9]

Integration of hamlet ties and norms into the collective farm can alleviate some of these problems. For example, some hamlet farms in Hikawa have revived the practice of unpaid communal farmland maintenance for all hamlet members, combining communal labor with social events such as barbecues (e.g., H-CF4; H-CF7). In Miyada Village, where virtually all paddy land is used collectively, land maintenance is still accepted as part of the owner's duties. Even non-farming members still feel obliged to carry out these tasks. The norm of communal farmland maintenance thus relieves the collective farm enterprise itself from some of the workload (M-O).

Hamlet-Based Collective Farming as a Social Strategy

In sum, resorting to the institutional repertoire in the hamlet allows aging, part-time farming hamlet members to adhere to national policy changes while still holding onto the lifestyle (and the benefits) of small-scale part-time farming. This includes continued access to state support, from paddy-field subsidies to cheap loans for large-scale machinery or storage facilities. Yet, as I have argued elsewhere in more detail, the meaning and functions of hamlet farming extend beyond extracting state support – they reproduce agriculture as a source of rural welfare as part-time farm households face an increasingly hostile socioeconomic and political environment (Jentzsch 2020a). Especially in more remote areas, there are (incorporated) hamlet-based farms that are more explicitly oriented toward revitalization of the area as a whole, with agricultural production only one of several fields of (social) activities (Yamamoto 2011, 2013; Kitagawa 2012; Matsunaga and Seki 2012). Taking the notion of communal integration even further, some hamlet-based farm enterprises also combine collective agricultural production with providing explicit eldercare (Iba and Sakamoto 2014). Yet, in Hikawa even hamlet farms that focus mainly on subsidy-productive paddy field farming tend to have important social functions, including, for example, opportunities for social exchange among the mostly elderly members beyond the realm of agricultural production, and the common motive to protect the hamlet against rural decline. Moreover, members of various hamlet farms have stressed that collectivization has improved their well-being, because it relieves aging households from some of the workload and financial risks, and provides a safety net in case of illness during busy seasons – which could mean the loss of an entire harvest for individual household farms (H-CF3; H-CF4; H-CF7; H-AL).

However, hamlet farming is not available to all hamlets equally. In many hamlets, the majority of households have already rented out or sold their land, or the hamlet lacks consensus, human resources, or information on subsidy policies and funding to set up a collective farm. This leads to a crucial argument: if and to what extent hamlet farms emerge in a certain locality is not only a matter of hamlet agency alone, but also a matter of how hamlets are embedded in the local agricultural regime.

Hamlet-Based Collective Farming in the Context of Local Agricultural Regimes

Government statistics and rural sociologists have often pointed to substantial regional differences in the proliferation of hamlet-based farming, which is particularly salient in parts of western Japan, Kyūshū, and the Hokuriku region. For example, these regional differences have been linked to a relatively high share of aging, part-time rice farmers and/or the mountainous topography, which tends to support high shares of hamlet-based farming.[10] Below the regional and prefectural level, however, there are also significant local differences, which can occur even between neighboring localities. These local "hot spots" have received less attention but are particularly relevant in the context of this book.[11]

Local Governments, Local Cooperatives, and the Proliferation of Hamlet-Based Farming

In principle, local administrations and local JA have good reasons to promote hamlet-based farming in their jurisdictions. For local administrations, promoting the formation of hamlet-based farms became a prolific means to implement national "bearer farm" policies and retain the inflow of state support to their jurisdictions. Since agricultural support became targeted more exclusively at certified "bearer farms," the promotion of hamlet-based collective farming allows local administrations to answer pressure from the central government to implement these reforms, even in the absence of business-minded agricultural entrepreneurs. Especially in remote and mountainous areas with an aging labor force and lack of well-developed arable land, collective farming often appears to be the only way to achieve the national policy goal of promoting farmland consolidation (Kitagawa 2008; JA Izumo 2010). Moreover, the turn toward less comprehensive agricultural subsidization in the mid-2000s coincided with a decline in the distribution of public investments to regional Japan.[12] Hamlet farming has long been related to implementation of public works projects. Many hamlet-based collective farms were founded in the context of prefectural or national land improvement projects to promote scale-enlargement and a more rational production structure in the context of earlier "bearer farm" policies in the 1990s (H-CF1; H-CF6; KB-CF; for Izumo City, see Tashiro 2010). Promoting hamlet-based farming continues to be a means for local governments to attract public investments in the agricultural infrastructure. Further, hamlet-based collective farming also facilitates the organization of rice production control targets, because these farms tend to follow the production quota en bloc in order to harvest the associated state support.

As an approach to structural change that includes aging part-time farm households, hamlet-based farming also appeals to the agricultural cooperative organization, which has an economic and political interest in retaining a high number of part-time (rice) farm households (Yamashita 2015b). Local co-ops are heavily involved in promoting hamlet-based farming throughout Japan by providing information, guidance, and practical support – often in close cooperation with local and prefectural governments.[13] In Izumo City, for example, JA Izumo provided detailed blueprints for setting up collective farms, pre-calculating necessary farm size, labor input, subsidies, and the expected annual revenue for maximum convenience (JA Izumo 2010). These calculations conveniently entail the handling fees for shipping the harvest to JA – and according to a local JA official, the majority of hamlet-based farms in Izumo actually applied the cooperative calculations (I-JA2). Founding a collective farm typically involves (subsidized) investments in new, large-scale machinery, which ties the farms to JA as the most common creditor in rural Japan. In some cases, the local co-op also directly acts as a shareholder (Tashiro 2010; Mitsui 2018). Once established, hamlet farms tend to remain closely associated with the local co-op, which for example continues to provide help with accounting, or information on the ever-changing subsidy schemes. In Hikawa, all hamlet farms have continued to market their paddy field products via the local cooperative. In Miyada, where all farm households belong to the village-wide collective farm, the farm and local cooperative branch de facto form an entity. All heavy machinery is owned cooperatively. In the words of a local JA official, there "is no wall between the collective farm and JA" (M-CF).

While there is no comprehensive national data on the social and economic ties between hamlet farms and JA, local evidence clearly suggests that promotion of hamlet-based farming has the potential to bind farm households and hamlets to JA socially and economically in times of an aging agricultural workforce and increasing regulatory freedom for farmers to operate outside the cooperative corset. Hamlet farming thus reinforces the institutional link between hamlets and the cooperative organization that had underpinned the power of the latter throughout the postwar era. Moreover, a large share of land in the hands of collective farms also blocks this land from access for other forms of (external, corporate) agri-business.

Although farm households, the cooperative, and local administrations share a common interest in hamlet-based farming throughout Japan, some local agricultural regimes display a share of collective farming that is not only much higher than in local, prefectural, and national comparison. I argue that such local "hot spots" do not emerge by coincidence. Rather, the extent to which hamlet-based farming takes hold as a comprehensive local strategy depends on how hamlet ties and norms are integrated into the local agricultural regime. Evidence from the local agricultural regime in Hikawa illustrates this argument particularly well.

The Proliferation of Hamlet-Based Farming in Hikawa

With more than 40 per cent of the total acreage cultivated collectively, in Hikawa there is a relatively high share of hamlet-based farming. The local administration and JA Hikawa have promoted hamlet-based farming since the early 1990s. From the beginning, the proliferation of hamlet-based farming was embedded in the local agricultural regime as a whole – and thus constitutes a vital element of its organized character. Akatsuki Farm – the pioneer collective farm in Hikawa – was founded in 1991 on the level of one *shinkōku*, i.e., three hamlets. Collectivization was pursued against the background of a large-scale national land improvement project, and the local cooperative and the administration guided the setup of the collective farm (H-GS1; H-CF1; H-CF1a). Subsequently, Akatsuki Farm served as a model for a wave of hamlets and/or *shinkōku* collectivizing land and machinery use once they received funding for land improvement projects and cheap loans to purchase the large-scale machinery for their remodeled plots under the umbrella of early "bearer farm" policies (H-GS1). Beyond the influence of administrative guidance or state policies, the local proliferation of collective farming also occurred via the dense network of social and/or organizational ties between the administration, the local JA, and the hamlets. The head of Green Support in Hikawa explained, "In every hamlet in Hikawa in which a collective farm is formed, there is a JA official or a member of the administration already living in the hamlet. In Hikawa, the presence of such leaders is important for the founding of hamlet-based farms" (H-GS1).

This mode of proliferation is not confined to Hikawa. Collective farms in Kami District and Hita City followed along similar patterns (Ht-CF; K-JA1; K-JA2). Other studies from throughout Japan have also shown that hamlet-based farms are typically led by cooperative "old boys," (former) members of the local administration, or assemblymen.[14] Such local social network ties provide detailed information on the formal proceedings for founding a hamlet-based collective farm, how to file for which kind of state support, and the social prestige to convince hamlet members to collectivize their land.

In Hikawa, however, the social ties between hamlets, JA, and administration were further institutionalized through integration of hamlets into the local agricultural regime via the *shinkōku* system, thus amplifying the proliferation of collective farming along these ties. As mentioned in the previous chapter, the spread of hamlet farming in Hikawa went hand-in-hand with proliferation of the notion of farmland as a collective resource – the normative underpinning of the emerging system of public farmland allocation through the Hikawa Nōgyō Kōsha. The Kōsha has displayed a preference for hamlet-based farming over other forms of cultivation that fall into the category of "bearer farms." Albeit implicitly, collective farming represents the ideal form of structural change in Hikawa, to which the development of non-collective large-scale (corporate) farming is supplementary.[15] The proliferation of collective cultivation is thus another means to contain the expansion of large individual farms, which also support smaller, less professional hamlet-based farms by taking over some or all the tasks that come with diverting paddy fields to other crops. Thus, under the Kōsha system the promotion of hamlet-based farming became an important element of organized control over the local farm sector. Tashiro (2010, 180) noted that hamlet farms in Hikawa tend to "act in accordance with the views of Nōkyō and the municipal administration."

The integration of hamlets and hamlet-based farming into the local agricultural regime also allowed for a swift and comprehensive reaction to the onset of more exclusive paddy-field subsidies in the mid-2000s. In 2004, there were already twenty-eight hamlet-based farms in Hikawa, more than half of which engaged in collective cultivation. At that time, however, none of the farms met the formal requirements for certification as "bearer farms" (Izumo City 2013, 21). Yet, anticipating the policy change to more exclusive subsidization, the agricultural administration began to push for formalization of existing farms in 2006, and also encouraged the foundation of several new hamlet-based farms. By December 2008, the number of hamlet farms that met the formal requirements to qualify as certified "bearer farms" had risen to thirty-two, thus securing a steady inflow of national subsidies to the town.

The Kōsha system allowed the foundation of new hamlet-based farms even against considerable resistance. In one case, a hamlet-based farm had obtained the use rights for several plots in the territory of an adjacent hamlet via the Kōsha system. The adjacent hamlet had originally decided against collective farming. In 2013, however, encouraged by the local administration and a lucrative new subsidy scheme, the hamlet members agreed to form a corporate collective farm. Their decision caused an inter-hamlet conflict, as members of the new farm reclaimed the use rights for some of the plots used by members of the neighboring hamlet-based farm, who refused to give up this land. In this deadlock, the Kōsha used its control over farmland exchange to enforce a compromise. The Kōsha redistributed three hectares from the older farm to the newly founded farm, and promised to compensate the former with the allocation of other plots over the coming years (H-JA4). This compromise was much to the dismay of the older farm (H-CF2). Yet, given the Kōsha's power over farmland allocation and the fact that the leader of the older farm himself was a former local JA official with close personal ties to the agricultural administration,[16] resistance seemed to be no option. This episode illustrates well how the Kōsha system enables the administration and JA to subject the interests of individual farm(er)s to their agenda.

Including the contested new hamlet farm, more than 1,000 of the 1,602 farm households in Hikawa were part of a hamlet-based collective farm by the end of 2013. Had their farmland instead been acquired by one of the emerging large-scale farms, the number of active farm households in Hikawa would have decreased far more drastically. The hamlet-based farms in town enabled the continuation of part-time farming as a lifestyle and a post-retirement source of additional income, as the operators are mainly or entirely retired members of (former) part-time farm households. The local agricultural regime was thus able to answer the national policy demand for structural reform far more comprehensively than other localities in Japan, while retaining the inclusive welfare character of the postwar agricultural support and protection regime, and expanding public and cooperative control over the process of structural change in the local agricultural sector.

Proliferation of Collective Farming in Comparison

The major difference between the role of collective farming in Hikawa and other localities is how and to what extent hamlets – and village institutions as a whole – are integrated into the local agricultural regime. In Izumo City, for example, the local co-op and the municipal government created organizational structures and informational resources to promote collective farming (JA Izumo 2010). Hamlet farms in Izumo have also formed through social ties between hamlets and the local JA (Tashiro 2010). Yet the local agricultural regime does not display the same level of institutionalization of ties between hamlets and the local administration/cooperative and lacks instruments to enforce collective cultivation (such as control over allocating land use rights). Thus, the proliferation of hamlet farming has not been as systematic as in Hikawa. This is also the case in Hita City. The largest collective farm in the city was also formed on the basis of a large-scale land improvement project, and alongside social ties between the local government, the co-op, and the local hamlet leaders. Yet there is no comprehensive framework to promote hamlet-based farming in the rest of the municipality (Ht-CF). The farm remains closely connected to JA and continues to rely on the cooperative for selling their harvest. For the co-op, the collective farm is an anchor in the area. After the local branch was closed in a cooperative merger, most other farm households reportedly stopped using cooperative services, or ceased farming commercially altogether. In this case, respondents suggested that the co-op might be more dependent on the collective farm than the other way around (Ht-CF).[17]

Meanwhile, some local agricultural regimes have produced even higher collectivization rates than Hikawa. In Kami District, virtually all paddy land was collectivized in sixty-nine hamlet-based collective farms in 2007 in response to the paddy field subsidization reform. Like in Hikawa, this sudden and comprehensive proliferation of hamlet farming did not occur spontaneously, but happened under the guidance of the local JA, which convinced all hamlets in town to follow the example of a model collective farm in order to qualify for the new subsidies.

The model farm itself was created in the hamlet in which the now managing director of the local co-op still lives (and farms part-time). The sudden collectivization in the mid-2000s also rested on preexisting subsidy-productive hamlet-level cooperation patterns in almost all hamlets in the district (K-JA1; K-JA2), in another parallel to Hikawa.

Miyada Village is a prominent (but not the only) example of a collective farm that formally covers the whole municipality. The shift toward all-encompassing collectivization was achieved on the basis of the preexisting local system to organize land use and block rotation in the context of the rice acreage reduction policy (see chapter 8). This foundation allowed for a swift and comprehensive local reaction to national policy changes in the mid-2000s. While some degree of collectivization had already been established by the early 2000s, these activities did not meet the formal requirements of the "certified farmer" scheme. Thus, in 2006 all farmland in the village was formally consolidated into one village-wide collective farm, as a direct answer to the onset of more exclusive subsidization. The institutional roots for this village-wide collectivization lie in the hamlet, where the collective use of farmland and machinery had long been practiced. The hamlets have remained the core units for organizing farmland use and exchange within the formal framework of the village-wide collective farm. Thus, integration of these hamlet-level patterns provided the resources to craft a local interpretation of national policies that supports small-scale part-time rice farming and secures the inflow of state support to the local agricultural regime. Like in Hikawa, collective farming also serves as control over the local agricultural sector. Over the years, Miyada has attracted younger, entrepreneurial farmers from outside the village, who typically engage in fruit production. The in-migration of younger farmers – while much-needed in demographic terms – has sometimes caused friction in Japanese communities, as the migrants' views, interests, and farming practices can clash with those of local farmers and their cooperatives (McGreevy 2012). In Miyada, however, all newcomers have to become members of the village-wide collective farm in order to receive land use rights. This ties them into the local agricultural regime formally and socially (e.g., because they attend regular meetings), and provides some control over their economic activities, as the newcomers cannot simply expand their acreage at the expense of incumbent local farm households (M-O).

Hamlet-Based Farms as Corporations

Despite its defensive potential for established local actors such as small-scale rice farms and local JA, hamlet-based farming should not be misunderstood as a mere obstruction to structural change in the Japanese farm sector. Rather, the proliferation of collective farming shapes institutional change – on the hamlet level and in local agricultural regimes. Change becomes particularly obvious in the incorporation of hamlet-based farms. After the hamlet-farming boom in the mid-2000s, the increase of incorporated hamlet farms – from 6.4 per cent in 2005 to 31 per cent in 2017 – indicates changes in the internal organizational structure of these farms (Shinagawa 2017). This development was induced not least by state policies. The 2005 "New Bearer's Management Stabilization Law" stipulates that hamlet-based farms must provide a plan to become corporations within five years in order to receive the subsidy-productive status of a certified "bearer farm." Thus, many hamlet farms that were founded in the context of the Across-Commodity Stabilization Countermeasure in 2007 had to consider incorporation in 2012.[18] The second Abe administration (2012–20) introduced additional policy incentives for collective farms to turn into corporations in the context of the introduction of farmland banks in 2014 (see below).

To some extent, ongoing incorporation suggests that the hamlet farming boom in the mid-2000s was an intermediate step on the path toward a more professional, large-scale, and diversified agricultural production structure (Hisano, Akitsu, and McGreevy 2018). Especially for local JA, this process is a double-edged sword. On the one hand, incorporation can stabilize hamlet-based farms against labor shortages and unstable access to farmland and state support. On the other hand, it entails the risk that farms turn their backs on the cooperative organization upon taking on a more professional and entrepreneurial character. Corporate farms tend to diversify their business and engage in the direct marketing of their products (Koike 2012; Koyama and Miyata 2012). Again, however, the transformation of hamlet-based collective farms into corporations and the impact of this process are also shaped by the institutional context of the respective hamlets, as well as their integration into the local agricultural regime.

Incorporation and the Hamlet

Incorporation alters the relation between the hamlet as a social unit and the farming operation – that is, the very social and normative foundation that was employed to turn the hamlet in a subsidy-productive form of agricultural production in the first place. As a crucial element of this process, incorporated hamlet farms gain the right to hold formal land use rights. Thus, when hamlet farms turn from voluntary associations into corporations, members typically rent their land to the newly founded legal entity. Moreover, incorporated hamlet farms can obtain land use rights from non-members as well, facilitating an expansion of the farm beyond hamlet boundaries.[19] Formalization of land use rights is closely related to the mode of distributing revenues. As mentioned before, voluntary associations distribute revenues according to the acreage each member provided to the collective farm. Upon turning into corporations, however, hamlet farms tend to reward contributing labor more than contributing land. That is, members who do not work for the farm might only receive the lease for the land they have rented to the farm. The potential financial impact for individual members should not be underestimated. For example, one of the largest hamlet farms in Hikawa was able to pay its members annual dividends of around ¥540,000 per hectare provided to the farm – even if they contributed only a marginal amount of labor (H-CF5). In late 2013, the farm was preparing its incorporation. Not surprisingly, this process was laden with conflict.[20] Beyond this example, the reorganization of dividends was a cause for worry in other collective farms in Hikawa at that time (H-CF2; H-CF6).

Once they turn into corporations, hamlet farms can issue formal employment contracts. Incorporation thus provides the formal ground to alleviate internal labor shortages. Although members and leaders of collective farms have consistently expressed the wish to run the farm as a strictly hamlet-based operation for as long as possible (H-CF2; H-CF3; H-CF4; H-CF5; H-CF5a; H-CF5b: H-CF5c), respondents have also acknowledged that they will have to rely on external labor eventually, as there are not enough successors within the hamlet (H-JA1; H-CF5; H-CF5d; H-CF6). More generally, formalization of land use rights and professionalization of labor relations can amount to a shift from "village logic" to "entrepreneurial logic" in hamlet-based collective farms (Koyama and Miyata 2012). This shift entails the social risk of alienating the farm from the hamlet, and particularly from landowners who are either unable or unwilling to invest regular labor. Even before incorporation, many hamlet farms take over land maintenance tasks from older or non-farming landowners. Upon incorporation, such practices are likely to increase, including the use of external labor. Turning social obligations into a paid service, however, potentially undermines members' commitment to communal labor. In turn, all aspects of management, cultivation, and land maintenance must be covered by regular (and thus costly) labor. Thus, while a more professional setup has the potential to alleviate the "moral hazard" of collective farming because it creates incentives to invest labor, it can also become a burden for the economic stability of the hamlet farm.[21]

This being said, incorporation does not automatically lead to the formation of independent, purely profit-oriented agri-businesses. Rather, in practice incorporation tends to produce an ambiguous institutional setup that can also reflect the aspiration to retain communal elements. The concrete relationship between hamlets and incorporated hamlet-based farms and the character of the latter depends on how members integrate hamlet ties and norms as resources to shape formal change. Some hamlet leaders in Hikawa were eager to organize incorporation in a way that minimizes alienation between hamlet and farm and sustains a sense of collective "ownership." For example, the head of one collective farm in the process of incorporation was explicitly worried that over-emphasizing labor input as the source for members' revenues would eventually undermine the objective to secure hamlet land as a collective resource. Moreover, professionalization would affect the oldest members of the farm the most, contradicting the original motives of founding the hamlet-based farms to support aging farm households. The farm was thus considering options to keep land-related dividends as high as possible to "maintain the hamlet spirit" that underlies collective cultivation (H-CF2).

Other hamlet farms in Hikawa have managed to retain a communal, welfare-oriented character despite formally operating as corporations over years (e.g., H-CF7; H-CF7a), while some have developed a form of double identity. For example, Akatsuki Farm, Hikawa's pioneer hamlet-based farm, became a corporation already in 2003. On this occasion, the farm invested in new greenhouses to grow strawberries and grapes, which eventually led to a departure from its original character as a strictly hamlet-based enterprise. The farm began to employ young, university-trained external workers to support the horticulture business. Moreover, the investment also allowed for partial emancipation from the local JA, as the farm markets at least some of its (processed) horticulture products directly. On the other hand, the farm continues to incorporate hamlet ties and norms into its organizational setup. For example, older women in the hamlet form work groups, reinforcing longstanding social ties within the three hamlets. These groups also provide a less costly labor force to support the professional horticulture production (H-CF1).

For other localities, incorporation of hamlet-based farms has also been discussed as a positive development for stabilizing rural livelihoods. Analyzing the trajectory of hamlet-based farms in Hiroshima Prefecture, Yamamoto found that incorporation can even sharpen the profile of hamlet farms as community-oriented "social enterprises" (instead of a more business-oriented profile), and such community orientation is more likely to occur in farms that include all hamlet members (Yamamoto 2011).

Corporate Hamlet Farming in Local Agricultural Regimes

Beyond the hamlet, local agriculture regimes shape how corporate farms emerge and which character they take on. In the organized local agricultural regime in Hikawa, the local JA and the Nōgyō Kōsha have monitored and guided the incorporation of hamlet-based farms closely. For example, officials from the JA Farm Management Center provide hamlets with legal information and standard business models and participate in hamlet meetings to prepare incorporation (H-JA2; H-CF6). In the context of the local agricultural regime, guiding hamlet farms toward incorporation has long served to maintain the inflow of state support as high as possible. In the mid-2000s, some small hamlets in town did not meet the acreage threshold required to receive the status of a certified "bearer farm." These hamlets were instead encouraged to form a corporate farm, which made them eligible for the certified farmers scheme, and thus for the full array of state support, regardless of their smaller size (H-GS1). Such cases of incorporation do not reflect a more entrepreneurial approach to farming, but rather are motivated by to perpetuate small-scale post-retirement rice farming – an especially vivid example for how much the interpretation of what corporate farming means (and if it is in the interest of the local co-op to support it) depends on the local institutional environment.

Until 2014, the Nōgyō Kōsha handled the transferring and formalizing of land use rights that comes with incorporation of hamlet farms. Landowning hamlet members yielded their land to the Kōsha under unconditional authority, and it then rented the land to the new hamlet-based agricultural corporation. This practice was subsidy-productive for both landowners and newly established corporations, as both sides received the national incentive payments for farmland consolidation (H-JA4). Moreover, the Kōsha could increase the share of farmland under its control with every incorporation. With the introduction of the farmland bank policy in 2014, the government expanded incentive payments for land transfers via the prefectural farmland banks. Noticeably, transferring land en bloc was rewarded with an extra payment – a strong incentive for farm households to establish an incorporated hamlet farm and rent their land to the new legal entity. These payments peaked in 2014 and 2015, and were subsequently reduced.[22] The Kōsha system allowed Hikawa to utilize the farmland bank system in 2014 and 2015 to a much greater extent than in prefectural and national comparison. Upon closer look, however, little land in Hikawa was actually consolidated in these two years. Instead, the local administration guided hamlets to use the new system for the highly subsidy-productive incorporation of existing hamlet-based collective farms. Thus, while the share of corporate hamlet farming in Hikawa increased sharply in 2014 and 2015, this increase hardly reflects a sudden turn toward agricultural entrepreneurship. Rather, it illustrates again that comprehensive control over farmland and farmers in the local agricultural regime in Hikawa has facilitated remarkably quick and subsidy-productive reactions to changes in national subsidy distribution.

The local agricultural regime in Miyada Village displays a similarly organized approach to corporate hamlet farming. In 2015, the all-encompassing village-wide collective farm formed a corporation. Yet, according to local officials, this step was motivated mostly by the generous incentive payments that were introduced in the context of the farmland bank reform. In practice, the local institutional configuration underlying collective land and machinery use in the village did not change with the transformation into a large-scale corporation (M-O; M-CF). The founding of the corporate farm was thus a subsidy-productive move toward reinforcing the local agricultural production structure rather than toward a more entrepreneurial approach to agricultural production. In other localities, incorporated hamlet farms also used the farmland bank system to extract subsidies for "concentrating" land that is already used collectively (Ht-CF; see also Shinagawa 2017) – but, other than in Hikawa or Miyada, not in the context of a comprehensive local strategy.

Even in organized local agricultural regimes, successful promotion of corporate collective farming can entail the risk of a loss of public/cooperative control over these farms. In Hikawa, prolific utilization of the farmland bank system to incorporate hamlet farms means that many land use contracts have come to be formally handled by the prefectural farmland bank, and not the local Kōsha. In 2016, the acreage exchanged under the farmland bank system overtook the acreage held by the Kōsha (Hikawa Town Agriculture and Forestry Office 2017, 17). Thus, at least formally, the Kōsha's control over farmland is not as comprehensive as before. In 2017, local officials stressed that in practice, the Kōsha has retained full control over the actual farmland *allocation* (H-JA4; H-O3), yet "outsourcing" land use rights to the farmland bank may still lead to loss of control in the future. Moreover, the growing number of corporate hamlet farms also increases the likelihood that some farms eventually develop a more business-minded, entrepreneurial character, as the pioneer Akatsuki Farm displayed in 2013. At least potentially, the foundation of the corporate farm in Miyada along with the use of the farmland bank system entails a similar risk of undermining public-cooperative control over the local farm sector – albeit this development was not on the horizon in the summer of 2017 (M-O).

In Iijima Town, however, hamlet-based collective farms have already developed into diversified, professional, and increasingly independent enterprises. All four large collective farms in town have founded corporations since the mid-2000s. While formalization was certainly also related to the objective of continued access to state support, the corporate farms have come to operate as professional enterprises, including use of external labor, diversification of their products, and processing and direct marketing. By 2017, the most prominent corporate farm in town marketed only 25 per cent of its products via JA (Ij-O). At the same time, however, the underlying hamlet-based collective structures still relieve the corporations from some of the workload, e.g., land maintenance tasks (Tashiro 2009; Hoshi and Yamazaki 2015). This ambiguous setup occurred in the context of Iijima's local system of comprehensive public control over land use and land exchange, which includes a set of formal incentives to encourage owners to maintain their land maintenance duties (see chapter 8). It shows that such local institutions to control farmland use shape, but do not necessarily prevent the onset of more entrepreneurial approaches to (collective) farming.

Interim Conclusion

Hamlet-based collective farming illustrates the role of village institutions in the changing agricultural support and protection regime particularly well. Based upon the integration of hamlet ties, norms, and practices, the local proliferation of hamlet-based collective farming can at least temporarily absorb farmland in the hands of (part-time) farm households instead of expanding agri-businesses. As such, hamlet-based farming can contribute to local manifestations of national reform that include small-scale part-time farm households and reinforce the position of the local cooperative within the local agricultural regime.

Taken together, the findings in part 4 reveal the dynamic role of village institutions in institutional change in the agricultural support and protection regime. Depending on how they have been built into local agricultural regimes throughout the postwar period, local social network ties and norms and practices in the use and exchange of farmland can support farmland consolidation in some local contexts and obstruct it in others. The protracted integration of village institutions into local agricultural regimes also shapes local interpretations of agricultural reform, as illustrated vividly in Hikawa, where successful farmland consolidation coincided with curtailing farmers' entrepreneurial freedom on behalf of the local agricultural administration and cooperative. To what extent and in whose interest village institutions shape the outcomes of formal change is thus also a matter of local institutional agency – that is, in the cases of Hikawa and Miyada the ability of local co-ops and administrations to build institutions for comprehensive public control over farmland and farmers. In the absence of such local institution-building processes, local actors – and especially local co-ops – can exert less control over the expansion and entrepreneurial aspirations of large (corporate) farms, and the latter become the local agents of institutional change. The local agricultural regimes in Izumo, Hita, and in the fruit-farming Kōfu Basin provide good examples in this respect. While a small number of entrepreneurial farms (potentially including "external" corporations) enjoy increasingly exclusive access to a variety of state support, more aging farm households give up farming without successors, and more land falls idle. Still, however, village institutions in these localities function as resources for local actors to access land and/or state support. Somewhat in the middle, the case of Yasu City shows that even in the absence of organized control over the local farmland market, local social ties and norms can to some extent support an interpretation of large-scale corporate farming that is marked by cooperation with the local co-op, the local administration, and hamlet-based collective farms. The local perspective has thus revealed how institutional change in the agricultural support and protection regime is shaped by local (re)combination of village institutions with the increasingly ambiguous macro-level regulatory framework. The remaining task is to put these findings in a broader context in order to understand the impact of local agency on the overall direction of institutional change in the agricultural support and protection regime.

Boundary Change: Decreasing Prospects for Comprehensive Local Institutional Agency

The case of Hikawa illustrates the potential of incumbent local actors such as local JA to shape the outcomes of agricultural reform in their interests. Yet, as noted in chapter 6, organized local agricultural regimes seem to be the exception rather than the rule. That is, while national reform has left incumbent local actors with some leeway to contain and control the outcomes of agricultural reform, in other localities this potential has not been exploited as much as in Hikawa. There are many reasons for this, ranging from lack of bargaining power of local JA, different priorities among local farms and landowners, to socioeconomic and topographical factors. While a systematic analysis of these factors is beyond the scope of this book, the trajectory of the local agricultural regime in Hikawa highlights the impact of one factor in particular: the Kōsha system was created and enforced within remarkably stable and relatively narrow local socio-spatial boundaries.

Therefore it is worthwhile to consider two interrelated macro-institutional developments that have altered the landscape of local socio-spatial organization in regional Japan since the 1990s. First, financial deregulation put economic pressure on local cooperative branches and accelerated local cooperative mergers since the early 1990s. Second, a series of decentralization reforms induced a wave of municipal mergers, which peaked between 2002 and 2006. Together, these processes have disrupted the socio-spatial boundaries of most postwar local agricultural regimes and created much larger, more heterogeneous local agricultural regimes. The wave of municipal mergers coincided with the heyday of agricultural reform in the Koizumi era, when responsibilities for structural reform and upholding access to state support were shifted toward local actors. Evidence from Hikawa and other localities suggests that stable socio-spatial boundaries support organized local responses to agricultural reform. In turn, I argue that boundary change has reduced the prospects of local actors to build institutions for controlling farmland and farmers and has thus amplified the neoliberal potential of agricultural reform.

Decentralization, Deregulation, and the Changing Cooperative and Administrative Landscape

While the number of municipalities remained strikingly stable after the Shōwa Amalgamation, local cooperative mergers have occurred throughout the postwar period, mostly following the mergers of former villages and towns into postwar municipalities. Throughout the postwar era, the number of local co-ops continued to exceed the number of municipalities, and only a small minority of cooperative districts covered more than one municipality (Tashiro 2018). Thus, earlier cooperative mergers have reinforced the overlap between municipal and cooperative boundaries rather than undermining it. This changed in the mid-1990s, however, when the number of local cooperatives began to decrease more rapidly again, and in more disruptive fashion in the overlap of cooperative and municipal boundaries. From 3,574 in 1991, the number of local co-ops dropped to a mere 634 in 2018 (JA Zenchū n.d.). Despite the sharp contraction in the number of municipalities in the 2000s, many local cooperative districts cover more than one municipality.

One political factor that accelerated cooperative mergers was related to agriculture only indirectly. In the early 1990s, the effects of a gradual financial deregulation began to undermine the benefits that co-ops enjoyed in their financial and insurance operations. Throughout the postwar period, the business activities of the co-ops shifted toward financial and insurance services for their increasingly non-agricultural members. In the heavily regulated postwar financial sector, the cooperative finance and insurance enterprises enjoyed regulatory benefits that provided particularly favorable conditions vis-à-vis their competitors (see chapter 2). Until the early 1990s, state intervention guaranteed that local cooperatives could generate stable profits from their role as deposit collectors (Gōdo 2001, 6–14). When the Ministry of Finance liberalized interest rates from the early 1990s onwards, local cooperatives were thrown into severe competition with other banking providers, and many local co-ops and prefectural credit federations came under financial pressure (Tashiro 2018, 18–21).[1] Against this background, and in the light of continued agricultural decline, the MAFF promoted the rationalization of the cooperative organization, including the plan to disband prefectural federations, and offering financial incentives for local co-op mergers in order to stabilize their economic basis through "scale merits." A drastic wave of mergers occurred between 1991 and 1996 (Gōdo 2001; George Mulgan 2000, 285; Tashiro 2018). Cooperative mergers typically downgrade formerly autonomous local co-ops into branches of the newly amalgamated cooperative. This often includes rationalization of the agricultural advisory staff in one core "agricultural management center" that serves the whole cooperative. In large amalgamated local co-ops, the once omnipresent organization retreats from the peripheries. Beyond decreasing agricultural and administrative functions, this can also include rationalization of services such as cooperative supermarkets, gas stations, or rice centers, which tends to be a social problem especially in remote areas with weak public service provision (Kitagawa 2008; Odagiri 2011, 2014; Matsunaga and Seki 2012). It is thus not surprising that cooperative mergers often happened against the will of the farming members, who tended to prefer smaller constituencies (George Mulgan 2000, 282–95). Moreover, financially more stable co-ops were particularly suspicious about merging with weaker ones, especially as it became apparent that financial stability and organizational efficiency did not necessarily improve after mergers (Gōdo 2001, 2009; George Mulgan 2000, 285–92).[2] Despite these potential problems, however, local cooperative mergers continue, thus creating even larger cooperative districts. As of 2018, in several prefectures – including Shimane – this has led to the formation of "local" co-ops that cover the whole prefecture (Tashiro 2018).

Municipal Mergers

In the mid-2000s, a wave of municipal mergers added to the redrawing of the boundaries of postwar local agricultural regimes. After four decades of remarkable stability, the "great wave of Heisei mergers" introduced a drastic and abrupt restructuring of the local administrative landscape. Between 2000 and 2006, the number of municipalities decreased from 3,229 to 1,821, with the bulk of the mergers occurring between 2002 and 2006. The average size of municipalities almost doubled in population and area (MIC 2010). The dominant form of local administration shifted from small towns and villages toward larger towns and cities. After 2006, the frequency of municipal mergers ebbed. In 2015, 1,718 municipalities were left, of which 745 were towns and a mere 183 were villages (Rausch 2016).

The "great wave of Heisei mergers" was the direct result of a series of decentralization reforms, which included reorganization of central-local fiscal relations. At least in principle, these reforms aimed at enhancing local autonomy.[3] In practice, however, the central government came to use fiscal decentralization mainly as an instrument to enforce municipal mergers to control public debt (Imai 2008). Between 1998 and 2001, the central government adjusted the distribution of intergovernmental transfers. Roughly at the same time, it introduced strong fiscal incentives for smaller municipalities to merge with each other or to become part of a larger city (Shimada 2014). From 2002 onward, the Koizumi administration intensified fiscal decentralization with the "trinity reforms." The reform package combined a cut in fiscal transfers to municipalities with enhanced autonomy for local governments to develop their own tax sources. Yet small villages and towns were rarely able to make use of their enhanced fiscal autonomy because of their critical socioeconomic situation.[4] In large parts of regional Japan, demographic shrinking and weak local economies had been forming a vicious circle for decades (Matanle, Rausch, and the Shrinking Regions Research Group 2011, 108–10). For much of the postwar era, the generous redistribution of state revenues to the peripheries via the local allocation tax, public infrastructural investments, and agricultural support programs had veiled the structural weakness of the rural and semi-urban peripheries. Yet economic recession and fiscal reforms since the late 1990s exacerbated these weaknesses (Song 2015). When the central government increased "the relative costs of being alone" for small municipalities, it effectively forced towns and villages to give up their administrative autonomy (Yamada 2012, 3). Consequently, small, aging municipalities in regional Japan were most likely to merge, while metropolitan areas saw few mergers or none at all (Rausch 2016).

The consequences of the decentralization reforms since the late 1990s have largely been viewed critically in the public and academic discourse.[5] Hundreds of formerly autonomous municipalities lost their local decision-making powers, and instead were forced to the margins of vast spatially and socioeconomically heterogeneous municipalities. In many of these amalgamated cities, peripheral areas that had been autonomous villages and towns until the mid-2000s are now located thirty to sixty minutes by car from the administrative center. Moreover, as the central political focus behind the decentralization reforms was cutting government expenditures, the mergers contributed to reduced public services in these peripheries. This often entailed further marginalization of the elderly population in the most remote parts of amalgamated municipalities, and a concentration of "town-making" efforts and infrastructural projects in the centers (Reiher 2014; Iba and Sakamoto 2014; Shimada 2014; Rausch 2014).

Diffusion of Socio-Spatial Boundaries in Amalgamated Local Agricultural Regimes

Cooperative and municipal restructuring have disrupted the socio-spatial and cooperative-administrative boundaries of most post-war local agricultural regimes. Reflecting their longstanding cooperation in local agricultural governance, municipal and cooperative districts have been changing somewhat synchronously in many cases. Yet, even where municipal and cooperative boundaries changed in sync, the arenas for local agricultural governance have become much more heterogeneous geographically and socioeconomically. Amalgamated local agricultural regimes thus often consist of several sub-regimes on the level of postwar cooperatives and/or former towns and villages. While these sub-regimes may retain distinct local rules and norms governing agricultural production, the congruence of socio-spatial and political-administrative boundaries that emerged over the postwar period has decreased substantially over the past two decades.

The example of the local agricultural regime in Izumo (excluding Hikawa) illustrates these changes well. In 1995, the seven local co-ops in pre-merger Izumo City and the surrounding municipalities (apart from JA Hikawa) merged into JA Izumo, which came to cover six different municipalities. The core administrative functions of the amalgamated JA moved to the central agricultural management center in Izumo City. Ten years later, the respective municipalities followed to merge into Izumo City, which reinstalled the overlap between cooperative and administrative boundaries, but on a much larger scale. For instance, the former towns/cooperative districts Hirata in the north and Sada in the south are almost an hour apart by car, and there are few common features or social links between them in land use or agricultural production. Moreover, in 2015 all local co-ops in Shimane (this time including JA Hikawa) became branches of the newly founded, prefecture-wide JA Shimane, and the cooperative headquarters moved to the prefectural capital Matsue City.

In the Kōfu Basin, municipal and cooperative mergers have been even more disruptive. In 2001, ten local co-ops merged into the large JA Fruits Yamanashi, which came to cover Enzan City, Katsunuma Town, and several other surrounding towns and villages. In the mid-2000s, the former overlap between municipal and cooperative boundaries was further diluted, as Katsunuma (reluctantly) joined Enzan City to form the newly founded Kōshū City, while some of the other towns and villages within JA Fruits Yamanashi merged with other municipalities *outside* the cooperative district. Today, the co-op covers a vast area, including the amalgamated cities of Kōshū and Yamanashi, and a small part of Fuefuki City, as part of a patchwork of local agricultural (sub-)regimes cutting through the Kōfu Basin.

Lasting Socio-Spatial Divisions and Local Agricultural Sub-regimes

The case of JA Fruits Yamanashi/Kōshū City illustrates particularly well that amalgamated local agricultural regimes can display lasting socio-spatial divisions between their constituent parts. Although Enzan and Katsunuma have both belonged to the same cooperative district and municipality since 2001 and 2005 respectively, social ties between grape farmers and wine producers were still strongly patterned by the former boundaries within the new city even in 2017. Respondents from Enzan pointed to an underlying sense of distrust or even hostility toward Katsunuma, while at the same time emphasizing the close ties among grape growers and wine makers in Enzan (KB-F1; KB-F12). Katsunuma has the reputation of being the center of Japanese wine (Kingsbury 2012) – a marketable image that Enzan as the largest part of the amalgamated Kōshū City has been eager to absorb, according to a respondent from Katsunuma (KB-F15). The social divide has concrete manifestations in the rules and norms that govern relations between farmers and wine producers, local marketing and promotional efforts, or land use. For example, the grape and wine industry in Katsunuma has retained exclusive access to certain prefectural and national subsidies that do not apply in other parts of the amalgamated city (KB-WT). One example of the resilience of the agricultural sub-regime in Katsunuma is the system that sets the annual price for Kōshū grapes negotiated by the Katsunuma chapter of JA Fruits Yamanashi, the local administration, and the Katsunuma Winery Association (see chapter 6). This system was created in 2000, i.e., before the municipal merger and in the last year of the independence of the Katsunuma agricultural cooperative. It is the successful local manifestation of a failed attempt to install a similar system at the prefectural level (Kingsbury 2012, 205). While the share of grapes marketed under the local system has been shrinking, it still works in marked contrast to Enzan, where there is no such system (KB-F14). Meanwhile, municipal policies since the merger have sometimes ignored and obscured preexisting local cooperation patterns. For example, Kōshū City has been trying to enforce a municipal standard for production of local wines since 2011. The standard applies the administrative boundaries of the amalgamated Kōshū City but disregards the lasting divide between Enzan and Katsunuma and the fact that many wineries in Katsunuma have a long history of sourcing grapes from farmers in neighboring Fuefuki City. The municipal standard has thus proven to be an inefficient tool for the marketing and local governance of high-quality grape and wine production (Kingsbury 2018). In 2019, the Katsunuma Wine Association, JA Fruits Yamanashi, and thirty hamlet-level grower cooperatives within the boundaries of Katsunuma and the former village of Yamato adapted the local system to govern grape supply to include more detailed information on the origins of the grapes in order to strengthen the local wine standard – thereby again excluding Enzan (KB-F1). Other wine-related marketing and promotional efforts have remained strikingly localized within the amalgamated Kōshū City. While a longstanding PR event organized by the Katsunuma Winery Association remains reserved for producers from the former town (KB-F1; KB-F15), a newer event organized by the seven wineries in Enzan since 2017 has remained exclusively an Enzan affair, as initial attempts to involve Katsunuma wineries were turned down (Jentzsch 2020b). The lack of mutual trust also complicates the exchange of farmland. Reportedly, farmers from Enzan have only little or complicated access to land in Katsunuma (KB-F14). In one case, a land use deal of a farmer from Enzan in Katsunuma was dissolved after lasting complaints of neighboring farmers (KB-F1).

As the formal boundaries of the local agricultural sub-regime in Katsunuma disappeared, however, not only the local grape supply scheme but also some of its other specific features are eroding. For example, the former town of Katsunuma invested in a large-scale tourist facility in the 1960s, which has become an important outlet for smaller grape and wine producers in town. After the municipal merger, the facility eventually (and reluctantly) had to be opened for wine-makers from Enzan as well, thus undermining its longstanding character as a mutual investment of local stakeholders in Katsunuma – to the dismay of some older growers in the former town (KB-F15; KB-F16).

Increasing Social and Normative Heterogeneity

More generally, I argue that boundary change has diffused the social and normative foundations of local agricultural regimes. Already in the late 1990s, George Mulgan argued that larger cooperative districts cause members to lose "the sense that the local [cooperatives] are their own associations" and create a greater distance "both psychically and physically." Consequently, the "traditionally close ties between villagers and their local cooperatives have been severed in some areas." Moreover, the "voice of farmers is less likely to be reflected" in larger cooperatives, reducing the efficiency of agricultural promotion through

Figure 11.1. Members (Including Associated Members) per Local Agricultural Cooperative, 1970–2011

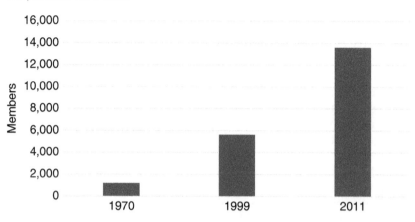

Sources: Ishida (2002); JA Zenchū (n.d.); Gōdo (2014d).

cooperative advisory staff (George Mulgan 2000, 288). The social distance between co-op and members has become even more pronounced since these observations were made. Between 1999 and 2011, membership in each local co-op more than doubled (see figure 11.1). Growing membership was accompanied by a higher share of non-farming "associated" members, who tend to have a thinner social and practical connection to the cooperative organization (H-GS1).

As one result of this development, the remaining farmers are frequently confronted with cooperative advisory staff from very different socio-spatial contexts (I-JA4; Ij-O), while their previously autonomous local cooperative branches lose all functions beyond banking and insurance services (I-JA3), or even shut down altogether. Fieldwork has shown that the boundaries of the former cooperative districts continue to form the basis for close social ties, local belonging, and cooperation patterns. For example in the case of the cooperative winery mentioned in chapter 9, the socio-spatial boundaries of the historical cooperative district still determine access to the facility, which was founded as a mutual investment of the nine constituent hamlets. Closely related, the nine hamlet-level shipping cooperatives continue to coordinate their activities within the former cooperative district (KB-F8; KB-JA2). In other localities, the former cooperative districts also retained some social and organizational functions (I-JA3; Ht-CF). Yet, within larger cooperative boundaries, these longstanding socio-spatial ties and cooperation patterns are less likely to add up to a coherent cooperative-wide network, in which members and co-op are tied to each other not only formally, but also through family relations, neighborhood, longstanding mutual investments, or other socio-spatial links. Local social ties have also not lost significance for accessing state support in amalgamated local agricultural regimes, e.g., when local cooperative leaders convince their own hamlet to form a collective farm (see chapter 10). Again, however, this is likely to happen in a less coherent fashion. Already in the mid-1990s wave of cooperative mergers, George Mulgan noted that in larger cooperative districts "priority is given to the interests and rights of the [co-op itself] and to the areas where their executives come from rather than to farmer members" (George Mulgan 2000, 288). As cooperative mergers continued, we can assume that local social ties and the associated benefits have become even more fragmented in the years following this observation.

Municipal mergers had similar effects. As municipalities grew in size, and formerly autonomous local governments lost most decision-making capabilities, local socio-spatial ties were diluted (MIC 2017, 3), and thus potentially became less productive in (informal) access to state support or information, especially in peripheral areas.[6] Personal contacts between local politicians and residents have substantially decreased in merged municipalities in Japan, which reduced the incentives for politicians to cater to the interests of residents in peripheral areas (Yamada and Arai 2017). Another effect is that local officials have less information on the actual situation in the former towns and villages, and residents have less means to voice their opinions (Kitagawa 2012, 15). This effect is reinforced through the practice of administrative rotation. Local officials in Japan are required to rotate to different positions regularly in order to prevent collusion. In amalgamated municipalities, local agricultural governance in previously relatively contained towns or villages is thus handled by "externals" with little or no personal ties to the local community (H-O1; H-O4), similar to the assignment of "external" cooperative farm management advisory staff to former cooperative districts mentioned above. Taken together, municipal and cooperative mergers have reduced the density of local social network ties to the extent that farmers in the same local agricultural regime may have little or no personal relations to each other, and thinner ties to the cooperative and the local administration.

The diffusion of local social ties is also associated with a diffusion of norms and practices. When small, agrarian localities are absorbed by larger, heterogeneous, and less agrarian cities, not only their local identities (Rausch 2006), but also their attitudes toward farmland are at risk of being marginalized – and thus less likely to become the normative foundation for local agricultural governance. Formally manifesting this development, municipal mergers require the respective agricultural committees – the local bodies overseeing farmland issues – to follow the redrawn administrative boundaries within three years. When agricultural committees merge, the number of elected and appointed members from each formerly autonomous locality decreases, while the overall constituency increases (Gōdo 2014a). As similar processes have been occurring throughout Japan, the formal representation of the former, more rural towns and villages in local farmland governance decreases, as does its social and normative embedding.

Extended Municipal and Cooperative Autonomy and the Trajectory of the Local Agricultural Regime in Hikawa in the 2000s

During the neoliberal heyday of agricultural reform in the mid-2000s, boundary change confronted incumbent local actors, including part-time rice farmers and local JA, with a new – and arguably worse – local socio-spatial environment to accommodate the changing regulatory framework and agricultural decline. Importantly, however, boundary change did not affect all localities equally. In some cases, cooperative and/or municipal boundaries persisted, thus contributing to relative socio-spatial stability in local agricultural regimes. This was the case in Hikawa, where the local agricultural regime retained both cooperative and municipal boundaries throughout the 2000s. It is thus a particularly productive case for which to examine the significance of stable socio-spatial boundaries during this crucial phase of national agricultural reform.

The boundaries of the local agricultural regime in Hikawa have not remained unchallenged. Yet, JA Hikawa resisted pressure to merge into JA Izumo in 1995 (JA Hikawa 2011), and the town withstood the wave of municipal mergers in 2003, when it chose independence over joining Izumo City in a local referendum. Only in October 2011 was the town absorbed by its larger neighbor. In 2015, JA Hikawa – like every other local co-op in Shimane – became a branch of the new prefectural JA Shimane (Tashiro 2018). As of 2017, however, the local agricultural regime still retained its distinct character and clear-cut boundaries, which still contain the system of farmland exchange via the Hikawa Nōgyō Kōsha. I argue that the extended stability of the local agricultural regime over the 2000s was a crucial factor in institution-building toward comprehensive public control over farmland and farmers in Hikawa. In the critical phase in national agricultural reform, the local agricultural regime retained its longstanding overlap of social, political, and territorial boundaries, within which the local agricultural administration (including JA Hikawa) held the bargaining power to establish the Kōsha system.

JA Hikawa's Quest for Local Autonomy

Hikawa Town's successful resistance against the municipal merger with Izumo in 2003 was not only a matter of willpower, but also of the town's relatively stable socioeconomic situation (see chapter 6). In contrast to other small municipalities in regional Japan, the town attracted several highly technology-intensive companies. Already in 1983, the manufacturer Murata opened a plant in Hikawa, followed by Fujitsu in 1990. The relatively stable local economy is also reflected in a positive demographic development (Hikawa Town 1997; Izumo City 2013). To a greater extent than weaker municipalities, Hikawa thus could regard a merger with Izumo City as a matter of choice rather than a matter of "fiscal and demographic necessity" (Shimizu 2013, 139). The local agricultural sector played an interesting role in the decision against joining Izumo City.

The merger with Izumo City came on the agenda in 2002 – a particularly critical time for the agricultural sector in Hikawa: the Kōsha system was still under construction, while the national policy turn toward more exclusive paddy field subsidization was already on the horizon. The agricultural administration and JA Hikawa had a strong interest in retaining decision-making power in local hands to prevent disruption of the institution-building process toward public farmland allocation. For JA Hikawa, the merger posed an existential threat. Because all other local cooperatives in the Izumo region had already merged into JA Izumo in 1995, JA Hikawa would have faced strong pressure to join the larger co-op in case of a municipal merger. Beyond the autonomy of the local co-op, the merger threatened the social, normative, and organizational foundations of the local agricultural regime. In late 2002, JA Hikawa issued a petition that reflects the distinct features of the local agricultural regime, and the significance of retaining its boundaries. The petition argued that the longstanding integration of the administration, JA Hikawa, and farmers had already brought outstanding results, including creation of large-scale hamlet-based collective farms and farmland consolidation "unmatched among the municipalities in Shimane" (JA Hikawa 2011, 133). A merger with Izumo would expose farmland use in town to the risk of "uninhibited development" – a thinly veiled criticism of the lack of control over farmland use and conversion in Izumo. Consequently, the local co-op demanded counter-measures to ensure promotion of the "town's own farmland consolidation project" in case of a merger (133). Eventually, public opinion was in favor of the cooperative position. A local referendum resulted in a vote for independence, after which Hikawa left the merger deliberation council in December 2003 (64; Morikawa 2011, 59).

This decision bought the agricultural administration and JA Hikawa more time to expand the Kōsha system under its own terms of trade. This concerned, for example, submission of the local agricultural committee to the Kōsha system and the comprehensive introduction of standardized leases in 2005 – a milestone toward comprehensive control over farmland and farmers in Hikawa (see chapter 7). Arguably, upholding the historically grown, clearly defined, and relatively narrow social, spatial, cooperative, and administrative boundaries enhanced the legitimacy of administrative and cooperative agency within these boundaries, including the informal bargaining power of influential actors like respondent H-GS1 over the local agricultural committee. The stability of these boundaries has also facilitated the shift of the norm of farmland as a collective resource from the hamlet level to the level of the whole town. The leitmotif of "One Town, One Field" was translated into formal rules to control farmland and farmers in the years after which Hikawa decided against the merger with Izumo.

The Local Agricultural Regime in Hikawa after the Mergers

When the merger with Izumo resurfaced on the local political agenda in 2010, the Hikawa Kōsha had already solidified its position as the undisputed local ordering force for farmland matters. In a second local referendum in 2010, a majority of the population now favored the merger with Izumo (JA Hikawa 2011, 82). This shift suggests that the concerns of farmers and the agricultural administration about the merger – although still a common theme among farmers and officials in 2013 – had lost salience over the course of the 2000s. Ironically, this development might well be related to the success of the Kōsha system itself. In the 2003 referendum, the majority against the merger was already narrow (Higashide n.d.). When public farmland reallocation gained momentum after 2003, hundreds of farm households yielded their land use rights to the Kōsha and stopped farming. Even if these households still own farmland, the long-term lease contracts under the Kōsha system can change – and potentially undermine – owners' attitudes toward their land (H-GS1; H-JA4). Moreover, non-farming landowners also are less involved with the local cooperative, fellow farmers, and the agricultural regime as a whole.[7] Against this background, it is no surprise that the local JA could not mobilize a majority against joining Izumo City again in 2010.

However, with the Kōsha system firmly in place, the local agricultural regime has remained remarkably stable since the merger. The social and normative underpinning of the local agricultural regime has remained strongly associated with the boundaries of the town and the local cooperative. In 2013 – two years after Hikawa eventually became a part of Izumo City – the head of the Hikawa Association of Hamlet-Based Collective Farms still emphasized different local attitudes toward farmland use implied in the petition issued by JA years before: In Izumo, people would regard farmland as a "private asset" and not as communal resource worth protecting. Against this background, he also expressed his "great concern" that the upcoming assimilation of the local agricultural committee with Izumo would harm farmland governance in Hikawa (H-CF6a). Other respondents also shared negative views of agricultural governance in Izumo (H-CF3; H-GS1). Considering its local characteristics in agricultural administration, the merger agreement granted the local administration in Hikawa a gradual integration into the broader administrative system over a period of ten years (Izumo City 2010, 24). The agricultural administration in Hikawa also delayed dissolution of the local agricultural committee until 2017, thus defending the formal and normative boundaries of the local agricultural regime. When the re-election was finally due, the candidate to represent Hikawa in Izumo's agricultural committee was the head of the agricultural corporation Green Support, the influential gray eminence behind the Kōsha system (H-GS1).

In the summer of 2017, the Hikawa agricultural sector was still firmly under local control – not only in farmland allocation, but also in organization of rice production control. While other aspects of local governance have reportedly become unified with Izumo City, local agricultural officials casually described Hikawa's agricultural sector as an "isolated country" (*sakoku*) – a flippant reference to the historical isolation of Japan in the Tokugawa period. Still, a gradual erosion of the local agricultural regime cannot be denied. In 2015, JA Hikawa had to give up its independence and became a branch of the prefecture-wide JA Shimane. In 2017, the head of the local cooperative branch in Hikawa – a long-term leading figure in the local agricultural regime and former board member of the Hikawa Nōgyō Kōsha – stated that the merger had not yet affected its position, not least because the prefecture-wide JA is so distant that it needs to grant its branches some organizational autonomy (H-JA4).[8] Yet, as the formal boundaries of the town, the agricultural committee, and JA Hikawa have all disappeared, even the head of Green Support has become doubtful about how much longer the distinct character of the organized local agricultural regime in Hikawa will hold (H-GS1).

Beyond Hikawa: Stable Boundaries in Comparison

Other examples confirm the significance of relatively stable socio-spatial boundaries for the trajectory of organized local agricultural regimes in the 2000s. Miyada Village has retained its status as an independent municipality. Together with Iijima Town and surrounding municipalities, Miyada belongs to the amalgamated local co-op JA Kami-Ina. However, according to local officials the Miyada branch has retained an unusual degree of autonomy (including, for example, the convention that the branch leadership has to come from Miyada Village), and has remained very closely associated with the village itself both personally and organizationally (M-O; M-CF). Consequently, the boundaries of the local collective land use system have remained clearly confined by the village boundaries. The history of Miyada Village sheds a particularly interesting light on the importance of stable socio-spatial boundaries. During the Shōwa amalgamation in the 1950s, the village was merged into the neighboring Komagane City. However, this merger met fierce resistance among many Miyada residents. Led, inter alia, by the Young Farmers' League within the Miyada agricultural cooperative, a local citizen movement eventually forced a revision of the merger decision – a very rare case of successful local resistance against the Shōwa amalgamation (Kramer 2015). The separation movement preceded the onset of the communal farmland governance approach in Miyada. According to local administrative and cooperative officials, this communal approach could not have been created had the village lost its autonomy in the 1950s (M-O; M-CF). The land use system in Iijima Town has emerged within similarly stable boundaries, as Iijima also withstood the wave of municipal mergers in the 2000s.

Ōyama also illustrates the significance of stable boundaries. The former town was merged into Hita City in 2005. Yet it still hosts an organized local agricultural regime with a community-oriented and cooperative-led interpretation of agricultural reform in general, and the "6th industrialization" in particular (Imamura 2015). Development of the local agricultural regime goes back to the initiative of the agricultural cooperative leader in the early postwar period, who then also served as mayor. Except for the town itself, the local co-op has retained its independence. According to a leader of the cooperative, the local approach to community-based agricultural production, processing, and marketing stands and falls with the autonomy of the local co-op, which has refused to join the surrounding amalgamated JA (O-JA). Regarding its political power, the co-op has even gained influence since the merger. In practice, the agricultural administration in Hita City grants the local co-op considerable authority to govern agricultural matters in Ōyama itself. The co-op has thus absorbed some functions of the former town administration (Ht-O; O-JA). Consequently, the local agricultural regime retained its socio-spatial boundaries and its distinct character despite the municipal merger.

In Kami District, where the agricultural production structure was transformed through swift and comprehensive proliferation of hamlet-based collective farming (see chapter 10), the local agricultural regime is also marked by relative stable socio-spatial boundaries. During the mid-2000s wave of municipal mergers, four of the five towns in the former Kami District merged into Kami Town, while the town of Shikama remained independent. After 1999, the four local co-ops in the district formed the amalgamated JA Kami Yotsuba, which since then covers the whole Kami District. According to local cooperative leaders, the cooperative merger was pursued on the basis of preexisting cooperation patterns between the branches within the district, and thus was perceived as a natural process by farmers and cooperatives. On the basis of its established role as serving the whole district, JA Kami Yotsuba came to provide a social and organizational platform for cross-municipal agricultural governance, which exceeds such cooperation in other local policy domains, according to local cooperative officials (K-JA1; K-JA2). Thus, despite covering two municipalities, the amalgamated JA Kami Yotsuba provides relatively stable, long-established socio-spatial boundaries for the local agricultural regime, within which the cooperative leadership was able to convince all hamlets in the district to adopt a subsidy-productive model for collective farming in 2007.

Decreasing Prospects for Organized Local Agricultural Regimes

The evidence discussed above shows that the effects of boundary change on the trajectory of local agricultural regimes must be analyzed in the local context. Under certain circumstances, the socio-spatial boundaries of local agricultural regimes can remain relatively stable even when the local co-op or municipality was subject to a merger. In general, however, boundary change has substantially altered – and expanded – the local arenas in which agricultural reform has been translated into practice.

Just when agricultural reform gained momentum in the mid-2000s, the conditions under which the Kōsha system in Hikawa was created and enforced – a local agricultural regime with a stable overlap of relatively narrow socio-spatial and political boundaries – turned from a common phenomenon into an exception. I argue that this has two main consequences for the trajectory of the agricultural support and protection regime as a whole.

First, the diffusion of local social ties and (farmland) norms in amalgamated local agricultural regimes has decreased the prospects for local actors such as co-ops to create and enforce local institutions to organize farmland consolidation and structural change in the agricultural sector in general. Supporting this argument, a number of studies have found that cooperative mergers have reduced the ability of local JA to lead in revitalization of rural communities (Kobayashi 2011), or to enforce community-oriented approaches to agricultural diversification in the context of national policies to promote the "6th industry" (Muroya 2013, 2016). Muroya (2013, 8) explicitly links the latter development to the increasing number of localities in which cooperatives and municipalities "are not congruent anymore," thus pointing to the significance of overlapping socio-spatial and administrative-cooperative boundaries for community-oriented interpretations of agricultural policies. This does not mean that such interpretations cannot emerge in amalgamated local agricultural regimes. As mentioned before, community-oriented, diversified hamlet-based farms have been found to emerge not least as a means to substitute for cooperative and administrative structures after mergers (Kitagawa 2008; Yamamoto 2013; Kitagawa 2012). However, such communal responses seem to be an expression of a growing need for hamlet-level self-help in the face of weakening public-cooperative control (Yamamoto 2013). As such, they differ from comprehensive, institutionalized, public and/or cooperative-led approaches to hamlet-based collective farming such as in Hikawa, Miyada, or Kami (Jentzsch 2020a).

Second, boundary change undermines the stability of *existing* local institutions for comprehensive local governance of farmland consolidation and agricultural production in general, as the formal boundaries in which these institutions were created are eroding. That is, even though the Kōsha system in Hikawa or the scheme to stabilize the price of wine grapes in Katsunuma may survive municipal and/or cooperative mergers for a time, they become increasingly vulnerable as local stakeholders lose their formal competencies and eventually their informal bargaining power within larger, more heterogeneous administrative and cooperative districts.

As a consequence, while agricultural reform has left local JA and small (part-time) household farms with opportunities to retain access to state support and control over farmland consolidation respectively, the parallel process of boundary change has reduced the prospects of local actors to exploit the non-liberal potential of the national agricultural reforms comprehensively. In turn, it has opened up maneuvering space for individual, entrepreneurial, and corporate approaches to agricultural production. Boundary change has thus amplified the neoliberal potential of agricultural reform.

Interim Conclusion

The first three chapters in this part have shown how village institutions can provide the foundation for creating and enforcing organized approaches to national agricultural reform. This chapter has argued that the disruption of the socio-spatial boundaries of most local agricultural regimes over the 2000s has rendered such institution-building less likely. The local perspective has thus revealed the crucial role of accompanying macro-institutional shifts, which have been mostly neglected: financial liberalization and fiscal decentralization and their impact on cooperative and municipal boundaries. Up to now, the 1994 electoral reform and the centralization of political decision-making have received most attention in agricultural politics, especially in the non-Japanese literature. While these changes have destabilized the postwar agricultural "iron triangle" of LDP, JA, and the MAFF, the ensuing reform has often been criticized as falling short of bringing about "real" change (i.e., liberalization) in the Japanese farm sector. Yet the slow and often inconsistent course of national reform is misleading if we consider the parallel process of boundary change. It is true that the Japanese government has never given up on agricultural intervention – yet it has shifted responsibilities for crucial tasks such as rice production control and farmland consolidation onto local co-ops, local governments, and farmers themselves. And it did so despite profound changes in local agricultural governance, which are marked by increasing social and spatial distance between farmers, hamlets, and their local co-ops and agricultural administrations – all of which has reduced the prospects for the defensive interpretation and the successful implementation of these national policies.

PART FIVE

Conclusions

The final part of this book is organized in two brief chapters. Chapter 12 summarizes the main findings and discusses their implications for the trajectory of Japan's agricultural support and protection regime, as well as the future of the agricultural sector as a whole. Chapter 13 puts the empirical findings into a broader theoretical context. It argues that a local perspective on institutional agency propels the theoretical debate on incremental institutional change in advanced political economies, in that it reveals the role of informal institutions as dynamic resources in such processes, and raises the attention to the significance of conditions under which local actors translate abstract macro policies into local practice, and how these conditions can change.

Chapter Twelve

Renegotiating Japan's Agricultural Support and Protection

The agricultural support and protection regime represents a crucial case to understand gradual institutional change in Japan's (formerly) "non-liberal" market economy. To an even greater extent than other policy fields, agricultural support and protection epitomizes the "syncretic" character of the ongoing transformation of Japan's postwar political economy (Kushida, Shimizu, and Oi 2013). From a macro perspective, the trajectory of the support and protection regime almost inevitably presents a vague, if not contradictory picture of change and stability. Offering a different view, the local perspective has revealed that the pace and direction of the agricultural support and protection regime hinges on the ways in which local actors translate the increasingly ambiguous regulatory framework into local practice.

Local institutional agency shapes the implementation and the interpretation of national agricultural policies. These policies have left space for strikingly different local interpretations. In the organized local agricultural regime in Hikawa, local protagonists were able to achieve a core policy objective – the distribution of land toward larger (subsidy-productive) farms – to an unusually high degree, while simultaneously muting the rise of independent agricultural entrepreneurship that the same national policies have been promoting. In less organized local agricultural regimes, entrepreneurial farmers can (and must) become drivers of institutional change, thereby taking advantage of the more market-liberal aspects of national reform. On the one hand, these different local manifestations of macro-level change are the result of protracted local processes. On the other hand, however, the local processes do not unfold independently from macro-institutional shifts that reach far beyond the realm of agricultural policy. The disruption of the socio-spatial boundaries of local agricultural regimes over the 2000s has reduced the prospects for incumbent actors to build and enforce organized local responses to national reform, which in turn has created more space (and pressure) for farmers to become independent agricultural entrepreneurs, while the majority of aging small-scale farm households abandon commercial agriculture.

Village Institutions and Local Agency

The findings emphasize that local social ties and norms and practices in agricultural production and farmland use – in short, village institutions – continue to play a crucial role in the trajectory of the agricultural support and protection regime. Village institutions continue to affect the consolidation of the agricultural production structure throughout Japan, e.g., in farmland exchange or the formation of hamlet-based collective farms. The latter illustrates particularly well that even seemingly obsolete agrarian norms and practices are dynamic resources, which local actors can (re)interpret or revive in response to socioeconomic and political challenges. In Hikawa and Miyada, village institutions have provided the social and normative foundation for the organization of the respective local regimes, as powerful local actors – such as representatives of the local co-op – used their local bargaining power to shift the norm of farmland as a collective resource from the hamlet level to that of the local agricultural regime. Through such local institution-building, farmland use in these organized local regimes has come to be determined not by individual economic interests alone, but by the "common interest" of the local agricultural sector and by extension the local administration and the local co-op – despite national market liberalization, farmland deregulation, and preferential policy support for agri-businesses.

Yet village institutions have not been integrated everywhere into local agricultural governance as comprehensively as in Hikawa or Miyada. Moreover, village institutions are not single-purpose tools for local actors to contain economic liberalization. To the contrary, they have also been employed to circumvent the formal constraints of postwar farmland regulations for private gains, and entrepreneurial farmers rely on local social ties for access to land, information, and other resources, while pursuing new paths of individual entrepreneurship beyond the influence of the local co-op.

These findings provide a fresh view on the role of local social ties and traditional norms and practices in the changing agricultural support and protection regime. Neither erosion nor persistence can fully capture this role. Rather, the local perspective shows that local agency shapes the trajectory and the role of hamlet ties and norms, and how they affect the outcomes of macro policy change. Of course, the influence of local actors is limited on the way in which traditional norms and practices are preserved, revived, and reinterpreted. Even in relatively narrow spatial contexts, the effects of de-agriculturalization and growing socioeconomic heterogeneity over the postwar decades cannot simply be reversed. Yet local agency has been shaping how these broader processes play out locally – with important consequences for political processes such as consolidation of the agricultural production structure.

Agricultural Reform and Local Agency in the Context of "Boundary Change"

The local perspective has helped to explain why organized interpretations of national reform are not more common. As the result of political processes outside agricultural policy-making, the relatively narrow and stable socio-spatial boundaries within which organized local regimes in Hikawa and elsewhere have emerged have become increasingly rare since the 1990s, and in particular over the 2000s. Cooperative restructuring and the wave of municipal mergers in the mid-2000s have created larger, more heterogeneous, and less "rural" local agricultural regimes. Arguably, this has further reduced the eroding (informal) organizational abilities of local co-ops, and thus also decreased their prospects to create and enforce organized local variants of the changing macro regime. In turn, farmers and corporate actors have gained leeway, and face more pressure, to develop diversified, professional forms of agricultural production. In this sense, far beyond gradual and inconsistent agricultural reform, the disruption of the socio-spatial boundaries of most local agricultural regimes has furthered the disorganization of Japan's agricultural sector, the consequences of which will be discussed below.

First, however, it is important to emphasize that the focus on boundary change has shed new light on how the transformation of the agricultural support and protection regime is intertwined with the transformation of the postwar political economy as a whole. Fiscal decentralization, financial deregulation, and agricultural reform all feed into a broader process through which the provision of social security in "regional Japan" depends increasingly on local acts of self-help and economic entrepreneurship – which at the same time has become the privileged avenue to access new forms of state support. Agricultural reform thus needs to be understood as an element of a broader shift from a developmentalist to a neoliberal approach to regional policies (Miyashita

2014; Tsukamoto 2012). This shift is also reflected in the former Abe administration's approach to "regional revitalization." While the government still employed public investments to foster regional economic growth, it also pushed for further deregulation of corporate farmland use and fishing rights while highlighting the commodification of "local resources" to revitalize local economies, and spurred inter-local competition for creating jobs and a positive demographic development – thus reinforcing the notion of "winners" and "losers" among and within the localities in regional Japan (Kanai and Yamashita 2015), and also among farm households, hamlets, and local cooperatives. This book has shown how local actors can shape the outcomes of these changes. Beyond agricultural production, the collectivized farm sectors in Miyada and Kami District also reproduce the postwar welfare character of the local support and protection regime, in that they sustain highly subsidized agricultural production in times of an aging and shrinking workforce, while allowing small, aging, part-time farm households to retain relatively stable access to state support. Beyond the realm of agriculture, other examples of successful community-based revitalization efforts also underscore the significance of protracted local institution-building within relatively narrow socio-spatial boundaries (Bu and Kim 2009; Odagiri 2014). At the same time, however, the findings in this book point to the limitations of comprehensive local responses in the context of the emerging larger, more heterogeneous arenas for local agency. In sum, the findings of this book support the notion that the changing administrative and socio-spatial landscape in regional Japan itself has been a crucial factor for the transformation of Japan's postwar political economy.

Quo Vadis, Japanese Agriculture? Limits of Intervention and Risks of Disorganization

What are the implications of these findings for Japan's agricultural support and protection regime, and the agricultural sector as a whole? The postwar support and protection regime will not recover. Proclaiming the ambitious goal to turn agriculture into a "growth industry," the Abe administration further promoted farmland deregulation, professionalization, and scale-enlargement. It was thus reinforcing the straying character of reform over the past years, in which deregulation and market liberalization had been intertwined with continued (but conditional) state support for the agricultural sector. Yet the findings presented in this book point to an increasing gap between national policy and the eroding local organizational abilities. This, in turn, amounts to a negative outlook on the prospects of resolving the structural crisis of Japanese farming with this policy mix. As rural areas continue to shrink, local disorganization is bound to lead to more abandoned land, limited efficiency gains for emerging large-scale farms due to farmland fragmentation, and an increasing presence of corporations that enter the agricultural sector seeking short-term economic gains, but not necessarily its long-term survival.

Even if successful, the promotion of large-scale, industrial agriculture is not an undisputed strategy. Around the globe, it is associated with ecological problems such as soil exhaustion and dependency on fossil energy (Chemnitz and Weigelt 2015; Woodhouse 2010), as well as social problems such as the exploitation of contract farmers on behalf of large corporations (Nelson and Kaptur 2015; Wolf 2014). In Japan, the growing number of labor migrants in the agricultural sector has recently raised concerns about exploitation and human rights violations (Ibusuki 2020) – a concern that will only grow if the number of agricultural corporations relying on wage labor increases, while demographic aging in rural areas progresses. Scale-enlargement in Japan is further complicated by geographical conditions, the effects of uncontrolled land development in the postwar period, and the peculiarities of the social process of exchanging farmland use rights. As shown in chapter 8, neither the expansion of local household farms nor the entry of external corporations per se increases the efficiency of agricultural production. Fragmented but large holdings are cost- and labor-intensive, as they require time and fuel to transport machinery from plot to plot. Other studies have shown that the productivity of corporate farm enterprises may remain (far) below average, such as when external investors can only access fragmented land with inferior soil quality (Sekine and Bonanno 2016, 122–3). It is thus highly questionable whether further farmland deregulation can enhance farmland utilization. In contrast, organized control over farmland consolidation such as in Hikawa can indeed make for more efficient use of land, in that the expanding farms can benefit from a more rational allocation of connected plots. To some extent, national policies have recognized these benefits – the Kōsha system in Hikawa has arguably inspired the national introduction of "farmland harmonization groups" and the subsequent farmland banks. However, these policies have failed to acknowledge either the local social and normative foundations of the Kōsha system, or the structural changes in local agricultural governance in the context of boundary change, or both – thus limiting the actual prospects of realizing a rational public redistribution of farmland.

As pointed out throughout this book, consolidation of the agricultural production structure is not only a functional challenge, but also a political process. The case of Hikawa shows particularly well that where incumbent actors such as local JA are successfully involved in farmland consolidation, the results will likely reflect the cooperative's conservative interests. Organized control over farmland transfers is not only a means to achieve scale-enlargement and land-use efficiency, but also a matter of control over the economic activities of farms, and the entry of external investors into local agricultural sectors. For proponents of agricultural liberalization, this is not an ideal scenario. They rather envision an agricultural sector freed from the influence of JA (Yamashita 2015a, 2015b). Yet, because national policy-makers have been shifting the responsibility to realize farmland consolidation to the local level since structural reform gained momentum in the 1990s, fulfilling this task requires a commonly accepted local ordering force. This task will not become easier soon. Given the rapid aging of the farming population, large amounts of farmland will have to be redistributed soon or fall idle. A comprehensive alternative to the ubiquitous cooperative organization to take over this role is not in sight in Japan. In this sense, not the continued strength, but the increasing weakness of the cooperative organization has been complicating the redistribution of farmland to fewer, more professional producers.

An Outlook on JA Reform

In this context, it is worth taking a brief outlook on the ongoing process of reforming the cooperative organization as the most ambitious agricultural policy project of the second Abe administration. JA continues to be framed as the biggest obstacle to structural change in the agricultural sector. After JA fought off several even harsher reform proposals, the revision of the Nōkyō Law went into force in April 2016. As a result, JA Zenchū lost the formal authority to provide guidance to local co-ops, and the legal right to audit their operations.[1] Local co-ops were allowed to take on other legal forms, such as stock companies or social (medicinal) welfare corporations (George Mulgan 2016; Tashiro 2017, 2018). More generally, the objective of the cooperative organization was altered to "raising the agricultural income" of its members. Parallel to revision of the Nōkyō Law, the MAFF issued a new directory for supervision of the cooperative organization. In line with the new legal objective to foster agri-business, the directory challenges the all-encompassing nature of local co-ops, in which the majority of the members are not farmers. Rather than providing a broad variety of services, including those that address the needs of non-farming members, local co-ops are now urged to specialize in supporting (full-time) farmers.

Accordingly, the board of each local co-op will be required to consist of a majority of certified "bearer farmers." These changes aim to undermine the cooperatives' postwar position as socially embedded local organizations that act on behalf of rural society as a whole, and instead seek to turn them into specialized, business-oriented agricultural service-providers (Tashiro 2017, 11–21).

In line with the overall direction of agricultural reform since the mid-1990s, JA reform is also marked by the familiar shift of responsibilities to the local level. Starting in 2016, the cooperative organization entered a five-year phase to investigate the situation of local co-ops to pursue "self-reform." While it is too early to sufficiently evaluate this process, the findings from this book strongly suggest that its actual impact will again depend on the social and normative embedding of co-ops in local agricultural regimes. Strong, socially embedded local JA are likely to be able to use their increasing autonomy in their interest. This may also include that more local JA act as entrepreneurial agri-businesses themselves (Maclachlan and Shimizu 2019). Overall, not least in the cooperative mergers moving toward the formation of "local" JA that cover whole prefectures (Tashiro 2018), JA reform is likely to further complicate the creation and enforcement of organized local responses to the growing impact of a neoliberal market logic in the agricultural sector. Considering the findings of this book, it remains highly questionable if this development will help to solve the structural crisis of Japanese agriculture.

Chapter Thirteen

Institutional Change through the Local Lens

The findings presented in this book also have important implications for our theoretical understanding of gradual institutional change. Developing a dynamic conception of institutional genesis and change has long been the crucial theoretical challenge for neo-institutionalist thought in general, and for understanding the pathways of liberalization in advanced capitalist political economies in particular. The debate has gained profoundly from approaches that capture institutional change as a constant that is shaped through the agency of micro-level actors. Yet, with the nation state as the most common unit of analysis, the concrete processes of *how* these actors exploit the gaps between formal rules and their enactment have mostly been left in the dark, despite some explicit attempts to address this gap theoretically (Berk and Galvan 2009) and empirically (Berk, Galvan, and Hattam 2013). By shifting the analytical focus to the local level, this book has opened the black box of institutional arrangements being renegotiated: the actors who inhabit a certain institutional arrangement make use of and adapt social norms, practices, and network ties as the "raw material" from which they construct local interpretations of changing (formal) macro rules. Moreover, the local perspective has revealed that we should pay careful attention to the specific conditions under which changing macro rules are (re)interpreted. These conditions – and how they change – can substantially affect the prospects and outcomes of local institutional agency.

Informal Institutions as Dynamic Resources

The local perspective allows for a more detailed understanding of the role of informal institutions in institutional change. The macro institutions that characterize non-liberal market economies in Europe and in Japan have often been found to be carried by shared beliefs, unwritten rules, and practices – informal foundations that can provide institutional stability despite formal change, or (less commonly) induce institutional change in times of formal stasis (Aoki 2001; Culpepper 2005; Streeck and Yamamura 2001). So far, however, the literature analyzing the transformation of these institutional arrangements has rarely focused on their informal foundations empirically or has treated them as seemingly intangible phenomena operating beyond the reach of conscious agency. From the latter perspective, informal change remains under the analytical radar until it reaches a tipping point, which can only be identified *ex post*, such as in the form of "joint belief shifts" (Culpepper 2005) or "paradigm shifts" (Röper 2017), which then either induce formal change or allow formal changes to take hold.

In contrast, the local perspective adopted in this book has uncovered the *dynamic* role that norms, practices, and social ties play in the very process of (re)negotiating macro-institutional arrangements. Against the conventional view of informal institutions, this role is subject to agency. Even in highly developed political economies such as Japan, traditional norms and practices do not simply gradually disappear. Rather, they can co-exist alongside or beneath alternative scripts for behavior – and local actors can revive and/or reinterpret "muted" or eroding norms and practices when they have an interest in doing so, e.g., as a reaction to changing state policies. This argument entails a fresh view on how informal institutions themselves change. Broader historical processes of norm erosion, cultural evolution, or changing social relations do not entirely unfold beyond actors' reach. Thus, while the impact of local actors on such processes is of course limited, it should not be dismissed as the background noise of larger (and allegedly more important) macro processes (Powell and Rerup 2017; K. Tsai 2006). Moreover – and more importantly – the book has shown that everyday acts of enforcing and (re)interpreting "how things should be done around here" are not just an end in themselves, nor should they be conceived as strictly localized acts. Rather, they relate directly to broader political and socioeconomic processes, and thus are a means of making sense of these processes, and of gaining discretion over their real-life outcomes.

The findings add empirical and theoretical substance to the claim that liberalization "always comes with, and is enveloped in, all kinds of countermeasures taken by 'society' – or by specific 'societies' in line with their respective traditions against the destructive effects of free, 'self-regulating' markets" (Streeck and Thelen 2005b, 4). This book has shown how local social norms or traditional practices can be employed to construct defensive local responses to a changing macro regime, such as to insulate local interests from increasing political and economic competition. But more importantly, it has shown that such local countermeasures are not necessarily a matter of institutional persistence, let alone stasis. Rather, the organized local agricultural regimes in Hikawa or Miyada were produced through the protracted (re)combination of traditional norms and practices within the changing regulatory framework of agricultural support and protection. In this sense, even defensive local agency is a crucial component of navigating institutional *change*.

This also suggests that there is nothing automatic about the role of informal institutions for the trajectory of changing coordinative (macro) institutions. They are not obstacles to formal institutional change *per se*, including market liberalization. On the contrary, the defensive potential of traditional norms and social ties needs to be unlocked by local actors who have an interest in doing so, and have the "bargaining power" to enforce their interpretations (Knight and Ensminger 1998). If they fail to do so, other actors may instead (re)utilize social networks, norms, and practices with different objectives, such as to create informal means to escape formal constraints and/or to expand their entrepreneurial freedom. These findings are not restricted to agriculture, or Japan. For example, Wank (1999) shows how emerging entrepreneurs in a coastal Chinese city have (re)utilized traditional social network ties (*guanxi*) in "commodifying communism."

The findings in this book suggest that traditional informal institutions need not disappear, erode, or fade to make way for formal institutional change, including market liberalization – much to the contrary, their constant (re)interpretation under changing socioeconomic and formal regulatory circumstances is precisely what shapes these processes. As deregulation, structural reform, and market liberalization have rendered the institutional arrangements governing (formerly) non-liberal or coordinated capitalist political economies increasingly ambiguous (Thelen 2014), the way in which local actors (re)combine local social norms and practices with changing macro rules determines what these rules mean in (local) practice, and thus also determines the pace and the direction of gradual institutional change from within.

Local Institutional Agency in Context

There is always the risk that a local perspective will mistake a potentially endemic phenomenon for the dominant direction of institutional change. That is, while we might find that local agency can exploit the non-liberal potential of a changing macro regime in one locality, this does not tell us if and to what extent similar processes happen in other localities. In general, comprehensive local countermeasures against liberalization are unlikely to be common. With few exceptions, the literature on institutional change in (formerly) non-liberal market economies has been very skeptical about the defensive capabilities of the coordinative or "non-liberal" institutions of the postwar era.[1]

This book is not meant to state the opposite. However, by illuminating precisely *how* local actors create, maintain, and enforce certain (informal) rules that constrain economic action in some cases, the local perspective also helps to explain why their abilities and motivation to do so are limited elsewhere. The playing field for institutional agency is by no means level. Actors that are typically subsumed under one category – be they small and medium-sized enterprises, multinational corporations, labor unions, or a national federation of cooperatives – operate in different local institutional arenas. These differences affect their abilities to create and enforce an interpretation of changing macro-level rules.[2] Several studies have argued that the explanation for how macro institutions change can be found in analyzing local differences within the same national institutional framework.[3] Refining this notion, the evidence in this book highlights the significance of the boundaries within which local institutional agency takes place. A stable overlap of local political and socio-spatial boundaries seems to support organized local interpretations of national regulatory change, under which actors are partially constrained by a "public interest" instead of pursuing short-term individual gains. Again, this finding is not limited to either agricultural reform or Japan. It relates directly to Tsai's (2007) study on the effects of decentralization in China, which has shown that overlapping social and political boundaries can produce "informal institutions of accountability" to commit village leaders to the common interest of their constituencies, instead of opportunistically pursuing their private rent-seeking interests.

It follows that understanding the impact of local institutional agency (or the lack thereof) requires close attention to how the arenas for local institutional agency are constituted, and how and why they change – and in particular, if they become less contained in social, political, or spatial terms, all of which can be assumed to obscure comprehensive, organized local responses to macro-level change. Notably, the boundaries for local institutional agency are likely to change as the result of processes that unfold beyond the reach of local actors, and even beyond the institutional domain in question. Consequently, the local perspective is a particularly promising analytical approach to refine the *meso-theory* of institutional change, in that it opens previously unexplored vantage points on how shifts in different domains of the political economy affect each other. The local perspective can thus expand the range of meso-level dynamics we have to consider for understanding how political economies change.[4]

Beyond Farming, beyond Japan

Admittedly, using spatially confined local institutional arenas as a unit of analysis is especially useful in a sector that is as bound to the land as agriculture. However, I argue that analyzing institutional agency in its specific local social and normative context can contribute to refining the theoretical debate on gradual deregulation, liberalization, and structural reform beyond agriculture. Take, for example, the Japanese innovation regime, another element of Japan's postwar model of non-liberal capitalism that has been undergoing gradual change. Over the 2000s, responsibilities for the development and marketization of new technologies have been gradually shifted toward regional innovation clusters, each of which constitutes distinct local institutional arenas within the changing macro-level innovation regime, shaped by intersecting municipal and prefectural formal competencies, but also by social relations and local practices (Rabe 2019). As another example, the emerging elderly care market in Japan since the introduction of long-term care insurance in 2000 has unfolded alongside subnational differences between urban and rural areas, and even within municipalities. In non-metropolitan areas, where the population is often aging disproportionally rapidly, provision of elderly care depends more on the activation of community ties and practices, because the private care market remains underdeveloped, and local administrations lack resources to supplement these deficits – especially in the aftermath of decentralization reforms and the Heisei municipal mergers (Heidt 2017). The effects of fiscal decentralization and municipal restructuring also provide an interesting angle for comparison between Japan and the United States and parts of Europe, where local administrative bodies with very different capacities struggle with the effects of state rescaling and "spatial austerity" in the aftermath of the financial crisis of 2008–9 (e.g., Peck 2012; Armondi 2017). Gradual institutional change in Germany's political economy is another case in which a local perspective is promising. As Germany's postwar non-liberal model of capitalism has been gradually transformed by financialization, the large sector of family-owned enterprises has remained relatively immune to increasing pressure to open up to global capital markets. Arguably, this "subvariety" of German capitalism has emerged because the "familial sector has conserved traditional Durkheimian institutions of solidarity and mutual obligation" (Lehrer and Celo 2017, 738). This has been linked to the local embedding of family firms, the majority of which are still "headquartered in rural regions" and retain a workforce and managers "with strong local family roots" (737, 740). Thus, the local social and normative embedding of family firms continues to shape the "bifurcated" trajectory of the German political economy. As another example, local industrial regimes in Germany have been found to display different ways to adapt to the pressures of globalization, including intensified cooperation within local inter-firm networks (Glassmann 2004, 2009).

A qualitative analysis of local institutional agency and how it is embedded in contrast and comparison with similar localities can be expected to produce a more fine-grained understanding of how gradual liberalization, deregulation, and structural reform interact and are (re) negotiated by the actors who inhabit these institutional arrangements. I hope that this book will contribute to establish the local perspective on institutional agency in the literature on comparative political economy.

Appendix A: Field Research

The arguments brought forward in this book rely crucially on information derived through participatory observation and interviews with farmers, local and prefectural officials, and representatives of local branches of the cooperative organization throughout Japan, and over a prolonged period of time.

Main Field Research Sites

Two longer periods of field research have provided the main empirical basis for this book, both of which were conducted in the context of my dissertation: March–June 2013 in the Kōfu Basin in Yamanashi Prefecture, and September–December 2013 in Hikawa Town and Izumo City in Shimane Prefecture. Field research in the Kōfu Basin was followed with numerous brief periods of participatory observation and interviews throughout 2017–19. It was preceded by several months of working experience with a local grape farmer (KB-F1) in early spring and summer 2010. Albeit not part of any official research program, this period has added to the insight in daily routines throughout the seasons and drawn attention to changes (e.g., regarding the farms' business model) over the years. Field research in the Kōfu Basin was further prepared with a two-day preliminary field trip in October 2012.

Field research in Hikawa/Izumo was prepared with a series of interviews with officials and farm visits on a three-day preliminary field trip in March 2013. Further information was sourced through interviews with officials and farm visits as well as document collection during a four-day follow-up trip in July 2017 and through several email exchanges with members of the local agricultural administration in Izumo City. Apart from Hikawa itself, field research also included interviews, data collection, and everyday observations in neighboring Izumo City, where I lived during my time in Shimane. The observations in Izumo added significantly to a deeper understanding of the specific character of the local agricultural regime in Hikawa.

Participatory Observation

Participatory observation in the Kōfu Basin entailed eleven weeks of daily farm labor, including two weeks of living in the household of KB-F1, and taking part in meetings between KB-F1 and local and prefectural officials. Apart from KB-F1, I worked with his employees, volunteers from Tōkyō, and several other farmers from the area. Additional participatory observation was carried out with a professional grape farmer from a semi-urban neighborhood in Kōfu City (KB-F2), where I also lived for most of the research period and was in daily contact with members of the local shipping cooperative. In May 2013, I attended a hearing of seventeen "bearer farmers" from Enzan (Kōshū City) with the governor of Yamanashi Prefecture, during which the farmers shared their opinions and concerns about land improvement and land use. Throughout 2017–19, I participated in events to promote the local wine industry. In March 2019, I participated in a meeting of a local committee to improve wine and grape production and information on farmland use in Kōshū City, chaired by KB-F1.

Participatory observation in Hikawa was carried out on several sites over the whole period of September–December 2013. A first phase of participatory observation (ten consecutive days, full-time) was carried out at a large incorporated farm (H-F1). Participatory observation covered the regular working day of the farmer and his staff (regular and part-time employees and young trainees), including morning meetings and visits off-hours, e.g., for a local festival. A second phase of participatory observation (ten consecutive days, full-time) was carried out at a hamlet-based collective farm (H-CF5). Again, this phase entailed regular farm labor (packing and drying rice, machine maintenance, land maintenance), and attending the daily morning meetings, in which the farmers discussed the upcoming tasks among themselves and with staff from JA Hikawa. A briefer period of participatory observation at an incorporated hamlet-based collective farm (H-CF1) included similar elements (two consecutive days). Moreover, I spent several weeks with occasional participatory observation at the Agricultural Production Corporation Green Support. I worked with the head of the company (H-GS1) and with the staff (harvesting, shipping to the country elevator, distributing implements), spent several days at the farm's office, and accompanied H-GS1 to meetings and on work-related trips. In

December 2013, I also attended the ceremony for the incorporation of a hamlet-based collective farm (H-CF6).

Participatory observation provided the basis for a broad variety of personal contacts and interviews – both formal (scheduled, semi-structured, and at times recorded) and in the form of countless ad hoc conversations (see appendix B). All hosts for participatory observation were aware of my role as researcher. While this might have induced caution among respondents, it also alleviated potential ethical problems and meant that I could routinely ask technical questions unconnected to the actual task at hand, e.g., regarding land use contracts, farm sizes, subsidy schemes, etc. Moreover, respondents were generally eager to introduce me to other local farmers, officials, or JA staff to support my research. The prolonged research periods and the element of participatory observation gave way to a depth of information on the practical details of farming, land use, agricultural governance, local social relations, attitudes, etc., that is virtually impossible to obtain with interviews alone.

Additional Field Research

The main periods of field research also provided the foundation for additional field research in other localities. This included a two-day field trip to Takasaki City in Gunma Prefecture (document collection and interviews with farmers and local officials, farm visits, December 2013), two field trips to Yasu City in Shiga Prefecture (document collection and interviews with the leader of a large corporate farm, members of the local agricultural committee and other local officials, farm visits, April 2017 and September 2019), a seven-day field trip to Nagano Prefecture (document collection and interviews with farmers, cooperative representatives, local officials in Iida City, Miyada Village, and Iijima Town, July 2017), a three-day field trip to Ōyama Town/Hita City in Ōita Prefecture (document collection and interview with cooperative representative in Ōyama, document collection and interviews with officials of the local agricultural administration in Hita City, interview and farm visit at a collective farm, November 2018), and a two-day field trip to Kami District in Miyagi Prefecture (document collection and interviews with cooperative representatives and stakeholders of the local "6th industry," February 2019). In all cases, field research was conducted against the background of the information obtained in the (already very different) cases of Hikawa/Izumo and the Kōfu Basin, which provided the basis and the framing for targeted questions on local differences in land use, agricultural production structure, the relations between different types of farms and the local co-ops, etc.

Appendix B: Interviews

The data from these field research periods are very heterogenous. Apart from the observations, they entail a number of conversations that were not recorded, nor did they follow a fixed structure. Still, however, a substantial part of the interviews was semi-structured, based upon a certain degree of preparation on behalf of the interviewer and following a (variable) set of guiding questions. For example, all interviews with farmers and collective farms included a relatively fixed set of questions on their agricultural operation (acreage under cultivation, legal status of the farm, history of the farm, management of the farm). Moreover, all interviews touched upon farmland use and consolidation, the (social) relations within the hamlet, other hamlets in the area, and the social and professional relations with the local administration and agricultural cooperative. Apart from these guidelines, interview questions varied according to the location and the respondents. Most interviews were conducted in informal settings, including the respondents' homes, public spaces such as cafés, or – most typically – on their land and in their offices. Interviews with officials and cooperative representatives were structured differently and often had a slightly greater degree of formality. Interviews lasted between twenty minutes and several hours. Many interviews included more than one respondent. Some respondents were interviewed twice, and a small number of core respondents were interviewed several times, including numerous ad hoc conversations (see list).

In the text, information and quotes from interviews are cited according to the following order:

Initial letter(s) specify location:

H	Hikawa Town (since 2011 part of Izumo City, Shimane Prefecture)
Ht	Hita City, Ōita Prefecture

I	Izumo City, Shimane Prefecture
Ii	Iida City, Nagano Prefecture
Ij	Iijima Town, Nagano Prefecture
K	Kami District (Kami Town and Shikama Town), Miyagi Prefecture
KB	Kōfu Basin, Yamanashi Prefecture; includes respondents from Kōshū City, Kōfu City, and Fuefuki City
M	Miyada Village, Nagano Prefecture
O	Ōyama Town (since 2005 part of Hita City), Ōita Prefecture
T	Takasaki City, Gunma Prefecture
Y	Yasu City, Shiga Prefecture

The following letters specify respondents:

CF	Members of hamlet-based collective farms or similar group farming entities, including voluntary associations and incorporated farms
F	Farmers, including household farms, members of household farms, and agricultural production corporations
GS	Representatives from Green Support Hikawa
JA	Representatives from local agricultural cooperatives
O(c,p)	Public officials from municipal (c) and prefectural (p) agricultural administrations

The numbers indicate that there are several respondents in the same category. Lowercase letters following a number indicate that more than one person of the same entity was interviewed separately, e.g., several family members of the same household or hamlet-based collective farm. The following list includes respondents from semi-structured interviews, not all of which appear in the text. Note that some respondents have numerous roles but are listed in only one category. Some core respondents (including the hosts for participatory observation, see above) were interviewed several times (formal interviews and informal conversations), some over a span of several years.

Farmers

| H-F1 | Full-time farmer, president of an incorporated household farm; two interviews and several informal conversations between October and November 2013, follow-up interview in July 2017 |
| H-F2 | Head of a household farm (full-time farmer) and his son-in-law; interview in November 2013 |

H-F3	Full-time farmer, household farm; interview in November 2013
H-F4	Full-time farmer, president of incorporated household farm; interview in October 2013
H-F4a	Wife of H-F4; interview in October 2013
H-F4b	Oldest son of H-F4, full-time farmer; interview in October 2013
H-F5	Part-time farmer, part-time worker at Green Support; interview in November 2013
I-F1	Full-time farmer, originally from Fukushima Prefecture, relocated to Izumo City in the aftermath of the earthquake, tsunami, and nuclear disaster in March 2011; interview in December 2013, follow-up interview in July 2017
I-F2	Part-time farmer; interview in October 2013
KB-F1	Kōshū City, full-time farmer, winemaker, president of incorporated household farm; two formal interviews and numerous informal conversations between March and June 2013 and between January 2017 and September 2019
KB-F2	Kōfu City, full-time farmer, president of incorporated household farm; one interview in April 2013 and several informal conversations between March and June 2013 and in 2018 and 2019
KB-F3	Kōshū City, full-time farmer, household farm; two interviews in May 2013
KB-F4	Kōfu City, full-time farmer, household farm; two interviews and several informal conversations between March and June 2013
KB-F4a	Wife of KB-F4; one interview and several informal conversations between March and June 2013
KB-F5	Kōfu City, full-time farmer, household farm; interview in May 2013
KB-F6	Yamanashi City, president of incorporated household farm; interview in May 2013, follow-up interview in November 2019
KB-F7	Fuefuki City, full-time farmer, household farm; interview in May 2013
KB-F8	Yamanashi City, full-time farmer, household farm, head of the agricultural practice union in his hamlet; interview in May 2013
KB-F8a	Son of KB-F8, full-time farmer, formerly employed at JA Fruits Yamanashi; interview in May 2013
KB-F8b	Wife of KB-F8; interview in May 2013

KB-F9	Kōshū City, part-time farmer, based mainly in Tōkyō; interview in April 2013, several informal conversations between March and June 2013
KB-F10	Fuefuki City, president of incorporated winery, which also cultivates grapes; interview in May 2013
KB-F11	Kōshū City, professionally trained winemaker, regularly employed at KB-F1; interview in May 2013, numerous informal conversations between March and June 2013
KB-F12	Kōshū City, regularly employed at KB-F1, co-organizer of an event to promote the local wine industry; numerous informal conversations between March and June 2013 and between January 2017 and September 2019
KB-F13	Kōfu City, former trainee at KB-F2, since 2014 full-time farmer in Tochigi Prefecture; interview in May 2013, several informal conversations between March and June 2013
KB-F14	Kōshū City, regular employee at KB-F1; numerous informal conversations between January 2017 and September 2019
KB-F15	Kōshū City, full-time farmer and winemaker; interview in April 2017
KB-F16	Kōshū City, full-time farmer and winemaker; interview in April 2017
T-F	President of corporate farm, member of the Takasaki City Agricultural Committee; interview in December 2013
Y-F1	President of corporate farm (as of April 2017), former member of the city council, former JA official; interview in April 2017
Y-F1a	Successor of Y-F1 as the president of the same corporate farm; interview in September 2019

Hamlet-Based Collective Farms

H-CF1	Incorporated hamlet-based collective farm; interview with the vice president (former president) and the acting president, November 2013
H-CF1a	Follow-up interview with the vice president of the same farm, November 2013
H-CF2	Hamlet-based collective farm; interview with the head of the farm (a former advisor for hamlet-based collective farms at JA Hikawa and full-time farmer) and his designated successor, December 2013
H-CF3	Incorporated hamlet-based collective farm; interview with the president of the farm, his brother, a member of the board

	(also member of the Izumo city council) and his brother, November 2013
H-CF4	Hamlet-based collective farm; interview with the head of the farm, November 2013
H-CF5	Hamlet-based collective farm (incorporated in 2015); interview with the head of the farm and H-JA1 (see below), March 2013
H-CF5a	Member of H-CF5, several informal conversations in October 2013
H-CF5b	Member of H-CF5, several informal conversations in October 2013
H-CF5c	Vice head of H-CF5, several informal conversations in October 2013
H-CF5d	Member of H-CF5, several informal conversations in October 2013
H-CF6	Hamlet-based collective farm (incorporated in December 2013); interview with the vice head of the farm, October 2013
H-CF6a	Member of H-CF6, head of the Hikawa Hamlet-Based Collective Farms Association, December 2013
H-CF7	Incorporated hamlet-based collective farm; Interview with eight members and the president of the farm, October 2013
H-CF7a	Follow-up interview with eight members of the same farm, July 2017
Ht-CF	Incorporated hamlet-based collective farm; interview with the president and the former president, November 2018
KB-CF	Hamlet-based collective farm (Kōshū City); interview with the head of the farm (also former head of the local land improvement district) and another member, May 2013
M-CF	Bureau chief of the incorporated collective farm Miyada, local JA official, July 2017

Representatives of Local JA

H-JA1	Head of JA Hikawa General Department, member of H-CF5; interview in November 2013, follow-up interview in July 2017 (then as president of the board of H-CF5)
H-JA2	JA Hikawa Farm Management Department, member of H-CF6; interview in November 2013
H-JA3	Retired JA Hikawa care worker, employed part-time at the farm of H-F1; interview in October 2013
H-JA4	Bureau Chief Hikawa Nōgyō Kōsha (as of 2013); head of the Farm Management Department of the Hikawa branch of JA

	Shimane (as of 2017); member of a hamlet-based collective farm in Hikawa; interview in March 2013, follow-up interviews in December 2013 and July 2017
H-JA5	JA Hikawa Farm Management Department; interview in March 2013
H-JA6	Head of JA Hikawa Farm Management Department; interview in March 2013
I-JA1	Vice head of JA Izumo Farm Management Department, head of JA Izumo Farm Management Planning Section; interview in November 2013
I-JA2	JA Izumo, farm management advisor; interview in November 2013
I-JA3	JA Izumo, head of the JA Izumo Ōtsu Branch; interview in November 2013
KB-JA1	Kōshū City, Farm Management Support Center, in charge of the local farmland harmonization group; interview in April 2013
KB-JA2	Yamanashi City, manager of a winery founded by the local agricultural cooperative; two interviews in May 2013
O-JA	Member of the executive board, Ōyama-Machi Nōkyō; interview in November 2018
K-JA1	Managing Director JA Kami Yotsuba, board member of an incorporated hamlet-based collective farm in Kami; interview in February 2019
K-JA2	Head of the Farm Management Center, JA Kami Yotsuba; interview in February 2019

Officials from Local and Prefectural Agricultural Administrations

H-O1	Izumo City, Hikawa Town, director of the Department for Industrial Promotion, in charge of local "bearer farm" promotion (as of 2013); transferred to the Industrial Revitalization Department in Izumo City in 2015; several interviews between October and December 2013 and in July 2017
H-O2	Bureau chief, Hikawa Nōgyō Kōsha; interview in July 2017
H-O3	Director, Hikawa Nōgyō Kōsha; interview in July 2017
H-O4	Staff at the Hikawa Nōgyō Kōsha; interview in July 2017
Ht-O	Interview with four representatives of the Agriculture and Forestry Division of Hita City, November 2018
KB-Oc1	Kōshū City, head of the Agriculture and Forestry Department
KB-Oc2	Kōshū City, Department for Industrial Revitalization, Agricultural Land Use; interview in April 2013

KB-Oc3　　　Kōshū City, inspector, Agriculture and Forestry Department; interview in April 2013

KB-Op1　　　Yamanashi Prefecture, Kyōtō Region Agricultural Office, head of Regional Agricultural Policies Department; interview in April 2013

KB-Op2　　　Yamanashi Prefecture, inspector, Kyōtō Region Agricultural Infrastructure Department; interview in May 2013

Ii-O1　　　　Head of the Iida City Agricultural Revitalization Center; interview in July 2017

Ii-O2　　　　Chief investigator, Iida City Farm Village Revitalization Section; interview in July 2017

Ij-O　　　　　Former member of the agricultural administration in Iijima Town, Iijima Town Hamlet-Based Collective Farming Manager, member of the Nagano Prefecture Agricultural Revitalization Committee; interview in July 2017

M-O　　　　　Head of the Agricultural Section, Miyada Village; interview in July 2017

T-O　　　　　Appointed member of the Takasaki City Agricultural Committee; interview in December 2013

Y-O1　　　　Interview with three members of the agricultural administration in Yasu City, including the vice head of the Environment and Economics Department and head of the Agricultural Committee Bureau, and chief investigator of the Yasu City Agricultural Section, April 2017

Y-O2　　　　Interview with the vice head of the Environment and Economics Department and head of the Agricultural Committee Bureau, and the chief investigator of the Yasu City Agricultural Section, September 2019

Green Support

H-GS1　　　Director of Green Support Hikawa, former official at JA Hikawa, member of the Agricultural Committee in Hikawa (as of 2013) and Izumo City (since autumn 2017); founding member of hamlet-based collective farm in Hikawa several formal interviews and informal conversations between October and December 2013 and in July 2017)

H-GS2　　　Full-time employee at Green Support, member of hamlet-based collective farm in Izumo City; several informal conversations between November and December 2013

Other Respondents

H-AL   Interview with five members of the Hikawa Hiroin Agri-Ladies, an association of farm wives in Hikawa. Four of them are members in different hamlet-based collective farms in Hikawa, one is H-F4a; November 2013

KB-WT   Interview with the founder and two co-founders of Yamanashi Wine Tourism, a wine tourism event in the Kōfu Basin, December 2017

PRIMAFF1   Researcher, Policy Research Institute of the MAFF; interview in April 2013

PRIMAFF2   Interview with three researchers (including PRIMAFF1), Policy Research Institute of the MAFF, February 2019

Additionally, I conducted a series of interviews and informal conversations with Gōdo Yoshihisa, professor of agricultural economy, Meiji Gakuin Daigaku, on several occasions between 2012 and 2019. Information that is sourced from these conversations is indicated as such in the notes.

Appendix C: Types of Farms in Japan

The MAFF distinguishes between several different types of farm households.

Farm household: Household engaged in farming and managing cultivated land of 10 ares (0.1 hectares) or more or earning more than ¥150,000 per year.

Apart from this basic definition, farms are classified by types of business, in commercial and non-commercial farm households.

Commercial farm household: Manages cultivated land of thirty ares or more *or* earns more than ¥500,000 per year from sales of agricultural products.

All households not satisfying these conditions are counted as *non-commercial farm households* or *self-consumption farm households*.

Commercial farm households are further differentiated by the scope of their business:

Business farm household: Main source of income (50 per cent or more) from farming and at least one family member under the age of sixty-five is engaged in (self-employed) farming for more than sixty days a year.

Semi-business farm household: Main source of income (50 per cent or more) derived from activities other than agriculture, but at least one family member under the age of sixty-five is engaged in (self-employed) farming for more than sixty days a year.

Side-business farm household: No household members under the age of sixty-five engaged in (self-employed) farming for more than sixty days a year.

Note that the term "commercial farm household" is not equivalent to "full-time farm household," which is defined as follows:

Full-time farm household: Farm household with no household member employed in non-farm employment for more than thirty days a year, or self-employed earning more than ¥150,000 per year.

Part-time farm household: Farm household with at least one household member engaged in non-farm employment. Part-time farm households are further classified into *Type 1* (majority of household income from farming) and *Type 2* (majority of household income from off-farm employment/off-farm self-employment).

Non-farming households possessing land: Household not actively engaged in farming, but possessing five ares or more of arable land, abandoned and/or under lease.

"Bearer Farm(er)s" and Certified Farm(er)s

Unlike the types of farm households, which are mainly statistical classifications, the terms "bearer farm(er)" (*ninaite*) and "certified farm(er)" are political categories that refer to the policy goal of farmland consolidation and the eligibility for certain agricultural support programs. A *"bearer farm(er)"* is a "farm management entity" aiming to be economically efficient and stable, i.e., a future "bearer" of agricultural production. The term includes farm households (part-time and full-time), certain forms of hamlet-based collective farms, and agricultural production corporations.

The term *certified farm*(er) (*nintei nōgyō-sha*, 認定農業者) refers to farm management entities formally recognized by the municipal agricultural administration based on so-called farm management improvement plans (*nōgyō keiei kaizen keikaku*, 農業経営改善計画). Certification is the formal precondition to access (additional) state support programs. It can be granted to full-time and part-time household farmers, but also hamlet-based collective farms (if they meet certain requirements to be recognized as "special agricultural group"), and agricultural production corporations. Municipalities can adjust the requirements for certification according to the local situation. For example, in 2013 the agricultural administration in Hikawa Town (Izumo City) defined the following conditions for obtaining the status of certified farm:

1 Annual income from farming above four million yen (of the main person engaged in agriculture per "farm management entity")
2 Annual farm labor exceeds 2,000 hours (of the main person engaged in agriculture per "farm management entity")

Focus management entities (*chiiki no chūshin to naru keieitai*, 地域の中心となる経営体) are a similar category, which was introduced additionally to the certified farmers scheme with the People and Farmland Plan in 2012. Focus management entities are formally acknowledged as "central" to local implementation of specific support policies (e.g., farmland consolidation, subsidized farm labor) under a local People and Farmland Plan. In practice, however, certified farms and focus management entities more or less refer to the same persons and/or farms.

A specific category of farms within the group of designated "bearer farms" are *agricultural production corporations*, which are defined as legal persons allowed to acquire ownership of agricultural land – in contrast to "general" corporations, which are only allowed to rent land (since 2009). Agricultural production corporations are eligible for special support under the certified farmers' scheme. Both farm households and hamlet-based collective farms can form agricultural production corporations. Agricultural production corporations must take the form of an unlisted stock company, a limited liability company, an unlimited partnership, a limited partnership, or a consolidated company. Activities of agricultural production corporations are subject to the oversight of local agricultural committees.

While there are important differences between the formal categories (e.g., certified farm, agricultural production corporation) and the less formal category of "bearer farm," they are often used synonymously. For example, official statistics on farmland consolidation in the hands of "bearer farms" include "certified farms or farms that meet the requirements for certification" (MAFF 2016a).

Sources: Gōdo (2014c); Hikawa Town Agriculture and Forestry Office (2013); Kimura and Martini (2009); Nihon Nōgyō Hōjin Kyōkai (n.d.).

Appendix D: Paddy Field Subsidies

This appendix gives an overview on the amount and different types of subsidies (¥/ten ares) that farmers participating in the rice production control program could obtain in Hikawa. It is based on information provided by the Agricultural Office in Hikawa in October 2013. In principle, it is applicable to all rice-farming areas in Japan at that time (apart from the local payments, see below). Some changes in the exact amount of payments and subsidized items notwithstanding, the subsidization scheme remained in place until 2018, with the notable exception of the direct income support payment for rice-farming households.

Direct income support for rice farming households: Between 2010 and 2013, every commercial rice-farming household received ¥15,000/ ten ares of direct income support. Eligibility was conditional on participation in the rice production control program, i.e., farm households who would refuse to follow rice production control targets could not receive the direct payment or the subsidies for paddy field diversion listed below. In 2014, the direct income support was cut in half. In 2018, rice production control became voluntary again, and the direct income support was abolished.

Support payments for diversion crops: There are two different types of national support payments for converting paddy fields to other crops in order to compensate farmers for the lower market prices of these crops: (1) income support, which depends on the amount and quality of diversion crops produced (e.g., for soy and wheat), and (2) additional support for cultivating certain "strategy crops" as diversion crops. Strategy crops are supported to boost Japan's food self-sufficiency, e.g., rice or rice straw for animal feed, rice for processing, or wheat and soy. The payments are not related to the actual amount and quality of the product, but only to the act of crop diversion itself. Cultivating more than one strategy crop in a row is supported with an additional payment ("second crop support"). Likewise, producing animal feed in cooperation with a livestock producer is also supported additionally. Moreover, municipalities can declare certain crops as "local specialties" – these crops are also subsidized in the context of the rice production control program under the "local produce fund." As of 2013 in Hikawa this included adlay and sunflowers, and certain vegetables designated as local "focus crops" (see below). Noticeably, the local produce fund also supports using paddy land for "fertility preservation" and "scenery" – that is, the land is not used for rice, but also not for a designated diversion crop, and maintained until the farm can grow rice again.

Local schemes: Apart from the national support programs listed above, farmers in Hikawa can also partake in a local program called the Hikawa Town Mutual Support Scheme (*Hikawa-chō tomo no hojokin*, 斐川町ともの補助金). This is a longstanding local scheme co-funded by the former municipality, the local co-op, and participating farmers. In contrast to national payments, the local scheme applies to all farmers who participate in crop diversion and is not restricted to commercial farms. Farmers who do not participate in crop diversion have to pay a fee of ¥15,000/10 ares. Other localities throughout Japan operate (or operated) similar local schemes. The local scheme provides basic support for participating in rice production control, and additional support for cultivating "focus crops," which are certain vegetables designated by the local administration (see above).

Depending on available machinery, labor resources, soil condition, etc., commercial rice farms in Hikawa can choose options for the subsidized diversion of their paddy land. Below is a list of examples of the "support menus" available in 2013 (¥/ten ares):

Two strategy crops:
– Hikawa Town mutual support scheme: ¥5,000 + strategy crop (wheat): ¥35,000 + second crop support (soy): ¥15,000 + income support (wheat, estimate): ¥20,000 + income support (soy, estimate): ¥20,000 = ¥95,000
– Hikawa Town mutual support scheme: ¥5,000 + strategy crop (feed): ¥35,000 + second crop support (feed): ¥15,000 + support for cooperation with livestock producer: ¥12,500 = ¥67,500

One strategy crop:
– Hikawa Town mutual support scheme: ¥5,000 + strategy crop (rice for animal feed, flour, or rice straw): ¥80,000 = ¥85,000
– Hikawa Town mutual support scheme: ¥5,000 + strategy crop (wheat): ¥35,000 + income support (wheat): ¥20,000 = ¥60,000

Strategy crop and focus crop:
- Hikawa Town mutual support scheme: ¥5,000 + strategy crop (wheat): ¥35,000 + local produce fund for focus crops (adlay): ¥10,000 + income support (wheat, estimate): ¥20,000 = ¥70,000
- Hikawa Town mutual support scheme: 5,000 + strategy crop (feed): ¥35,000 + local produce fund for focus crops (sunflower): ¥20,000 + support for cooperation with livestock producer: ¥12,500 = ¥62,500

Only focus crops:
- Hikawa Town mutual support scheme: ¥5,000 + local produce fund (two types of designated vegetables): ¥14,000 + Hikawa Town mutual support scheme focus crops (two types of designated vegetables): ¥10,000 = ¥42,500

No conversion crops:
- Hikawa Town mutual support scheme: ¥5,000 + local produce fund (fertility preservation, scenery): ¥2,000 = ¥7,000

Idle paddy land:
- Hikawa Town mutual support scheme: ¥5,000

As mentioned above, apart from the Hikawa Town Mutual Support Scheme, these support payments were available for all commercial rice farms participating in rice production control in Japan as of 2013. Larger holdings and hamlet-based collective farms can maximize subsidies through "block rotation" of certain diversion crops. Within the organized local agricultural regime in Hikawa, access to state support for rice production control was additionally enhanced through the coordination of crop diversion among smaller producers and large-scale farms (including Green Support) under the Kōsha system, so that even land in the hands of part-time farm households and small hamlet-based collective farms unable to produce diversion crops could be used in the most subsidy-productive way (see chapters 8–10).

A major change in the subsidization scheme occurred in 2018, when rice production control became voluntary again, and the direct income support for rice farmers was abolished. In turn, the support for "strategy crops" such as rice for animal feed or processing or wheat was expanded. Thus, the change affected mostly small and aging rice farmers who lack the resources to cultivate the designated strategy crops. In Hikawa, these effects were again counterbalanced by the Kōsha system.

Notes

Part 1. Introduction: Institutional Change in Japan's Agricultural Sector

1 Adlay – also known as Job's tears – is a grain that has become rare in contemporary Japan. In Hikawa, it has been rediscovered and branded as a "local specialty" and is grown on paddy fields diverted from rice cultivation.

Chapter 1. Japan's Agricultural Support and Protection Regime

1 See Hisano, Akitsu, and McGreevy (2018) on Japan; Commission of the European Community (2015) on the EU; United States Department of Agriculture (2017) on the United States.
2 In a number of case studies, Tashiro (2009) emphasizes the need for local cooperation patterns between farmers, hamlets, local co-ops, and administrations as a means to accommodate the effects of "straying" national agricultural policies in the context of transnational agricultural liberalization. For similar cases, see also K. Taniguchi (2009); Hoshi and Yamazaki (2015). See chapter 5 for details on the reform process.

Chapter 2. Toward a Local Perspective on Gradual Institutional Change

1 Beyond the field of comparative political economy, the stability bias of neo-institutionalist thought has also been challenged by political scientists, see, e.g., Berk and Galvan (2009, 2013), in organizational studies; see, e.g., Lawrence, Suddaby, and Leca (2009); Powell and Rerup (2017), and in social movement studies; see, e.g., Fligstein and McAdam (2012).
2 For critical reviews of the "stability bias" in neo-institutionalist thought (and historical institutionalism in particular), see Thelen (2004, 32–1);

Streeck and Thelen (2005b, 2–9); Mahoney and Thelen (2010b, 5–7). See also Deeg and Jackson (2007); Hall and Thelen (2009).

3 In contrast, functional or "rational-choice" approaches principally assume that institutions are "either efficient or obsolete" (March and Olsen 1984) and thus do not leave conceptual space for agency. In sociological approaches, institutions are typically seen as shared scripts of behavior or norms that are taken for granted (even beyond conscious scrutiny, e.g. Jepperson 1991; Zucker 1991) – and thus also appear immune to agency. For a more detailed discussion, see Streeck and Thelen (2005b); Mahoney and Thelen (2010a).

4 For details on the "modes" of endogenous change and the role of relative power and coalitions, see Thelen (2004); Streeck and Thelen (2005a); Mahoney and Thelen (2010a, 17–18).

5 In the words of Etienne and Schnyder (2014), there are only "sketches of a theory" linking agency and institutions. For a similar view, see also Berk and Galvan (2009), and Powell and Rerup (2017).

6 See, for example, Berk and Galvan (2009, 2013), who propose to understand institutional change as a constant process of "creative syncretism." Similarly, scholars in organizational studies have emphasized the significance of micro-level agency for producing institutional change and stability; see, e.g., Lawrence, Suddaby, and Leca (2009) and Powell and Rerup (2017). Despite their different empirical focus, these studies have been an important source of inspiration for this book.

7 For the United Kingdom, see, e.g., Kennett et al. (2015); Peck (2012); for Japan, see, e.g., Matanle, Rausch, and the Shrinking Regions Research Group (2011); Iba and Sakamoto (2014); Sekine and Bonanno (2016).

8 See Crouch and Keune (2005, 84). The notion of institutional heterogeneity does not necessarily correspond to subnational political divisions, but can also apply to preexisting (dormant or marginalized) institutional legacies; see, e.g., Crouch and Keune (2005).

9 In Hikawa, the core case of this book, the town and the co-op together cover an area of roughly eighty square kilometers. While some local agricultural regimes are even smaller, many others have become larger due to cooperative and municipal mergers in the 2000s. See chapter 11 for details.

10 See, e.g., Papachristos, Hureau, and Braga (2013); Heinze, Soderstrom, and Heinze (2016); Grischow (2008); Johnston and Pattie (2011); Zimmerbauer and Paasi (2013).

11 See, e.g., Knoke (1994, 119–48); L. Tsai (2007); Small (2006); Papachristos, Hureau, and Braga (2013). On local economies, see Crouch and Voelzkow (2004). On villages and access to micro-finance, see Jackson (2014). On neighborhoods as "elaborate and enduring framework for social life" in Japan, see, e.g., Bestor (1989).

12 Among many examples, see, e.g., Aoki (2001); North (1993, 2005); Roland (2004); Culpepper (2005); Greif (2006).

13 A few examples include Helmke and Levitsky (2006); K. Tsai (2006); L. Tsai (2007); O'Donnell (2006); Cousins (2007); Grischow (2008); Chavance (2008); Morris and Polese (2015); Estrin and Mickiewitz (2010).

14 For studies that focus on informal institutions in industrialized democracies, see, e.g., Azari and Smith (2012) on the United States, or Farrell (2012) on Italy and Germany.

15 See, e.g., Aoki (2001); Culpepper (2005) for studies that include changes regarding norms and practices in their analysis on change in political economy institutions.

16 A notable exception is K. Tsai (2006), which will be discussed below. Other studies on endogenous institutional change have addressed informal institutions vaguely as "implicit understandings held by the relevant community" (Mahoney and Thelen 2010b, 13), which can play a role in the enactment of formal rules (Onoma 2010).

Chapter 3. Institutional Change in Japanese Agricultural Support and Protection through the Local Lens

1 See the appendix for details on field sites and interviewees.

2 My own calculation based on data directly obtained from the MAFF in November 2019. See chapter 6 (figure 6.2) for details.

3 For this reasoning, see, e.g., Flyvbjerg (2006); George and Bennett (2005); Beach and Pedersen (2013).

4 The official name is Hikawa Town Agricultural Public Corporation (斐川町 農業公社).

5 Beyond the Japanese case, numerous studies have shown that and how social ties between farmers, local governments, or cooperatives, and the norms and practices carried by these ties enable or constrain farmers' entrepreneurial aspirations. See, e.g., Fitz-Koch et al. (2018); Ferguson and Hansson (2015); Harris-White, Mishra, and Upadhyay (2009); Dias, Rodrigues, and Ferreira (2019).

6 Numerous accounts approach social networks as informal institutions; see Hall (1986); Ansell (2006); Beaman (2012); Jackson (2014); Ballester, Calvó-Armengol, and Zenou (2006).

7 For example, during fieldwork I encountered situations in which my own labor became a proxy for that of my main respondents. They would explicitly or implicitly expect me to pay them back for their help by helping them and also would "pay back" their own obligations toward other farmers by sending me as a helper instead.

8 On the concept of village institutions, see also Jentzsch (2017b, 2020a).

9 See, e.g., Odagiri, Ouchi, and Tsuboi (2009). For a statistical overview, see MAFF (2012). For a case study on multiple functions in a contemporary hamlet, see Hiraguchi, Nishihashi, and Morozumi (2010).

10 *Shinkōku* (振興区) are local administrative units located between the farm hamlet level and the municipal level in Hikawa. The *shinkōku* system will be discussed in more detail in chapters 6–8.

Part 2. Japan's Agricultural Support and Protection over Time

Chapter 4. Postwar Evolution of Support and Protection

1 For more detailed accounts of the land reform and its effects, see Dore (1984); Kawagoe (1999); George Mulgan (2000); Kelly (2007).

2 For overviews on the postwar legal development of the ALL, see, e.g., McDonald (1997); George Mulgan (2000); Kimura and Martini (2009); Tashiro (2009).

3 Interview Professor Gōdo Yoshihisa, March 2014.

4 Additionally, specialized co-ops (*senmon nōkyō*) focus on certain crops. While not all farmers belong to a specialized co-op, members almost certainly belong to "their" local multi-purpose cooperative; see George Mulgan (2000, 52–4).

5 For details, see George Mulgan (2000, 55–8). In response to growing political and economic pressure, the cooperative organization began rationalization in the 1990s. In the process, some prefectural federations were disbanded, and the number of local cooperatives has been declining sharply. On the effects of cooperative mergers, see chapter 11.

6 In the first years after the passage of the ALL, the agricultural committees competed with Nōkyō over the role of main political representative of farmers. However, given Nōkyō's all-encompassing membership and its organizational penetration of the committees, Nōkyō soon dominated them (and their prefectural and national federations) as the political voice of rural Japan. For details, see George Mulgan (2000, 69–72).

7 General MacArthur, the supreme commander of the Allied Powers, referred to the land reform as "the most successful land reform program in history" (Kawagoe 1999, 1).

8 For the effects of SNTV in Japan and beyond, see, e.g., G. Cox and Niou (1994); Ramseyer and Rosenbluth (1997); C.-H. Tsai (2005); Rosenbluth and Thies (2010).

9 George Mulgan (2000, 415–37) provides a detailed discussion of the multi-faceted electoral activities of Nōkyō and its affiliated groups.

10 See George Mulgan (2006c) for a fascinating account of such a political career.

11 In 1950, Japan had almost 6.2 million farm households (Dore 1984, 176).

12 On the relation between part-time farming and economic growth/industrialization in Japan, see, e.g., Francks (2000, 2005).

13 See the appendix for the definitions of different types of farm households. On part-time farming in Japan, see Jussaume (1991, 2003). For an anthropologic perspective on part-time farm households in postwar Japan, see, e.g., Kelly (1990a, 1990b).

14 On the Japanese "construction state," see, e.g., McCormack (1996); Kerr (2001); Black (2004). On the link between construction and agriculture, see, e.g., Kelly (1990b); George Mulgan (2001, 2006c).

15 Analyzing the institutional configuration of welfare states is crucial for understanding how different models of capitalism operate; see Estevez-Abe, Iversen, Soskice (2001); Thelen (2004); Estevez-Abe (2008).

16 On the *gentan*, see, e.g., George Mulgan (2000); Hayami (1991); Wood (2012); Tashiro (2014b).

17 According to George Mulgan (2000, 6), approximately 80 per cent of all agricultural commodities "have been subject to administered pricing systems of one kind or the other." However, the degree of politicization has been especially high with respect to rice, paddy field diversion crops, and livestock products.

18 See esp. George Mulgan (2000, 458–73). See also Sasada (2008); Horiuchi and Saito (2010).

Chapter 5. Gradual Change and Increasing Institutional Ambiguity in Agricultural Support and Protection

1 With the percentage producer support estimate, the OECD measures the percentage of support payments of gross farm receipts. Transfers to agricultural producers are measured at the farm gate level. The index includes factors like market price support, budgetary payments and the cost of revenue foregone. For details, see OECD (2016).

2 For a similar view, see Tashiro (2014b).

3 On the electoral reform and the (expected and actual) consequences, see, e.g., Amyx and Drysdale (2003); K. Cox and Schoppa (2002); Horiuchi and Saito (2003); McElwain, Reed, and Shimizu (2009); Rosenbluth and Thies (2010); Krauss and Pekkanen (2011).

4 On the comparatively weak position of the Japanese prime minister before the reforms, see, e.g., Hayao (1993). For a chronological account of the administrative reform process since 1996, see, e.g., Shinoda (2013). On the

centralization of the policy process since the mid-1990s, see Rosenbluth and Thies (2010).

5 Among the most important new features in the policy-making process is the Council on Economic and Fiscal Policy (CEFP). Koizumi used the CEFP to avoid consultation with the respective policy specialists and subcommittees. Arguably, Koizumi could follow this strategy because his election as LDP president depended less on factional support as the result of a reform of the inner-LDP leadership selection process in 2001; see e.g. Shinoda (2013, 78–87).

6 The term "straying" (meisō) is borrowed from Shōgenji (2012). Similarly, Tashiro (2009) uses the term "chaotic" (konmei) to describe the inconsistency of agricultural policies over the 2000s.

7 See Honma et al. (2000) for an English translation of the full text of the NBL. For detailed discussions and interpretations of the NBL, see, e.g., Shōgenji (2000); George Mulgan (2006b); Honma (2010).

8 The concept of targeted support for a designated group of farmers to improve the production structure already surfaced in the 1980s, see George Mulgan (2006b, 56).

9 Municipal administrations typically lack the capacities – both in personal and information resources – to monitor rice production control, not least because practically it has never been their task; interview with Gōdo Yoshihisa, March 2014.

10 In everyday parlance, rice farmers and local officials have never stopped talking about the gentan when referring to rice production control.

11 Municipalities can move some responsibilities around by "trading" production target rates among each other according to the local production structure (fieldwork, October–December 2013, Hikawa Town).

12 Strictly speaking, the MAFF had started to depart from uniform subsidization before the Staple Food Law – but only very carefully. In 1991, the rice price was first calculated based on the production costs of "larger" (i.e., >1.5 hectare) farms; see George Mulgan (2006b).

13 The rationale for such spending was the WTO accession and the resulting need to "improve" the competitiveness of Japanese farming.

14 For details on the 2007 reform, see, e.g., Honma (2010, 156–62); Gōdo (2010, 132–6).

15 The direct payments were set at ¥15,000 per 0.1 hectares. A "commercial farm household" is defined as a farm household that manages more than thirty ares of land or earns more than ¥500,000 per year from agriculture; see Hikawa Town Agriculture and Forestry Office (2013, 18). See the appendix for an overview of different types of farms in Japan.

16 Under the direct income support system, group farming continued to pay off for hamlet-based collective farms. The payment granted ¥15,000 per 0.1

hectares (reduced to ¥7,500 in 2014, abolished in 2018). If every farmer in the hamlet grows rice individually, 0.1 hectares of the acreage *per household* are subtracted from the support payment, because it is assumed that they are cultivated for "self-consumption." However, if the hamlet members form a hamlet-based collective farm, it counts as one "farm management entity." As a result, only 0.1 hectares of the *total* acreage in the hamlet are subtracted for "self-consumption": see Hikawa Town Agriculture and Forestry Office (2013, 16).

17 Cited in Yamashita (2008).
18 The following section contains material originally published in Jentzsch (2017a) and Jentzsch (2017c). Reused with permission.
19 Land sales were uncommon. Moreover, the public agencies typically had to take on the financial risk of obtaining intermediate ownership of farmland, not knowing if and when a "certified farmer" would buy the land; see Takahashi (2013).
20 Before 2014, incentive payments were granted for both owners and users. Under the new Farmland Bank scheme, the payments have been restricted to owners offering land (Andō 2014). See also below.
21 In the 2013 budget, support programs for new farm labor (including agricultural start-ups) accounted for ¥23.3 billion, of which ¥5.8 billion were reserved for supporting corporate farm labor (MAFF 2013).
22 For a list of some of the largest and most prominent operations, see Komoto (2015, 55).
23 The term "6th industry" is derived from the combination of the primary, secondary, and tertiary sector (1 + 2 + 3 = 6). It was originally coined by the agricultural economist Imamura Naraomi in the 1990s; see JA Communications (2017).
24 The Law Promoting Farmland Intermediary Management Institutions of December 2013 added a new legal route for farmland transfers, which was supposed to become the main route from then on. For details, see, e.g., Kobari (2015, 26–7).
25 There are, however, market-stabilization programs to compensate farmers against falling prices. For example, following target rates formulated by the MAFF, farmers together with local cooperatives control production, mainly through culling; see Ito and Dyck (2010).
26 The effects of this boundary change will be discussed in more detail in chapter 11.
27 For a similar argument (albeit in different context), see Höpner (2007).
28 See Hisano, Akitsu, and McGreevy (2018) for a discussion of the various manifestations of the "neoliberal transformation" of Japanese agriculture.

Part 3. Local Agricultural Regimes and Village Institutions

Chapter 6. Different Local Manifestations of Macro-Level Change

1 All information that is directly sourced from interviews is indicated with a code, which specifies the location (e.g., H = Hikawa), the inter-viewees' position/role (e.g., O = official, F = Farmer, CF = member[s] of a hamlet-based collective farm, etc.) and uses a number to distinguish between several interviewees of the same category. See the appendix for a legend and a full list of interviewees and additional information on data collection.

2 Data obtained via email from the agricultural promotion office in Izumo City, June 2019.

3 See, e.g., Tashiro (2009, 206–10); Maclachlan and Shimizu (2019); Mitsui (2018).

4 Yamanashi Prefecture produces only 0.3 per cent of the nation's rice out-put (MAFF 2016c). This rice is grown mostly in the southern parts of the prefecture, i.e., not in Kōfu Basin.

5 In 2015, 82 per cent of the 2,665 remaining farm households in Kōshū City were classified as commercial farm households. Yet the average farm size was below 0.8 hectares; see Zenkoku Nōgyō Kaigijo (2016).

6 The fiscal strength is an index provided by the Statistics Bureau of Japan. It measures the actual fiscal resources of each municipality, thereby, e.g., excluding fiscal transfers from the central government. For a detailed explanation of the index, see Portal Site of Official Statistics of Japan (n.d.).

7 Shinagawa (2017) makes a similar point by analyzing the qualitative changes within hamlet-based collective farms that are concealed by quan-titative data such as the agricultural census.

Chapter 7. The Postwar Formation of Local Agricultural Regimes and Village Institutions

1 This is also reflected in numerous publications on local agricultural gov-ernance in Japan, see, e.g., Tashiro (2009); N. Taniguchi (2014); Muroya (2016).

2 A detailed discussion of the internal organization of hamlets over the course of history is beyond the focus of this work. For details, see, e.g., Dore (1984, 351–4); Fukutake (1980); Marshall (1984).

3 The Occupation authorities viewed hamlet and neighborhood associations as "designed for the execution of war" and ordered their dissolution, see Fukutake (1980, 90).

4 More recently, rural sociologists point to the problems of equating contemporary hamlets with Tokugawa administrative villages and/or the subunits in the Meiji administrative system, which might not only be spatially inaccurate, but also poses the risks of confusing the different institutional logic of superimposed administrative structures and naturally evolved settlements. For a summary of the debate, see, e.g., Shōji (2012, 5–16).

5 See, e.g., Dore (1984, 354–7) for the immediate postwar years.

6 For detailed accounts of the often quite puzzling coexistence of several forms of social organization on the sub-municipal level and how they relate to "agricultural settlements" counted in the agricultural census, see, e.g., Hiraguchi, Nishihashi, and Morozumi (2010); PRIMAFF 2017.

7 *Shinkōku* are referred to as "community-level administrative bodies for agricultural promotion" (Izumo City 2013, 11).

8 Field research in Kōfu City, Yamanashi Prefecture (March–May 2013); interview with Professor Gōdo Yoshihisa, March 2014.

9 See also Nagata (1994); Odagiri, Ouchi, and Tsuboi (2009); Andō (2012).

10 Similarly, the argument that urban neighborhood associations have directly evolved from rural (communal) traditions has been criticized for its "undynamic concept of culture" (Bestor 1985, 123), and for transporting an ideologically charged notion of a distinct "Japanese" character of social organization (as, for example, in Nakane 1967, 1972). For a more thorough discussion of the pitfalls of "traditionalism" concerning both the Japanese village and urban neighborhoods, see, e.g., Marshall (1984); Bestor (1989); Ivy (1995).

11 Japanese sociologists usually refer to this process as *konjūka* – literally the mixing of regional society; see, e.g., Fukutake (1980); Tokuno, Tsutsumi, and Yamamoto (2008, 164–84).

12 Reflecting ongoing de-agriculturalization and the growing share of farmland under lease contracts, a revised definition of the MAFF (adopted for the census in 2010) counts even hamlets in which no active farmers reside as "agricultural settlements," as long as there is farmland and/or agriculture-related facilities (such as irrigation channels, ponds) within their boundaries (Andō 2012, 75–6).

13 For example, several municipalities in the Ina Valley rely on historical administrative villages as a social unit to support the administration of agriculture-related issues like collective farming and farmland exchange; see, e.g., Tashiro (2009). For other examples of organizational patterns, including several hamlets, see, e.g., Bu and Kim (2009); Odagiri (2014); K. Taniguchi (2009); Hiraguchi, Nishihashi, and Morozumi (2010); PRIMAFF 2017.

14 Fieldwork, Hikawa and Izumo, October–December 2013.

15 Ostracism and other informal enforcement mechanisms on the hamlet level were associated with Nōkyō's embedding into hamlet structures in

earlier publications; see Dore (1984); R. Smith (1961). For a more recent example of social exclusion due to a person's refusal to join JA from the Kōfu Basin, see Kingsbury (2012, 152).

16 The coexistence of potentially conflicting norms in rural communities is not only a postwar phenomenon. Farmland norms – and hamlet relations in general – have been subject to change long before the postwar land reform, especially since the concept of private ownership rights gained momentum in the nineteenth century. A detailed discussion of these changes is beyond the scope of this book. For details, see, e.g., Dore (1984); Fukutake (1980); Hasegawa (1993); Iwamoto (2003); Haley (2010); Shōji (2012).

17 Harris-White, Mishra, and Upadhyay (2009) describe a similar process in the ongoing capitalist transformation of a rural region in northern India.

18 On the continued relevance of the territorial character of local support bases after the electoral reform, see George Mulgan (2006c); Krauss and Pekkanen (2011).

19 Block rotation means crop diversion on an annually moving block of connected plots to enhance productivity.

Part 4. Village Institutions as Dynamic Resources: Local Renegotiation of Agricultural Support and Protection

Chapter 8. Farmland Consolidation as a Social Process

1 The following chapter is partly adapted from Jentzsch (2017a, 2017c).

2 On the practical and normative aspects of land abandonment, see also Tokuno, Tsutsumi, and Yamamoto (2008, 187–98); Matanle, Rausch, and the Shrinking Regions Research Group (2011).

3 For details on the economic costs of farmland fragmentation, see, e.g., Kimura and Martini (2009); Kawasaki (2010).

4 On the character of such agreements in the Kōfu Basin, see also Kingsbury (2012, 155).

5 In one case during fieldwork in Kōshū City, the owner of a plot of land became angry when the land user dispatched "foreign" volunteers to work the land (including the author). The tenant had to settle the conflict with several phone calls. Eventually, he gave up the plot to avoid further conflicts (KB-F1).

6 This problem has become a source for grave concern in many localities across Japan, as it affects not only farmland, but also forest land and residential estates; see, e.g., Gabanansu (2017a).

7 Basic farmland maintenance typically includes weeding and maintaining the ridges between rice fields and cleaning channels for irrigation and drainage (*sui kanri*).

8 The land handled by the Kōsha peaked in 2013. Since 2014, the new pre-fecture-level farmland bank has handled a growing share of farmland con-tracts. Yet this is mainly a formal change – the task to organize and allocate farmland use in Hikawa remains with the Kōsha. See below for details.

9 The only exception is a man from Fukushima Prefecture, who moved to Izumo under a national disaster relief program in 2012. He started a small vegetable farm close to the river that separates Hikawa from Izumo. In 2016, he rented a small plot in Hikawa via the Nōgyō Kōsha – as of July 2017, he remained the only case of an "outsider" renting land in town (I-F1).

10 Some hamlets in Hikawa have even developed collective cultivation pat-terns before the *gentan* was launched in 1970 (H-JA1).

11 Referred to as *rippa na hito* and *sonkei no hito* by H-GS1.

12 For this argument, see also Jentzsch (2017c).

13 Even direct contact between actors from both localities is not unlikely – one of the main architects of the Kōsha system used to head the National Association of Agricultural Land Holding Rationalization in Tōkyō, an organization for the inter-municipal exchange of information on farmland governance (H-GS1).

14 Interview with Professor Gōdo Yoshihisa, April 2017.

15 See MAFF (2011b) for a complete list of municipal farmland harmoniza-tion groups.

16 Interview with Professor Gōdo Yoshihisa, April 2017. See also Andō (2014); Kobari (2015).

17 Interview Professor Gōdo Yoshihisa, April 2017.

18 Interview with Professor Gōdo Yoshihisa, March 2014.

19 Interview with researchers at the Policy Research Institute of the MAFF, February 2019. See also Makidaira (2011).

20 The increase of solar panels was a common problem raised by Japan's mayors in a nationwide questionnaire. For an overview on the debate on land use in Japan, see, e.g., Gabanansu (2017a).

21 Apart from individual talks, the topic was raised as a major issue of concern in a formal hearing of "bearer farmers" and land improvement district leaders from Enzan (Kōshū City) with the governor of Yamanashi Prefecture in May 2013, which the author attended.

Chapter 9. Local Variations of Agricultural Entrepreneurship

1 Ōgata Village was founded on the basis of a land reclamation project in the 1960s and populated with settlers from all over Japan. Each household received 10 hectares, i.e., a large amount of land in national comparison. The settlers became famous for their defiance against the *gentan* policy in the 1980s, which they saw as a constraint on their entrepreneurial aspira-tions as large-scale rice farmers; each see Wood (2012).

2 In 2015, only 1,959 farms in Japan cultivated more than fifty hectares, which is little more than 0.1 per cent of all farms (MAFF 2016b).

3 Some farms in Hikawa – including hamlet-based collective farms – market vegetables and horticulture products directly. In 2017, H-F1 had begun to market a minor share of his rice directly in Izumo City and in Tokyo. Green Support has also engaged in a small contract-farming operation that bypasses JA.

4 This is not least expressed in the fact that Green Support is managed by H-GS1, a former JA official, longstanding member of the local agricultural committee, and a major architect of the Kōsha system.

5 Email survey among the seven wineries in Enzan, April 2017.

6 KB-F15; KB-F16; email survey among wineries in Enzan, April 2017.

7 See chapter 8 on the effects of cooperative and municipal mergers and local agricultural sub-regimes.

8 Apart from two local employees, KB-F1 has hired a female winemaker trained in France and the United States, and a former *salariman* from Tokyo.

9 Fieldwork in April and November 2017. There are several events, from the professionally organized annual "Yamanashi Wine Tourism" tour to a small festival in Enzan, organized by the winemakers themselves.

10 The farmer ships table grapes directly to customers (often per web order), which yields higher prices than selling to JA. Yet he occasionally relies on JA to sell surplus table grapes.

11 Observation and informal conversations with KB-F1, April–June 2013. Participation in a hearing of local "bearer farmers" with the prefectural governor, May 2013; participation in meeting of a local committee to promote local wine and grape production, chaired by KB-F1 (March 2019).

12 KB-F1 remains a JA member and has no plans to leave the co-op. Yet he uses JA only for practical reasons, e.g., to dump otherwise unmarketable grapes. His personal opinion of the organization is very low.

13 Material obtained during an interview with Y-F1 in April 2017.

14 For details on the promotion of hamlet-based collective farming as a local strategy, see chapter 10.

15 The boundaries of the local agricultural regime have undergone several changes since the 1990s. Chūzu Town and Yasu Town, which together formed the Yasu District, were merged into Yasu City in 2004. The district was disbanded. Already in 1997, the local cooperative branches in Chūzu Town, Yasu Town, and neighboring Moriyama City were merged into JA Ōmifuji; see (JA Ōmifuji 2017, 5). For details on the process of "boundary change" in local agricultural regimes, see chapter 11.

Chapter 10. Hamlet-Based Collective Farming and Village Institutions

1 This chapter is adapted from Jentzsch (2020a). The author thanks *Pacific Affairs* for permission to reuse parts of the material in this book.
2 On hamlet-level decision-making practices, see Marshall (1984); Fukutake (1980).
3 For this argument, see also Jentzsch (2017b).
4 The merger of hamlet-based collective farms was a debated topic in Hikawa (follow-up visit, July 2017), Hita City (November 2018), and Kami District (February 2019). The trend for such mergers has already been visible for several years, and is likely to increase further; see, e.g., Koike (2012).
5 This motive has been reported by all hamlet farms interviewed in Hikawa. It is also reflected in the Japanese literature on hamlet-based farming; see, e.g., Kitagawa (2008); Tashiro (2009).
6 Albeit there are no comprehensive statistics, this development seems more salient in incorporated farms, which hold full land use rights. See also Shōji (2009).
7 Interviews conducted in Hikawa in October–December 2013. Some farms pay slightly higher for operating machinery than for less skill-intensive tasks. Also there are different practices regarding which work is paid, and what remains unpaid, i.e., part of informal "hamlet duties." In some cases, the hourly wages also entail a gender gap – women sometimes participate in group farming activities without pay, or receive less pay per hour than the male "operators" (H-CF1; H-CF5; H-CF7; H-CF8).
8 On moral hazard in Japanese hamlet-based collective farms, see Nakajima and Tahara (2009); Shōji (2009). Relatedly, Verdery (2003) vividly describes the demise of a farming association in rural post-socialist Romania, which was due partly to the lack of a normative commitment of the members to the association.
9 With very few exceptions, all interviewed hamlet farms reported acute or imminent labor shortages due to aging and a lack of successors. National-level data show the same picture (MAFF 2017).
10 See, e.g., Yamamoto (2010, 2011) on Hiroshima Prefecture; Kitagawa (2014) on Fukui Prefecture; Shinagawa (2017) on Saga Prefecture; Kitagawa (2008) on Kyōto Prefecture.
11 Hamlet-based farming is typically analyzed on the prefectural level or on the hamlet or sub-municipal level. Statistical data by the MAFF reveal regional and prefectural differences but do not display the details of local distribution; see, e.g., Hashizume (2013); MAFF (2017).
12 On the decline of local-national (fiscal) transfers and public investments in the context of rising urban-rural inequality, see, e.g., Song (2015).

13 For the important role of hamlet-based farming in the strategy of the national JA Zenchū, see, e.g., JA Zenchū (2011, 2013).
14 For case studies that mention the (former) occupation of hamlet-farm leaders, see, e.g., Tashiro (2010, 2013); Shōji (2009).
15 Interview with Professor Gōdo Yoshihisa, March 2013. See also Jindai (2008, 82).
16 Together with H-GS1, the leader of H-CF2 was, inter alia, involved in the founding of Akatsuki Farm, the pioneer collective farm in Hikawa.
17 Relatedly, other studies have shown that hamlet-based collective farms have come to substitute cooperative functions after cooperative mergers; see, e.g., Kitagawa (2008, 2012); Yamamoto (2013).
18 There are several legal forms for corporate hamlet-based farms. Hamlet farms can become either agricultural cooperative corporations (*nōji kumiai hōjin*) or agricultural production corporations. In the latter case, the farm can also become a joint-stock company (*kabushiki gaisha*). In any case, incorporation formally allows the farm to rent and own farmland under the Agricultural Land Law. For details, see Nihon Nōgyō Hōjin Kyōkai (n.d.).
19 Technically, voluntary associations can also cultivate land beyond hamlet boundaries, e.g., when members of a hamlet-based collective farm bring in land that they rent from other owners individually.
20 Incorporation was a prominent issue among members at that time. However, members would only discuss the issue of changing revenue redistribution with me (as a participant observer) when the head of the cooperative was out of earshot. Many hamlet farms in Hikawa were undergoing a similar process in 2013 or had already become corporations in 2012.
21 This finding is backed by research in other areas as well; see, e.g., Shōji (2009); Kitagawa (2008).
22 If one or several hamlets could transfer more than 80 per cent of the land *en bloc*, the transfer was subject to the maximum incentive payment, i.e., ¥36,000 per ten are. Thus, a hamlet farm of thirty hectares could receive eleven million yen for transferring the land use rights to a newly founded corporation (Andō 2014, 7). By 2018, the maximum incentive payment for *en bloc* transfers had been cut to only half of the sum in 2014/15; see Hikawa Town Agriculture and Forestry Office (2015).

Chapter 11. Boundary Change: Decreasing Prospects for Comprehensive Local Institutional Agency

1 Gōdo (2001) provides detailed data on the decline of cooperative profits in the 1990s.
2 Financial liberalization coincided with the collapse of the real-estate market in the context of the burst of the "bubble economy." As a main

investor, the cooperative prefectural credit federations suffered heavy losses from the bankruptcy of several mortgage-lending firms in 1996 and eventually had to be bailed out by the Ministry of Finance; see Bullock (1997). However, Gōdo (2001) argues that financial liberalization rather than the scandal was the "more fundamental reason" for the decline of the cooperative organization's economic and eventually political power.

3 Apart from fiscal decentralization, another major element of decentralization reform was elimination of the system of mandatory delegation of administrative functions from the national government to local authorities in 2000, which formally released governors and mayors form their direct subordination to the central bureaucracy; see, e.g., Schmidt (2009); Hüstebeck (2014).

4 For details on the "trinity reforms," see, e.g., Mochida (2008); Imai (2008); Ihori (2009); Hüstebeck (2014); Reiher (2014).

5 See, e.g., Gabanansu (2017b) for an overview on the critique of the mergers. See also Imai (2008).

6 Evidence from other countries supports the finding that peripheral areas in merged municipalities tend to lose representation; see, e.g., Voda and Svačinová (2019).

7 Non-farming households typically remain "associated members" of JA to enjoy services like banking and insurance. The overall number of JA Hikawa members has been even increasing after 2003 and has long surpassed the number of active farmers (JA Hikawa 2011, 188). This is consistent with the national trend; see George Mulgan (2013, 224).

8 For details on the case of the prefecture-wide JA Shimane, see Tashiro (2018).

Part 5. Conclusions

Chapter 12. Renegotiating Japan's Agricultural Support and Protection

1 On the peculiarities and the history of the cooperative audit system, see Gōdo (2015).

Chapter 13. Institutional Change through the Local Lens

1 See Streeck (2009). For a summary of the debate on the "inevitability" of liberalization, see, e.g., Thelen (2012). For an exception, see Etienne and Schnyder (2014).

2 On the local embedding of multinational corporations on the shop-floor level and its consequences, see Dörrenbächer and Geppert (2012).

3 See, for example, Crouch and Keune (2005); Crouch and Voelzkow (2004a, 2009a).
4 On the significance of the meso-level for understanding institutional change in the varieties of capitalism, see, e.g., Streeck (2009); Deeg and Jackson (2007).

References

Amyx, Jennifer, and Peter Drysdale, eds. 2003. *Japanese Governance: Beyond Japan Inc.* London: Routledge.

Andō, Mitsuyoshi. 2012. *Nōgyō Kōzō Hendō No Chiiki Bunseki: 2010 Nen Sensasu Bunseki to Chiiki No Jittai Chōsa* [Regional analysis of structural change in agriculture: Analysis of the 2010 census and regional field surveys]. Tōkyō: Nōsangyōsonbunka Kyōkai.

– 2014. "Nōchi Chūkan Kanri Kikō Ha Kinō Suru Ka? Kadai to Tenbō" [Do intermediary farmland management organizations work? Issues and prospects]. In *JC Sōken Report No. 30*, edited by Japan Cooperative Alliance, 2–10. Tōkyō: Japan Cooperative Alliance.

Ansell, Christopher. 2006. "Network Institutionalism." In *The Oxford Handbook of Political Institutions*, edited by R.A.W. Rhodes, Sarah A. Binder, and Bert A. Rockman, 75–89. Oxford: Oxford University Press.

Aoki, Masahiko. 2001. *Toward a Comparative Institutional Analysis.* Cambridge, MA: MIT Press.

Armondi, Simonetta. 2017. "State Rescaling and New Metropolitan Space in the Age of Austerity: Evidence from Italy." *Geoforum* 81:174–9. https://doi.org/10.1016/j.geoforum.2017.03.008.

Asakawa, Yoshihiro. 2009. "Nōkyō Ga Doko Ka Warui No Ka" [Where does Nōkyō go wrong?]." *Agri-Business*, 1 September. https://agri-biz.jp/item/detail/6510.

Azari, Julia R., and Jennifer K. Smith. 2012. "Unwritten Rules: Informal Institutions in Established Democracies." *Perspectives on Politics* 10 (1): 37–55. https://doi.org/10.1017/S1537592711004890.

Babb, James. 2004. "Making Farmers Conservative: Japanese Farmers, Land Reform and Socialism." *Social Science Japan Journal* 8 (2): 175–95. https://doi.org/10.1093/ssjj/jyi037.

Ballester, Coralio, Antoni Calvó-Armengol, and Yves Zenou. 2006. "Who's Who in Networks. Wanted: The Key Player." *Econometrica* 74 (5): 1403–17. https://doi.org/10.1111/j.1468-0262.2006.00709.x.

Beach, Derek, and Rasmus B. Pedersen. 2013. *Process-Tracing Methods: Foundations and Guidelines.* Ann Arbor: Michigan University Press.

Beaman, L.A. 2012. "Social Networks and the Dynamics of Labour Market Outcomes: Evidence from Refugees Resettled in the U.S." *Review of Economic Studies* 79 (1): 128–61. https://doi.org/10.1093/restud/rdr017.

Berk, Gerald, and Dennis Galvan. 2009. "How People Experience and Change Institutions: A Field Guide to Creative Syncretism." *Theory and Society* 38 (6): 543–80.

– 2013. "Processes of Creative Syncretism." In Berk, Galvan, and Hattam, *Political Creativity*, 29–54.

Berk, Gerald, Dennis C. Galvan, and Victoria Hattam, eds. 2013. *Political Creativity: Reconfiguring Institutional Order and Change.* Philadelphia: University of Pennsylvania Press.

Bestor, Theodore C. 1985. "Tradition and Japanese Social Organization: Institutional Development in a Tokyo Neighborhood." *Ethnology* 24 (2): 121–35. https://doi.org/10.2307/3773554.

– 1989. *Neighborhood Tokyo.* Stanford: Stanford University Press.

Black, William. 2004. "The *Dango* Tango: Why Corruption Blocks Real Reform in Japan." *Business Ethics Quarterly* 14: 603–23. https://doi.org/10.5840/beq200414442.

Bu, Hye-Jin, and Doo-Chul Kim. 2009. "Coping with Depopulation and Demographic Ageing in Japan: From Government to Local Governance." *Journal for Geography* 4 (1): 77–88.

Bullock, Robert. 1997. "Nokyo: A Short Cultural History." JPRI Working Paper No. 41. Oakland, CA: Japan Policy Research Institute. http://www.jpri.org/publications/workingpapers/wp41.html.

– 2003. "Redefining the Conservative Coalition: Agriculture and Small Business in 1990s Japan." In *The State of Civil Society in Japan*, edited by Susan J. Pharr and Frank J. Schwartz, 175–94. Cambridge: Cambridge University Press.

Chavance, Bernard. 2008. "Formal and Informal Institutional Change: The Experience of Postsocialist Transformation." *European Journal of Comparative Economics* 5 (1): 57–71.

Chemnitz, Christine, and Jes Weigelt, eds. 2015. *Bodenatlas 2015: Daten und Fakten über Acker, Land und Erde.* http://www.iass-potsdam.de/sites/default/files/files/bodenatlas2015_deutsch.pdf.

Clemens, Elisabeth S., and James M. Cook. 1999. "Politics and Institutionalism: Explaining Durability and Change." *Annual Review of Sociology* 25: 441–66. https://doi.org/10.1146/annurev.soc.25.1.441.

Commission of the European Community. 2015. "Statistiken über die Struktur landwirtschaftlicher Betriebe." http://ec.europa.eu/eurostat/statistics-explained/index.php/Farm_structure_statistics/de.

Cousins, Ben. 2007. "More Than Socially Embedded: The Distinctive Character of 'Communal Tenure' Regimes in South Africa and Its Implications for Land Policy." *Journal of Agrarian Change* 7 (3): 281–315. https://doi.org /10.1111/j.1471-0366.2007.00147.x.

Cox, Gary W., and Emerson Niou. 1994. "Seat Bonuses under the Single Nontransferable Vote System: Evidence from Japan and Taiwan." *Comparative Politics* 26 (2): 221–36. https://doi.org/10.2307/422269.

Cox, K.E., and L.J. Schoppa. 2002. "Interaction Effects in Mixed-Member Electoral Systems: Theory and Evidence from Germany, Japan, and Italy." *Comparative Political Studies* 35 (9): 1027–53. https://doi.org/10.1093 /acprof:oso/9780199286652.003.0006.

Crouch, Colin. 2005. *Capitalist Diversity and Change: Recombinant Governance and Institutional Entrepreneurs*. Oxford: Oxford University Press.

Crouch, Colin, and Maarten Keune. 2005. "Changing Dominant Practice: Making Use of Institutional Diversity in Hungary and the United Kingdom." In Streeck and Thelen, *Beyond Continuity?*, 83–102.

Crouch, Colin, and Helmut Voelzkow, eds. 2004a. *Changing Governance of Local Economies: Responses of European Local Production Systems*. Oxford: Oxford University Press.

– 2004b. "Introduction." In Crouch and Voelzkow, *Changing Governance of Local Economies*, 1–11.

–, eds. 2009a. *Innovation in Local Economies: Germany in Comparative Context*. Oxford: Oxford University Press.

– 2009b. "Introduction." In Crouch and Helmut Voelzkow, *Innovation in Local Economies*, 1–21.

Culpepper, Pepper D. 2005. "Institutional Change in Contemporary Capitalism: Coordinated Financial Systems since 1990." *World Politics* 57 (2): 173–99. https://doi.org/10.1353/wp.2005.0016.

Curtis, Gerald L. 1999. *The Logic of Japanese Politics: Leaders, Institutions, and the Limits of Change*. New York: Columbia University Press.

Davis, Christina. 2004. "International Institutions and Issue Linkage: Building Support for Agriculture Trade Liberalization." *American Political Science Review* 98 (1): 153–69. https://doi.org/10.1017/S0003055404001066.

Davis, Christina, and Jennifer Oh. 2007. "Repeal of the Rice Laws in Japan: The Role of International Pressure to Overcome Vested Interests." *Comparative Politics* 40 (1): 21–40. https://doi.org/10.5129 /001041507X12911361134352.

Deeg, Richard, and Gregory Jackson. 2007. "Towards a More Dynamic Theory of Capitalist Variety." *Socio-Economic Review* 5 (1): 149–79. https://doi.org /10.1093/ser/mwl021.

Dias, Claudia S.L., Ricardo G. Rodrigues, and João J. Ferreira. 2019. "What's New in the Research on Agricultural Entrepreneurship?"

Journal of Rural Studies 65: 99–115. https://doi.org/10.1016
/j.jrurstud.2018.11.003.

Dore, Ronald. 1978. *Shinohata: A Portrait of a Japanese Village.* New York: Pantheon Books.

– 1984. *Land Reform in Japan.* London: Athlone.

Dörrenbächer, Christoph, and Mike Geppert. 2012. "Politics and Power in the Multinational Corporation: An Introduction." In Dörrenbächer and Geppert, *Politics and Power in the Multinational Corporation*, 3–38.

Esham, Mohamed, Hajime Kobayashi, Ichizen Matsumura, and Alif Alam. 2012. "Japanese Agricultural Cooperatives at Crossroads: A Review." *American-Eurasian Journal of Agriculture and Environmental Science* 12 (7): 943–53. https://doi.org/10.5829/idosi.aejaes.2012.12.07.1759.

Estevez-Abe, Margarita. 2008. *Welfare and Capitalism in Postwar Japan.* Cambridge: Cambridge University Press.

Estevez-Abe, Margarita, Torben Iversen, and David Soskice. 2001. "Social Protection and the Formation of Skills: A Reinterpretation of the Welfare State." In *Varieties of Capitalism: The Institutional Foundations of Comparative Advantage*, edited by Peter A. Hall and David Soskice, 145–83. Oxford: Oxford University Press.

Estrin, Saul, and Thomasz Mickiewitz. 2010. "Entrepreneurship in Transition Economies: The Role of Institutions and Generational Change." Discussion Paper No. 4805. Bonn: Institute for the Study of Labor. http://ftp.iza.org /dp4805.pdf.

Etienne, Julien, and Gerhard Schnyder. 2014. "Logics of Action and Models of Capitalism: Explaining Bottom-up Non-Liberal Change." *Swiss Political Science Review* 20 (3): 365–87. https://doi.org/10.1111/spsr.12082.

Farrell, Henry. 2012. *The Political Economy of Trust: Institutions, Interests, and Inter-Firm Cooperation in Italy and Germany.* Cambridge: Cambridge University Press.

Feldhoff, Thomas. 2017. "Japan's Electoral Geography and Agricultural Policy Making: The Rural Vote and Prevailing Issues of Proportional Misrepresentation." *Journal of Rural Studies* 55: 131–42. https://doi.org /10.1016/j.jrurstud.2017.08.005.

Feldhoff, Thomas, and Daniel Kremers. 2020. "Local Renewables: Japan's Energy Transformation and Its Potential for the Remaking of Rural Communities." In *Japan's New Ruralities*, edited by Wolfram Manzenreiter, Ralph Lützeler, and Sebastian Polak-Rottmann, 103–23. Abingdon, UK: Routledge.

Ferguson, Richard, and Helena Hansson. 2015. "Measuring Embeddedness and Its Effect on New Venture Creation: A Study of Farm Diversification." *Managerial and Decision Economics* 36 (5): 314–25. https://doi.org/10.1002 /mde.2671.

Fitz-Koch, Sarah, Mattias Nordqvist, Sara Carter, and Erik Hunter. 2018. "Entrepreneurship in the Agricultural Sector: A Literature Review and

Future Research Opportunities." *Entrepreneurship Theory and Practice* 42 (1): 129–66.

Fligstein, Neil, and Doug McAdam. 2012. *A Theory of Fields*. Oxford: Oxford University Press.

Flyvbjerg, Bent. 2006. "Five Misunderstandings about Case-Study Research." *Qualitative Inquiry* 12 (2): 219–45. https://doi.org/10.1177/1077800405284363.

Francks, Penelope. 2000. "Japan and an East Asian Model of Agriculture's Role in Industrialization." *Japan Forum* 12 (1): 43–52. https://doi.org/10.1080/09555800050059450.

– 2005. "Multiple Choices: Rural Household Diversification and Japan's Path to Industrialization." *Journal of Agrarian Change* 5 (4): 451–75. https://doi.org/10.1111/j.1471-0366.2005.00108.x.

Freiner, Nicole L. 2018. *Rice and Agricultural Policies in Japan: The Loss of a Traditional Lifestyle*. Basingstoke, Hampshire: Palgrave Macmillan.

Fukutake, Tadashi. 1980. *Rural Society in Japan*. Tōkyō: University of Tōkyō Press.

Gabanansu. 2017a. "Jinkō Genshō Jidai No Jichitai Tochiseisaku" [Municipal land use policies in the era of population decline]. *Gabanansu* 196 (8): 13–40.

– 2017b. "Saiko Jichitai-Kan Kyōsō" [Rethinking inter-administrative unit competition]. *Gabanansu* 199 (11): 14–35.

Gao, Xiaoping. 2013. *Study of Public Goods Provision in Rural Areas Based on the Japanese Experience*. Institute of Developing Economies, Japan External Trade Organization, V.R.F. Series No. 479. http://www.ide.go.jp/library/English/Publish/Download/Vrf/pdf/479.pdf.

George, Alexander L., and Andrew Bennett. 2005. *Case Studies and Theory Development in the Social Sciences*. Cambridge, MA: MIT Press.

George Mulgan, Aurelia. 2000. *The Politics of Agriculture in Japan*. London: Routledge.

– 2001. "'Japan Inc.' in the Agricultural Sector: Reform or Regression?" Asia Pacific Economic Papers No. 314. Canberra: Australia-Japan Research Centre. https://crawford.anu.edu.au/pdf/pep/pep-314.pdf.

– 2003. "Agricultural Policy and Agricultural Policymaking: Perpetuating the Status Quo." In *Japanese Governance: Beyond Japan Inc.*, edited by Jennifer Amyx and Peter Drysdale, 170–93. London: Routledge.

– 2005. "Where Tradition Meets Change: Japan's Agricultural Politics in Transition." *Journal of Japanese Studies* 31 (2): 261–98. https://doi.org/10.1353/jjs.2005.0053.

– 2006a. "Agriculture and Political Reform in Japan: The Koizumi Legacy." Asia Pacific Economic Papers No. 360. Canberra: Australia-Japan Research Centre. https://crawford.anu.edu.au/pdf/pep/pep-360.pdf.

– 2006b. *Japan's Agricultural Policy Regime*. London: Routledge.

- 2006c. *Power and Pork: A Japanese Political Life.* Canberra: Asia Pacific Press.
- 2011. "Agricultural Politics and the Democratic Party of Japan." http://
  japaninstitute.anu.edu.au/sites/default/files/u5/Japan_Agricultural
  _Politics_DPJ.pdf.
- 2013. "Farmers, Agricultural Policies, and the Election." In *Japan Decides
  2012: The Japanese General Election,* edited by Robert Pekkanen, Steven Reed,
  and Ethan Scheiner, 213–24. London and New York: Palgrave Macmillan.
- 2016. "Loosening the Ties That Bind: Japan's Agricultural Policy Triangle
  and Reform of Cooperatives (JA)." *Journal of Japanese Studies* 42 (2): 221–46.
  https://doi.org/10.1353/jjs.2016.0039.
- 2017. "Japan's General Election." East Asia Forum. https://www.eastasiaforum
  .org/2017/10/31/abes-big-gamble-2/.
Gimpel, James, and Celeste Lay. 2005. "Party Identification, Local Partisan
  Contexts, and the Acquisition of Participatory Attitudes." In *The Social Logic
  of Politics: Personal Networks as Contexts for Political Behavior,* edited by Alan
  S. Zuckerman, 209–28. Philadelphia: Temple University Press.
Glassmann, Ulrich. 2004. "Refining National Policy: The Machine-Tool
  Industry in the Local Economy of Stuttgart." In Crouch and Voelzkow,
  Changing Governance of Local Economies, 46–73.
- 2009. "Rule-Breaking and Freedom of Rules in National Production Models:
  How German Capitalism Departs from the 'Rhenish Equilibrium.'" In
  Crouch and Voelzkow, *Innovation in Local Economies,* 22–42.
Gōdo, Yoshihisa. 2001. "The Changing Economic Performance and Political
  Significance of Japan's Agricultural Cooperatives." Asia Pacific Economic
  Papers No. 318. Canberra: Australia-Japan Research Centre. https://
  crawford.anu.edu.au/pdf/pep/pep-318.pdf.
- 2007. "The Puzzle of Small Farming in Japan." Asia Pacific Economic Papers
  No. 365. Canberra: Australia-Japan Research Centre. https://eaber.org
  /wp-content/uploads/2011/05/AJRC_Godo_07.pdf.
- 2009. "The Changing Political Dynamics of Japanese Agricultural
  Cooperatives." Paper presented at the International Association of
  Agricultural Economists Conference, Beijing 16–22. http://ageconsearch
  .umn.edu/bitstream/51400/2/20090620GodoIAAE.pdf.
- 2010. *Sayonara Nippon Nōgyō* [Farewell Japanese agriculture]. Tōkyō: NHK
  Shuppan.
- 2013. "The History of Japan's Post-Pacific-War Rice Policy." FFTC
  Agricultural Policy Platform. http://ap.fftc.agnet.org/ap_db.php?id=107.
- 2014a. "Agricultural Commissions in Japan." FFTC Agricultural Policy
  Platform. http://ap.fftc.agnet.org/ap_db.php?id=146.
- 2014b. "Non-Agricultural Companies' Entry into the Agricultural Industry
  in Japan." FFTC Agricultural Policy Platform. http://ap.fftc.agnet.org/ap
  _db.php?id=192.

– 2014c. "An Outlook on Japanese Farm Households." FFTC Agricultural Policy Platform. http://ap.fftc.agnet.org/ap_db.php?id=66.

– 2014d. "The Significance of Non-Farmers in Japanese Agricultural Cooperatives." FFTC Agricultural Policy Platform. http://ap.fftc.agnet.org/ap_db.php?id=264.

– 2015. "External Audit System of Japanese Agricultural Cooperatives." FFTC Agricultural Policy Platform. https://ap.fftc.org.tw/article/909.

Gōdo, Yoshihisa, and Daisuke Takahashi. 2012. "Evaluation of Japanese Agricultural Policy Reforms under the WTO Agreement on Agriculture." Poster presented at the International Association of Agricultural Economists Triennial Conference, Foz do Iguaçu, Brazil, 18–24 August. http://ageconsearch.umn.edu/bitstream/125102/2/20120609GodoIAAE_AESPoster.pdf.

Greif, Avner. 2006. *Institutions and the Path to the Modern Economy*. Cambridge: Cambridge University Press.

Grischow, Jeff. 2008. "Rural 'Community,' Chiefs and Social Capital: The Case of Southern Ghana." *Journal of Agrarian Change* 8 (1): 64–93. https://doi.org/10.1111/j.1471-0366.2007.00163.x.

Haley, John O. 2010. "Rivers and Rice: What Lawyers and Legal Historians Should Know about Medieval Japan." *Journal of Japanese Studies* 36 (2): 313–49. https://doi.org/10.1353/jjs.0.0196.

Hall, Peter A. 1986. *Governing the Economy: The Politics of State Intervention in Britain and France*. New York: Oxford University Press.

Hall, Peter A., and Kathleen Thelen. 2009. "Institutional Change in Varieties of Capitalism." *Socio-Economic Review* 7 (1): 7–34. https://doi.org/10.1093/ser/mwn020.

Harada, Yutaka. 2012. "Can Japanese Farming Survive Liberalization?" http://www.tokyofoundation.org/en/articles/2011/farming-survive-liberalization.

Harris-White, Barbara, Deepak Mishra, and Vandana Upadhyay. 2009. "Institutional Diversity and Capitalist Transition: The Political Economy of Agrarian Change in Arunachal Pradesh, India." *Journal of Agrarian Change* 9 (4): 512–47. https://doi.org/10.1111/j.1471-0366.2009.00230.x.

Hasegawa, Akihiko. 1993. *Nōson No Kazoku to Chiiki Shakai: Sono Ronri to Kadai* [Logic and challenges of the farm village and regional society]. Tōkyō: Ochanomizu Shobō.

Hashizume, Noboru. 2013. "Shūraku Einō Hatten-Ka No Nōchi Riyō No Henka to Chiikisei" [Changes and regional characteristics of farmland use under the development of hamlet-based collective farming]. In *Shūraku Einō Hatten-Ka No Nōgyō Kōzō: 2010 Sensasu Bunseki* [The agricultural structure under the development of hamlet-based collective farming: Analysis from the 2010 agricultural census], edited by PRIMAFF, 110–31. Tōkyō: Policy Research Institute, Ministry of Agriculture, Forestry and Fisheries.

- 2018. "2015 Nen Nōgyō Sensasu Ni Miru Kōzō Hendō No Tokuchō to Tenkai Hōkō" [Characteristics of structrual change and development directions in the 2015 agricultural census]. In *Nihon Nōgyō Nōson Kōzō No Tenkai Katei: 2015 Nen Nōgyō Sensasu No Sōgō Bunseki* [The development of the Japanese agricultural structure: General analysis of the 2015 agricultural census], edited by PRIMAFF, 229–36. Tōkyō: Policy Research Institute, Ministry of Agriculture, Forestry and Fisheries.

Hayami, Yujirō, and Saburō Yamada, eds. 1991. *The Agricultural Development of Japan*. Tōkyō: University of Tōkyō Press.

Hayao, Kenji. 1993. *The Japanese Prime Minister and Public Policy*. Pittsburgh: University of Pittsburgh Press.

Heidt, Vitali. 2017. *Two Worlds of Aging: Institutional Shifts, Social Risks, and the Livelihood of the Japanese Elderly*. Baden-Baden: Nomos.

Heinze, Kathryn L., Sara Soderstrom, and Justin E. Heinze. 2016. "Translating Institutional Change to Local Communities: The Role of Linking Organizations." *Organization Studies* 37 (8): 1141–69. https://doi.org/10.1177/0170840615622068.

Helmke, Gretchen, and Steven Levitsky. 2004. "Informal Institutions and Comparative Politics: A Research Agenda." *Perspectives on Politics* 2 (4): 725–40. https://doi.org/10.1017/S1537592704040472.

–, eds. 2006. *Informal Institutions and Democracy: Lessons from Latin America*. Baltimore, MD: Johns Hopkins University Press.

- 2006. "Introduction." In *Informal Institutions and Democracy: Lessons from Latin America*, edited by Gretchen Helmke and Steven Levitsky, 1–32. Baltimore, MD: Johns Hopkins University Press.

Higashide, M. n.d. Homepage. "Todōfuken Shikuchōson (Izumo-Shi)" [Prefectures and municipalities (Izumo City)]." http://uub.jp/upd/updind.cgi?N=16135.

Hikawa Town. 1997. *Hikawa No Nōgyō* [Agriculture of Hikawa]. Hikawa Town: Hikawa Town Administration.

Hikawa Town Agriculture and Forestry Office. 2013. *Heisei 24 Nendo Einō Zadankai Shiryō* [Heisei 24 Documents Symposium on Agriculture]. Izumo City.

- 2015. *Heisei 26 Nendo Einō Zadankai Shiryō* [Heisei 26 Documents Symposium on Agriculture]. Izumo City.

- 2017. *Heisei 28 Nendo Einō Zadankai Shiryō* [Heisei 28 Documents Symposium on Agriculture]. Izumo City.

Hiraguchi, Yoshinori, Shun Nishihashi, and Kazuo Morozumi. 2010. "Nōsanson Chiiki No Iji-Teki Hatten Ni Hatasu Shūraku Soshiki No Kinō to Yakuwari: Iwate-Ken Rikuzentakata-Shi O-Chiku Wo Jirei Ni Shite" [The functions and the role of hamlet organizations for the sustainable development of mountainous farm village areas: The case of O District in

Rikuzentakata City, Iwate Prefecture]. *Nōgyō Keiei Kenkyū Hōkoku* 41 (2): 49–68.

Hisano, Shuji, Motoki Akitsu, and Steven R. McGreevy. 2018. "Revitalising Rurality under the Neoliberal Transformation of Agriculture: Experiences of Re-Agrarianisation in Japan." *Journal of Rural Studies* 61: 290–301. https://doi.org/10.1016/j.jrurstud.2018.01.013.

Hita City. 2017. *Hita-Shi Nōgyō Shinkō Bijon* [Vision for the revitalization of agriculture in Hita City]. Hita City.

Honma, Masayoshi. 2010. *Gendai Nihon Nōgyō No Seisaku Katei* [The agricultural policy-making process in contemporary Japan]. Tōkyō: Keio Gijuku Daigaku Shuppankai.

– 2015. "The TPP and Agricultural Reform in Japan." In *The Political Economy of Japanese Trade Policy*, 94–122. Basingstoke, UK: Palgrave Macmillan.

Honma, Masayoshi, and Aurelia George Mulgan. 2018. "Political Economy of Agricultural Reform in Japan under Abe's Administration." *Asian Economic Policy Review* 13:128–44.

Honma, Masayoshi, Ray Trewin, Jennifer Amyx, and Allan Ray, eds. 2000. *A Way Forward for Japanese Agriculture*. Asia Pacific Economic Papers No. 300. Canberra: Australia-Japan Research Centre. https://crawford.anu.edu.au/pdf/pep/pep-300.pdf.

Höpner, Martin. 2007. "Coordination and Organization: The Two Dimensions of Nonliberal Capitalism." MPIfG Discussion Paper No. 07/12. Cologne: Max-Planck Institute for the Study of Societies.

Horiuchi, Yusaku, and Jun Saito. 2003. "Reapportionment and Redistribution: Consequences of Electoral Reform in Japan." *American Journal of Political Science* 47 (4): 669–82. https://doi.org/10.1111/1540-5907.00047.

– 2010. "Cultivating Rice and Votes: The Origins of Agricultural Protectionism in Japan." *Journal of East Asian Studies* 10 (3): 425–52. https://doi.org/10.1017/S1598240800003684.

Hoshi, Tsutomo, and Ryōichi Yamazaki, eds. 2015. *Inadani No Chiiki Nōgyō Shisutemu* [Local agricultural systems in Ina Valley]. Tōkyō: Tsukuba Shobō.

Hüstebeck, Momoyo. 2014. *Dezentralisierung in Japan: Politische Autonomie Und Partizipation Auf Gemeindeebene*. Wiesbaden: Springer VS.

Iba, Haruhiko, and Kiyohiko Sakamoto. 2014. "Beyond Farming: Cases of Revitalization of Rural Communities through Social Service Provision by Community Farming Enterprises." In Wolf, *The Neoliberal Regime in the Agri-Food Sector*, 129–49.

Ibusuki, Shōichi. 2020. "Gaikokujin Rōdōsha Wo Meguru Seisaku Kadai" [Policy problems regarding foreign workers]. *Nihon Rōdō Kenkyū Zasshi* 715:42–8.

Ihori, Toshihiro. 2009. "Political Decentralization and Fiscal Reconstruction in Japan." In *Decentralization Policies in East Asian Development*, edited by Shinichi Ichimura and Roy Bahl. 55–84. Singapore: World Scientific Publishing.

Ikeda, Toshio. 1972. "Hikawa No Seikatsu Kankyō" [Living environment in Hikawa]. In *Hikawa-Chō-Shi* [History of Hikawa Town], edited by Hikawa Education Committee, 1–40. Hikawa Town: Hikawa Town Mayor.

Imai, Akira. 2008. *Heisei Daigappei No Seijigaku* [Politics of the great Heisei mergers]. Tōkyō: Kōjinsha.

Imamura, Naraomi. 2015. *Watashi No Chihō Sōsei-Ron* [My approach to regional creation]. Tōkyō: Nōsangyōsonbunka Kyōkai.

Isaka, Yumi. 2015. "Shakai Kankei Kara Mita Nōchi Shūseki No Jittai" [The reality of farmland consolidation from the perspective of social relations]. *Tochi to Nōgyō* 45: 66–93.

Ishida, Masaaki. 2002. "Development of Agricultural Cooperatives in Japan: Agricultural Cooperatives of Today." *Bulletin of the Faculty for Bioresources, Mie University* 28:19–34.

Ito, Kenzo, and John Dyck. 2010. "Fruit Policies in Japan." USDA Fruits and Tree Nuts Outlook No. 341-01. Washington: United States Department of Agriculture. https://www.ers.usda.gov/webdocs/outlooks/37032/8707_fts34101_1_.pdf?v=7489.

Ivy, Marilyn. 1995. *Discourses of the Vanishing: Modernity, Phantasm, Japan.* Chicago: University of Chicago Press.

Iwamoto, Noriaki. 2003. "Local Conceptions of Land and Land Use and the Reform of Japanese Agriculture." In *Farmers and Village Life in Twentieth-Century Japan*, edited by Ann Waswo and Yoshiaki Nishida, 221–43. London: Routledge.

Izumo City. 2010. "Izumo-Shi Hikawa-Chō Shin-Shi Kihonkeikaku" [New municipal basic plan for Izumo City and Hikawa Town]. http://www.city.izumo.shimane.jp/gappeihk/keikaku/image/kihonkeikaku.pdf.

– 2013. "Nōchi Shūseki De Tegakeru Nōgyō Shinkōsaku" [Policies to produce agricultural revitalization through farmland consolidation]. Presentation, Izumo City.

– 2017. "Izumo-Shi No Nōgyō" [Agriculture in Izumo City]. http://www.maff.go.jp/chushi/mokuji/attach/pdf/180116-8.pdf.

Jackson, Gregory, and Arndt Sorge. 2012. "The Trajectory of Institutional Change in Germany, 1979–2009." *Journal of European Public Policy* 19 (8): 1146–67. https://doi.org/10.1080/13501763.2012.709009.

Jackson, Matthew O. 2014. "Networks in the Understanding of Economic Behaviors." *Journal of Economic Perspectives* 28 (4): 3–22. https://doi.org/10.1257/jep.28.4.3.

JA Communications. 2017. "Imamura Naraomi Ima JA Ni Nozomu Koto" [What Imamura Naraomi now expects from JA]. http://www.jacom.or.jp/noukyo/rensai/cat620/.

JA Hikawa. 2011. *Hikawa-Chō Nōgyō Kyōdō Kumiai: Gappei 50 Shūnen Kinenshi* [50 years JA Hikawa: Commemorative publication]. Hikawa Town: JA Hikawa.

JA-IT Kenkyūkai. 2014. "JA Kami-Ina Iijima-Chō Ni Okeru Chiiki Nōgyō No Genjō to Kongo No Torikumi" [Present situation and future approach of local agriculture in Iijima Town, JA Kami-Ina]. http://ja-it.net/wpb/wp-content/uploads/PDF/seminar_report/36report1.pdf.

JA Izumo. 2010. *Nōgyō Shinkō Bijon: Heisei 22 Nendo-Heisei 24 Nendo* [Vision for the revitalization of agriculture: 2010–2012]. Izumo City: JA Izumo.

JA Ōmifuji. 2017. *JA Ōmifuji No Genkyō 2017" [JA Ōmifuji disclosure 2017].* Moriyama City: JA Ōmifuji.

Japan Times. 2014. "U.S. Agrees to Let Japanese Tariffs Stand on Rice, Wheat," 17 April. https://www.japantimes.co.jp/news/2014/04/17/business/u-s-agrees-to-let-japanese-tariffs-stand-on-rice-wheat/.

JA Zenchū. n.d. Homepage. "JA Kazu No Suii" [Change in the number of local JA]. https://org.ja-group.jp/find/transition.

– 2011. *Nōgyō Fukken Ni Muketa JA Gurūpu No Teigenan [JA Group proposal for the restoration of agriculture].* Tōkyō: JA Zenchū.

– 2013. *Katsuryoku Aru Nōgyō - Chiiki Zukuri Ni Mukete - 26 Nendo Ikō Shinnōsei Ni Kan Suru Teigen* [Towards a vital agriculture and building the countryside: Proposal for new agricultural policies from 2014]. Tōkyō: JA Zenchū.

Jentzsch, Hanno. 2017a. "Abandoned Land, Corporate Farming, and Farmland Banks: A Local Perspective on the Process of Deregulating and Redistributing Farmland in Japan." *Contemporary Japan* 28 (2): 1–16. https://doi.org/10.1080/18692729.2017.1256977.

– 2017b. "Subsidized Tradition, Networks, and Power: Hamlet Farming in Japan's Changing Agricultural Support and Protection Regime." In *Feeding Japan: The Cultural and Political Issues of Dependency and Risk*, edited by Andreas Niehaus and Tine Walravens, 413–42. New York: Palgrave Macmillan.

– 2017c. "Tracing the Local Origins of Farmland Policies in Japan: Local-National Policy Transfers and Endogenous Institutional Change." *Social Science Japan Journal* 20 (2): 243–60. https://doi.org/10.1093/ssjj/jyx026.

– 2020a. "Japan's Changing Regional World of Welfare: Agricultural Reform, Hamlet-Based Collective Farming, and the Local Renegotiation of Social Risks." *Pacific Affairs* 93 (2): 327–51. https://doi.org/10.5509/2020932327.

– 2020b. "Regional Revitalization as a Contested Arena: Promoting Wine Tourism in Yamanashi." In *Japan's New Ruralities: Coping with Decline in the Periphery*, edited by Wolfram Manzenreiter, Ralph Lützeler, and Sebastian Polak-Rottmann, 159–74. Abingdon, UK: Routledge.

Jepperson, Ronald L. 1991. "Institutions, Institutional Effects, and
    Institutionalism." In *The New Institutionalism in Organizational Analysis*,
    edited by Paul DiMaggio and Walter Powell, 143–63. Chicago: University of
    Chicago Press.

Jindai, Hideaki. 2008. "Shimane-Ken Hiikawa-Gun Hikawa-Chō Ni Okeru
    Nōchi No Men-Teki Shūseki No Torigumi to Sono Kōka" [The approach to
    farmland consolidation and its results in Hikawa Town, Hiikawa District,
    Shimane Prefecture]. In *Ninaite Kara Mita Nōchi No Men-Teki Shūseki Kōka Ni
    Kan Suru Jittai Chōsa Hōkokusho* [Factual investigation report on the effects of
    farmland consolidation from the perspective of "ninaite"], edited by Nōsei
    Chōsakai, 80–102. Tōkyō: Nōsei Chōsakai.

Johnson, Chalmers. 1995. *Japan, Who Governs? The Rise of the Developmental
    State.* New York: Norton.

Johnston, Ron, and Charles Pattie. 2011. "Social Networks, Geography, and
    Neighborhood Effects." In *The SAGE Handbook of Social Networks*, edited by
    Scott John, 301–11. London: SAGE.

Jussaume, Raymond. 1991. *Japanese Part-Time Farming: Evolution and Impacts.*
    Ames: Iowa State University Press.

– 2003. "Part-Time Farming and the Structure of Agriculture in Postwar
    Japan." In *Farmers and Village Life in Twentieth-Century Japan,* edited by Ann
    Waswo and Yoshiaki Nishida, 199–220. London: Routledge.

Kanai, Toshiyuki, and Yusuke Yamashita. 2015. *Chihō Sōsei No Shōtai* [The true
    character of regional creation]. Tōkyō: Chikuma Shinsho.

Kawagoe, Toshihiko. 1999. "Agricultural Land Reform in Postwar Japan:
    Experiences and Issues." World Bank Policy Research Working Paper
    No. 2111. https://elibrary.worldbank.org/doi/abs/10.1596/1813-9450-2111.

Kawamura, Kazunori. 2011. "Rieki-Dantai Nai No Dōtai to Seiken-Kōtai:
    Nōgyō Hyō No Yūkai [Change of government and dynamic within interest
    groups: The decline of the farm vote]. *Nenpō Seijigaku* 2:33–51.

Kawasaki, Kentaro. 2010. "The Costs and Benefits of Land Fragmentation
    of Rice Farms in Japan." *Australian Journal of Agricultural and Resource
    Economics* 54:509–26. https://doi.org/10.1111/j.1467-8489.2010.00509.x.

Keizai Hōrei Kenkyūkai, ed. 2011. *6jisangyō-Ka to JA No Arata Na Yakuwari* [The
    "6th industrialization" and JA's new role]. Tōkyō: Keizai Hōrei Kenkyūkai.

Kelly, William. 1990a. "Japanese Farmers." *Wilson Quarterly* 14 (4): 34–41.

– 1990b. "Regional Japan: The Price of Prosperity and the Benefits of
    Dependency." *Daedalus* 119 (3): 209–27.

– 2007. "Why Is Japanese Farming Culturally Central and Economically
    Marginal? Rice Revolutions and Farm Families in a Tohoku Region." *Asia
    Pacific Journal: Japan Focus* 5 (6): 1–20.

Kennett, Patricia, Gerwyn Jones, Richard Meegan, and Jacqui Croft. 2015.
    "Recession, Austerity and the 'Great Risk Shift': Local Government

and Household Impacts and Responses in Bristol and Liverpool." *Local Government Studies* 41 (4): 622–44. https://doi.org/10.1080/03003930.2015.1036986.

Kerr, Alex. 2001. *Dogs and Demons: Tales from the Dark Side of Japan.* New York: Hill and Wang.

Kimura, Shingo, and Roger Martini. 2009. "Evaluation of Agricultural Policy Reform in Japan." Paris: OECD Publishing. https://www.oecd.org/japan/42791674.pdf.

Kingsbury, Aaron. 2012. "Re-Localizing Japanese Wine: The Grape and Wine Clusters of Yamanashi Prefecture, Japan." PhD. diss., University of Hawaii.

– 2014. "Constructed Heritage and Co-Produced Meaning: The Re-Branding of Wines from the Kōshū Grape." *Contemporary Japan* 26 (1): 29–48. https://doi.org/10.1515/cj-2014-0002.

– 2018. "Are We Embracing Our Terroir or Just Branding Our Own Piles of Dirt? Negotiating Definitions of Locality in the Yamanashi Wine Cluster." What Is the 'Local'? Rethinking the Politics of Subnational Spaces in Japan, Symposium, German Institute for Japanese Studies, Tōkyō, 19 October.

Kitagawa, Taichi. 2008. *Nōgyō, Mura, Kurashi No Saisei Wo Mezasu: Shūraku Gata Nōgyō Hōjin* [Towards the revitalization of agriculture, villages, and livelihood: Community-type agricultural corporations]. Tōkyō: Zenkoku Nōgyō Kaigijo.

– 2012. "Chiiki No Kōeki-Teki Katsudō Wo Ninau Shūraku Einō" [Hamlet-based collective farms taking on activities for the regions' public good]. *Nōgyō to Keizai* 78 (5): 14–23.

– 2014. "Fukui-Ken Ni Okeru Chiiki Nōgyō No Dōkō to Ninaite: Shūraku Einō Soshiki Wo Chushin Shite" [Trends and bearers of regional agriculture in Fukui Prefecture: Focusing on hamlet-based collective farms]. In *Nōgyō Kōzō No Hendō to Chiiki-Sei Wo Fumaeta Nōgyō Seisan Shutai No Keisei to Saihen: Kaku Chiiki No Genjo Bunseki* [The formation and reorganization of agricultural production subjects with consideration of agricultural structural change and regional characteristics], edited by PRIMAFF, 15–28. Tōkyō: Policy Research Institute, Ministry of Agriculture, Forestry and Fisheries.

Knight, Jack, and Jean Ensminger. 1997. "Changing Social Norms: Common Property, Bridewealth, and Clan Exogamy." *Current Anthropology* 38 (1): 1–24. https://doi.org/10.1086/204579.

– 1998. "Conflict over Changing Social Norms: Bargaining, Ideology, and Enforcement." In *The New Institutionalism in Sociology*, edited by Mary Brinton and Victor Nee, 105–27. Stanford: Stanford University Press.

Knoke, David. 1994. *Political Networks: The Structural Perspective.* Cambridge: Cambridge University Press.

Kobari, Miwa. 2015. "Nōchi Chūkan Kanri Kikō Shonendo Ni Okeru Nōchi Shūseki No Dōkō" [Farmland concentration trends in the first year of the intermediary farmland management organization]. *Nōrin Kinyū* 68 (7): 20–34. http://www.nochuri.co.jp/report/pdf/n1507re2.pdf.

Kobayashi, Hajime. 2011. "Nōsanson Saisei to JA No Kanōsei" [The revitalization of mountainous farm villages and JA's potential]. In *Nōsanson Saisei No Jissen* [The revitalization of agricultural mountain villages in practice], edited by Tokumi Odagiri, 264–80. Tōkyō: Nōsangyōsonbunka Kyōkai.

Koike, Tsuneo. 2012. "Shokuryō Seisan No Sekinin to Kitai" [Responsibilities and expectations regarding food production]. *Nōgyō to Keizai* 78 (5): 5–14.

Komoto, Keishō. 2015. "Nō No 6jisangyō-Ka He No Ryūtsū Senryaku" [Toward a distribution strategy for the "6th industrialization" of agriculture]. In *Nō No 6jisangyō-Ka to Chiiki Shinkō* [The "6th industrialization" of agriculture and regional revitalization], edited by Isao Kumakura and Takefumi Yoneya, 52–77. Tōkyō: Shumpusha Publishing.

Konno, Masashi, and Yasuhiko Kudō. 2014. "6jisangyō-Ka Ni Okeru Shōkibo Torikumi No Jittai to Seisaku No Kadai: Hokkaidō '6jisangyō-Ka Jittai Haaku Chōsa' Kekka Kara" [The situation and policy challenges concerning small-scale approaches to the "6th industrialization": Evidence from a survey on the status of the "6th industry" in Hokkaido]. *Review of Agricultural Economics* 69:63–76.

Koyama, Akiko, and Tsuyoshi Miyata. 2012. "Chūsankan Chiiki Ni Okeru Shūraku Einō No Unei Kanri" [Operational management of hamlet-based collective farms in hilly and mountainous areas]. *Nōgyō Keiei Kenkyū* 50 (1): 35–40. https://doi.org/10.11300/fmsj.50.4_39.

Kramer, Sven. 2015. "Shōwa Dai Gappei Ni Okeru Gappei Hantai, Bunshi Undō to Shimin Ishiki - Nagano-Ken Kamiina-Gun Miyada-Mura Wo Jirei Ni" [Opposition and separation movements and local identity in the Shōwa mergers: The case of Miyada Village, Kamiina District, Nagano Prefecture]. *Nihonshi Kenkyū* 636:26–53.

Krauss, Ellis, and Robert Pekkanen. 2011. *The Rise and Fall of Japan's LDP.* Ithaca, NY: Cornell University Press.

Kushida, Kenji E., and Kay Shimizu. 2013. "Syncretism: The Politics of Japan's Financial Reforms." *Socio-Economic Review* 11 (2): 337–69. https://doi.org /10.1093/ser/mwt003.

Kushida, Kenji E., Kay Shimizu, and Jean C. Oi, eds. 2013. *Syncretism: The Politics of Economic Restructuring and System Reform in Japan.* Stanford, CA: Walter H. Shorenstein Asia-Pacific Research Center.

Latz, Gil. 1989. *Agricultural Development in Japan: The Land Improvement District in Concept and Practice.* Geography Research Paper 225. Chicago: Committee on Geographical Studies, University of Chicago.

Lawrence, Thomas B., Roy Suddaby, and Bernard Leca. 2009. *Institutional Work: Actors and Agency in Institutional Studies of Organization.* Cambridge: Cambridge University Press.

Lechevalier, Sébastien, ed. 2014. *The Great Transformation of Japanese Capitalism.* London: Routledge.

Lehrer, Mark, and Sokol Celo. 2017. "German Family Capitalism in the 21st Century: Patient Capital between Bifurcation and Symbiosis." *Socio-Economic Review* 14 (4): 729–50. https://doi.org/10.1093/ser/mww023.

Lewis, Leo. 2015. "Japan: End of the Rice Age." *Financial Times,* 21 September. http://www.ft.com/cms/s/0/f4db3b26-6045-11e5-a28b-50226830d644.html#axzz3uZXUqk6y.

Maclachlan, Patricia L. 2011. *The People's Post Office: The History and Politics of the Japanese Postal System, 1871–2010.* Cambridge, MA: Harvard University Press.

Maclachlan, Patricia L., and Kay Shimizu. 2016a. "Japanese Farmers in Flux: The Domestic Sources of Agricultural Reform." *Asian Survey* 56 (3): 442–65. https://doi.org/10.1525/as.2016.56.3.442.

– 2016b. "The Kantei vs the LDP: Agricultural Reform, the Organized Vote, and the 2014 Election." In *Japan Decides 2014,* edited by Robert J. Pekkanen, Steven R. Reed, and Ethan Scheiner, 170–82. Basingstoke, UK: Palgrave Macmillan.

– 2019. "Cultivating Institutional Change in Japan." Japanese Political Economy Workshop, Tōkyō, 18 June.

MAFF. 2007. "Nōchi Seisaku No Tenkai Hōkō Ni Tuite" [On the direction of farmland policies]. http://www.maff.go.jp/j/press/keiei/koukai/pdf/071106-01.pdf.

– 2011a. "2010 Nen Sekai Nōringyō Sensasu Kekka No Gaiyō" [Outline of the results of the 2010 world census on agriculture and forestry]. http://www.maff.go.jp/j/tokei/census/afc/about/pdf/kakutei_zentai.pdf.

– 2011b. "Shichōson-Betsu Nōchiryūdōka Enkatsukadantai Ichiran" [Overview of farmland harmonization groups in municipalities]." http://www.maff.go.jp/j/keiei/koukai/ryuudouka/enkatuka/other/3_e_dantai_9matsu.xls.

– 2013. "Hito to Nōchi No Mondai No Kaiketsu Ni Muketa Shisaku" [Measures towards resolving the problems associated with people and farmland]. http://www.maff.go.jp/j/keiei/koukai/pdf/250204_2.pdf.

– 2015a. "Heisei 27 Nendo 6jisangyô-Ka Kanren Jigyō No Yosan Gaiyō" [2015 outline of budget related to 6th industry projects]. http://www.maff.go.jp/j/shokusan/sanki/6jika/yosan/pdf/27_yosan_gaiyo.pdf.

– 2015b. "Ippan Kigyō No Nōgyō He No Sannyū" [The entry of general corporations into agriculture]." http://www.maff.go.jp/j/keiei/koukai/sannyu/attach/pdf/kigyou_sannyu-4.pdf.

– 2015c. "Nōchi Wo Hoyū Dekiru Hōjin (Nōgyō Seisan Hōjin) No Jōken-Nado No Minaoshi" [Adjustments concerning the requirements for corporations that can obtain farmland (agricultural production corporations)]. http://www.maff.go.jp/j/keiei/koukai/nouchi_seido/pdf/nouchi_taihi.pdf.

- 2016a. "2015 Nen Nōrin Sensasu Kekka No Gaiyō" [Outline of the results of the 2015 agriculture and forestry census]. http://www.maff.go.jp/j/tokei/census/afc/2015/pdf/census_15k_20160427.pdf.
- 2016b. "FY 2015 Annual Report on Food, Agriculture and Rural Areas: Summary." https://www.maff.go.jp/e/data/publish/attach/pdf/index-38.pdf.
- 2016c. "Yamanashi-Ken Nōringyō" [Agriculture and forestry in Yamanashi Prefecture]. http://www.maff.go.jp/kanto/to_jyo/nenpou/pdf/27_19_yamanashi_03b.pdf.
- 2017. "Heisei 29 Shūraku Einō Jittai Chōsa" [Hamlet farm survey 2017]. http://www.maff.go.jp/j/tokei/kouhyou/einou/attach/pdf/index-1.pdf.

Mahoney, James, and Kathleen Thelen, eds. 2010a. *Explaining Institutional Change: Ambiguity, Agency, and Power*. Cambridge: Cambridge University Press.
- 2010b. "A Theory of Gradual Institutional Change." In Mahoney and Thelen, *Explaining Institutional Change*, 1–37.

Makidaira, Tatsuhiro. 2011. "Chiiki Nōgyō, Nōson No '6jisangyō-Ka' to Sono Shintenkai" [The "6th Industrialization" of regional agriculture and farm villages and its new development]. In *Nōsanson Saisei No Jissen* [The revitalization of agricultural mountain villages in practice], edited by Tokumi Odagiri, 70–96. Tōkyō: Nōsangyōsonbunka Kyōkai.

March, James G., and Johan P. Olsen. 1984. "The New Institutionalism: Organizational Factors in Political Life." *American Political Science Review* 78 (3): 734–49. https://doi.org/10.2307/1961840.

Marshall, Robert C. 1984. *Collective Decision Making in Rural Japan*. Michigan Papers in Japanese Studies 11. Ann Arbor: Michigan University Press.

Matanle, Peter, Anthony Rausch, and the Shrinking Regions Research Group. 2011. *Japan's Shrinking Regions in the 21st Century: Contemporary Responses to Depopulation and Socioeconomic Decline*. Amherst, NY: Cambria.

Matsunaga, Keiko, and Mitsuhiro Seki, eds. 2012. *Shūraku Einō: Nōsanson No Shōrai Wo Hiraku* [Hamlet-based collective farms: Opening up the future of mountain farm villages]. Tōkyō: Shinhyōron.

McCormack, Gavan. 1996. *The Emptiness of Japanese Affluence*. Armonk, NY: M.E. Sharpe.

McDonald, Mary. 1997. "Agricultural Landholding in Japan: 50 Years after Land Reform." *Geoforum* 28 (1): 55–78. https://doi.org/10.1016/S0016-7185(97)85527-3.

McElwain, Kenneth M., Steven Reed, and Kay Shimizu, eds. 2009. *Political Change in Japan: Electoral Behavior, Party Realignment, and the Koizumi Reforms*. Stanford: Shorenstein APARC.

McGreevy, Steven R. 2012. "Lost in Translation: Incomer Organic Farmers, Local Knowledge, and the Revitalization of Upland Japanese Hamlets."

Agriculture and Human Values 29 (3): 393–412. https://doi.org/10.1007/s10460-011-9347-5.

MIC. n.d. Homepage. "Shichōsonkazu No Hensen to Meiji Shōwa No Daigappei No Tokuchō" [Development in the number of municipalities and characteristics of the Meiji and Shōwa waves of municipal mergers]. http://www.soumu.go.jp/gapei/gapei2.html.

– 2010. "Heisei No Gappei Ni Tuite No Kōhyō" [Official announcement on Heisei municipal mergers]." www.gappei-archive.soumu.go.jp/heiseinogappei.pdf.

– 2017. "Chihō Gikai Giin Ni Kan Suru Kenkyūkai Hōkokusho" [Report of the Research Group on Local Assemblies and Assembly Members]. http://www.soumu.go.jp/main_content/000495620.pdf.

Mitsui, Hisao. 2018. "Hōjin-Ka De Nōka No Shōtoku Zōdai" [Raising the incomes of farm families through incorporation]. *Gekkan JA* 765:20–3.

Miyashita, Seishi. 2014. "Chiiki Seisaku No Rekishi-Teki Tenkai to Gendai Chiiki Seisaku No Tokushitu (Shimo)" [The history and characteristics of contemporary regional politics in Japan: Part 2]. *Nagano Daigaku Kiyō* 36 (2): 77–92.

Mochida, Nobuki. 2008. *Fiscal Decentralization and Local Public Finance in Japan.* London: Routledge.

Morikawa, Hiroshi. 2011. "Chūgoku Chihō 5 Ken Ni Okeru 'Heisei No Daigappei' Hikaku Kōsatsu" [Comparative analysis of the "Great Heisei Merger" in the five Chūgoku prefectures]. The Japan Research Institute for Local Government Report No. 387. Tōkyō: Japan Research Institute for Local Government. http://jichisoken.jp/publication/monthly/JILGO/2011/01/hmorikawa1101.pdf.

Morris, Jeremy, and Abel Polese, eds. 2015. *Informal Economies in Post-Socialist Spaces: Practices, Institutions and Networks*, Basingstoke, UK: Palgrave Macmillan.

Muroya, Arihiro. 2013. "6jisangyô-Ka No Genjō to Kadai" [Present situation and challenges of the "6th industrialization"]. *Nōrin Kinyū* 66 (5): 2–21.

– 2016. "Nōkyō to 6jisangyō-Ka" [Nōkyō and the "6th industrialization"]. *Nōrin Kinyū* 69 (2): 2–16.

Nagata, Keijiro. 1994. *Evolution of Land Improvement Districts in Japan.* Colombo, Sri Lanka: International Irrigation Management Institute.

Nakajima, Shinsaku, and Kengo Tahara. 2009. "The Choice of Participation Forms in Community-Based Group Farming and Efficiency in Team Production." Paper presented at the International Association of Agricultural Economists Conference, Beijing, 16–22 August. http://ageconsearch.umn.edu/record/51640/files/Contributed%20Paper_Reference%20number%20_370__The%20Choice%20of%20Participation%20Forms%20in%20Community-Based%20Group%20Farming%20and%20Production%20in%20Team.pdf?version=1.

Nakane, Chie. 1967. *Kinship and Economic Organization in Rural Japan*. London: Athlone.

– 1972. *Japanese Society*. Berkeley: University of California Press.

Nelson, Willie, and Marcy Kaptur. 2015. "U.S. Poultry Farmers' Rights Are under Siege." *Washington Post*, 7 July. https://www.washingtonpost .com/opinions/us-poultry-farmers-rights-are-under-siege/2015/07/07 /cce6ad60-23fc-11e5-b77f-eb13a215f593_story.html.

Nihon Nōgyō Hōjin Kyōkai. n.d. Homepage. "Nōgyō Hōjin to Ha" [What is an agricultural corporation?]. http://hojin.or.jp/standard/what_is/what _is.html.

Nikkei Asian Review. 2016. "Japan's Abe Gets Cracking on Fiscal 2016 Spending," 30 March. https://asia.nikkei.com/Politics-Economy /Economy/Japan-s-Abe-gets-cracking-on-fiscal-2016-spending.

– 2017. "Can Mushrooms and Solar Power Fill Japan's Vacant Farmland?" 5 September. https://asia.nikkei.com/Japan-Update/Can-mushrooms -and-solar-power-fill-Japan-s-vacant-farmland?page=1.

– 2019. "Winemakers Double Vineyards as 'Japanese Wine' Takes Root," 25 May. https://asia.nikkei.com/Business/Business-trends/Winemakers -double-vineyards-as-Japanese-wine-takes-root?utm_campaign=RN %20Subscriber%20newsletter&utm_medium=JP%20update%20 newsletter&utm_source=NAR%20Newsletter&utm_content=article%20link.

North, Douglass. 1990. *Institutions, Institutional Change and Economic Performance*. New York: Cambridge University Press.

– 1993. "Toward a Theory of Institutional Change." In *Political Economy: Institutions, Competition, and Representation*, edited by William A. Barnett, Melvin Hinich, and Norman J. Schofield, 61–70. New York: Cambridge University Press.

– 2005. *Understanding the Process of Economic Change*. Princeton, NJ: Princeton University Press.

Odagiri, Tokumi, ed. 2011. *Nōsanson Saisei No Jissen* [The revitalization of agricultural mountain villages in practice]. Tōkyō: Nōsangyōsonbunka Kyōkai.

– 2014. *Nōsanson Ha Shōmetsu Shinai* [The mountain village does not disappear]. Tōkyō: Iwanami Shinsho.

Odagiri, Tokumi, Masatoshi Ouchi, and Nobuhiro Tsuboi, eds. 2009. *Gendai No Mura: Mura-Ron to Nihon Shakai No Tembō* [The village today: Village theory and the prospects of Japanese society]. Tōkyō: Nōsangyōsonbunka Kyōkai.

OECD. 2014. *Agricultural Policy Monitoring and Evaluation 2014: OECD Countries*. Paris: OECD Publishing. https://doi.org/10.1787/22217371.

– 2016. "OECD's Producer Support Estimate and Related Indicators of Agricultural Support." https://www.oecd.org/agriculture/topics /agricultural-policy-monitoring-and-evaluation/documents/producer -support-estimates-manual.pdf.

– 2017. *Agricultural Policy Monitoring and Evaluation 2017*. Paris: OECD Publishing. http://dx.doi.org/10.1787/agr_pol-2017-en.

– 2020. *Agricultural Policy Monitoring and Evaluation 2020*. Paris: OECD Publishing. https://doi.org/10.1787/928181a8-en.

Ōizumi, Kazunuki. 2018. "A New Direction for Agriculture in Japan." In *Economic Challenges Facing Japan's Regional Areas*, edited by Tatsuo Hatta, 9–17. Singapore: Palgrave Pivot.

Okubo, Mika, Abrar J. Mohammed, and Makoto Inoue. 2016. "Out-Migrants and Local Institutions: Case Study of a Depopulated Mountain Village in Japan." *Asian Culture and History* 8 (1): 1–9. https://doi.org/10.5539/ach.v8n1p1.

Onoma, Ato K. 2010. "The Contradictory Potential of Institutions: The Rise and Decline of Land Documentation in Kenya." In Mahoney and Thelen, *Explaining Institutional Change*, 63–93.

Organization to Secure a Stable Rice Supply. n.d. Homepage. "Kome No Kakaku Kanren Jōhō" [Rice price information]. http://www.komenet.jp/jukyuudb/830.html.

Papachristos, Andrew, David Hureau, and Anthony Braga. 2013. "The Corner and the Crew: The Influence of Geography and Social Networks on Gang Violence." *American Sociological Review* 78 (3): 417–47. https://doi.org/10.1177/0003122413486800.

Peck, Jamie. 2012. "Austerity Urbanism: American Cities under Extreme Economy." *City* 16 (6): 626–55. https://doi.org/10.1080/13604813.2012.734071.

Pekkanen, Robert. 2006. *Japan's Dual Civil Society: Members without Advocates*. Stanford: Stanford University Press.

Pierson, Paul. 2004. *Placing Politics in Time: History, Institutions, and Political Analysis*. New York: Princeton University Press.

Portal Site of Official Statistics of Japan. n.d. Homepage. "Kōmoku Teigi – D: Gyōsei Kiban" [Item definitions – D: administrative base]. https://www.e-stat.go.jp/koumoku/koumoku_teigi/D#D2201.

Powell, Walter, and Claus Rerup. 2017. "Opening the Black Box: Micro-Foundations of Institutional Theory." In *The SAGE Handbook of Organizational Institutionalism*, 2nd ed., edited by Royston Greenwood, Christine Oliver, Thomas B. Lawrence, and Renate E. Meyer, 311–37. London: Sage Publications.

PRIMAFF, ed. 2017. *Heisei 28 Nendo Kōiki-Teki Renkei Ni Yoru Nōgyō Shūraku No Saisei Ni Kan Suru Kenkyū Hōkokujo. Kumamoto-Ken, Wakayama-Ken, Nagano-Ken Ni Okeru "Kōiki Chiiki Soshiki" No Genchi Chōsa Kekka* [2016 research report on the revitalization of agricultural settlements in the context of wider-area cooperation: Survey results on "wider-area organizations" from Kumamoto Prefecture, Wakayama Prefecture, and Nagano Prefecture].

Tōkyō: Policy Research Institute, Ministry of Agriculture, Forestry, and Fisheries.

Rabe, Benjamin. 2019. "Institutional Change in Japan's Innovation System: The Case of Regional Innovation Clusters in Yamagata." Annual Conference of the Association for Asian Studies, Denver, 23 March.

Ramseyer, J.M., and Frances M. Rosenbluth. 1997. *Japan's Political Marketplace.* 2nd ed. Cambridge, MA: Harvard University Press.

Rausch, Anthony. 2006. "The *Heisei Dai Gappei*: A Case Study for Understanding the Municipal Mergers of the Heisei Era." *Japan Forum* 18 (1): 133–56. https://doi.org/10.1080/09555800500498558.

– 2014. "Japan's Heisei Municipal Mergers and the Contradictions of Neo-liberal Administrative Planning." *Asia Pacific Journal of Public Administration* 36 (2): 135–49. https://doi.org/10.1080/23276665.2014.911490.

– 2016. "The Heisei Municipal Mergers: Measures of Sustainability, Equality and Identity." In *Sustainability in Contemporary Rural Japan: Challenges and Opportunities,* edited by Stephanie Assmann, 35–48. New York: Routledge.

Reiher, Cornelia. 2014. *Lokale Identität und ländliche Revitalisierung: Die japanische Keramikstadt Arita und die Grenzen der Globalisierung.* Bielefeld: Transcript Verlag.

Roland, Gerard. 2004. "Understanding Institutional Change: Fast-Moving and Slow-Moving Institutions." *Studies in Comparative International Development* 38 (4): 109–31. https://doi.org/10.1007/BF02686330.

Röper, Nils. 2017. "German Finance Capitalism: The Paradigm Shift Underlying Financial Diversification." *New Political Economy* 14 (4): 1–25.

Rosenbluth, Frances M., and Michael Thies. 2010. *Japan Transformed: Political Change and Economic Restructuring.* Princeton: Princeton University Press.

Saitō, Yuriko. 2005. "Shūraku Soshiki No Henyō to Kaikaku Hōkō" [Changes and objectives for reform of hamlet-level organization]." *Nōrin Kinyū* 12:18–34.

Sarker, Ashutosh, and Tadao Itō. 2001. "Design Principles in Long-Enduring Institutions of Japanese Irrigation Common-Pool Resources." *Agricultural Water Management* 48: 89–102. https://doi.org/10.1016/S0378-3774(00)00125-6.

Sasada, Hironori. 2008. "Japan's New Agricultural Trade Policy and Electoral Reform: Agricultural Policy in an Offensive Posture." *Japanese Journal of Political Science* 9 (2): 121–44. https://doi.org/10.1017/S1468109908002958.

Scheiner, Ethan. 2013. "The Electoral System and Japan's Partial Transformation: Party System Consolidation without Policy Realignment." In *Japan under the DPJ: The Politics of Transition and Governance,* edited by Kenji E. Kushida and Phillip E. Lipscy, 73–102. Stanford, CA: Walter H. Shorenstein Asia-Pacific Research Center.

Schmidt, Carmen. 2009. "The Changing Institutional Framework for Local Democracy in Japan." In *Quality of Life and Working Life in Comparison,* edited by György Széll and Ute Széll, 57–70. Frankfurt am Main: P. Lang.

Sekine, Kae, and Alessandro Bonanno. 2016. *The Contradictions of Neoliberal Agri-Food: Corporations, Resistance, and Disasters in Japan.* Morgantown: West Virginia University Press.

Sheingate, Adam. 2001. *The Rise of the Agricultural Welfare State: Institutions and Interest Group Power in the United States, France, and Japan.* Princeton, NJ: Princeton University Press.

Shimada, Keiji. 2014. "Kesareta Chōson: Heisei Daigappei No Ketsumatsu" [Liquidated towns and villages: The result of the Heisei mergers]. *Japanese Research Institute for Local Government Monthly* 434:46–72.

Shimane Prefectural Government. 2008. "Nōchi No Hoyū to Riyō Wo Bunri Shite Menteki No Shūseki" [Farmland consolidation through the separation of ownership and use]. http://www.pref.shimane.lg.jp/industry/norin /nougyo/seido/kousakuhoukiti/jirei2103.data/0811hikawa.pdf.

Shimizu, Kay. 2013. "Electoral Consequences of Municipal Mergers." In *Japan under the DPJ: The Politics of Transition and Governance,* edited by Kenji E. Kushida and Phillip E. Lipscy, 127–56. Stanford, CA: Walter H. Shorenstein Asia-Pacific Research Center.

Shinagawa, Masaru. 2017. "Kyūshū Suiden Chitai Ni Okeru Nōgyō Kōzō No Hendō to Shūraku Einō" [Agricultural structural change and community-based farms in rice paddy areas in Kyūshū]. *Nōgyō Mondai Kenkyū* 48 (1): 29–38. https://doi.org/10.24808/nomonken.48.1_29.

Shinoda, Tomohito. 2013. *Contemporary Japanese Politics: Institutional Changes and Power Shifts.* New York: Columbia University Press.

Shōgenji, Shinichi. 2000. *Nōsei Daikaikaku: 21 Seiki He No Teigen* [Major agricultural policy reforms: A proposal for the 21st century]. Tōkyō: Ie no Hikari Kyōkai.

– 2012. "Meisō Suru Nōsei to Hito Nōchi Puran: Nōson Genba No Shitataka Na Taiō No Tame Ni" [Straying agricultural policies and the people and farmland plan: For strong support to the farm village]. https://www.tkfd .or.jp/research/detail.php?id=2255.

Shōji, Shunsaku. 2009. "Kyōto-Fu Kameoka-Shi Ni Okeru Shūraku-Gata Nōgyō Seisan Hōjin No Tenkai to Kadai" [Present situation and problems of community-based collective farms in Kameoka City, Kyōto Prefecture]. *Bulletin of the Institute for the Study of Humanities & Social Sciences, Doshisha University* 85:147–85.

– 2012. *Nihon No Sonraku to Shutai Keisei* [The Japanese village and independent organization]. Tōkyō: Nihon Keizai Hyōronsha.

Small, Mario L. 2006. "Neighborhood Institutions as Resource Brokers: Childcare Centers, Interorganizational Ties, and Resource Access among the Poor." *Social Problems* 53 (2): 274–92. https://doi.org/10.1525/sp.2006.53 .2.274.

Smith, Charles. 1988a. "The High-Yield Farm Lobby." *Far Eastern Economic Review*, 17 November, 24–5.

– 1988b. "Rich Harvest in Downtown Yokohama." *Far Eastern Economic Review*, 17 November, 26–31.

Smith, Robert J. 1961. "The Japanese Rural Community: Norms, Sanctions, and Ostracism." *American Anthropologist* 63 (3): 522–33. https://doi.org /10.1525/aa.1961.63.3.02a00050.

Snyder, Richard. 1999. "After Neoliberalism: The Politics of Reregulation in Mexico." *World Politics* 51 (2): 173–204. https://doi.org/10.1017 /S0043887100008169.

Song, Jiyeoun. 2015. "Japan's Regional Inequality in Hard Times." *Pacific Focus* 30 (1): 126–49. https://doi.org/10.1111/pafo.12043.

Statistics Bureau of Japan. n.d. Homepage. "Regional Statistics Database." https://www.e-stat.go.jp/en/regional-statistics/ssdsview.

– 2012. "Report on Results of 2010 World Census of Agriculture and Forestry in Japan." http://www.e-stat.go.jp/SG1/estat/ListE.do?bid=000001037762 &cycode=0.

– 2016. "Statistical Handbook of Japan 2016." http://www.stat.go.jp/english /data/handbook/pdf/2016all.pdf.

Streeck, Wolfgang. 2009. *Re-Forming Capitalism: Institutional Change in the German Political Economy*. Oxford: Oxford University Press.

Streeck, Wolfgang, and Kathleen Thelen, eds. 2005a. *Beyond Continuity: Institutional Change in Advanced Political Economies*. Oxford: Oxford University Press.

– 2005b. "Introduction: Institutional Change in Advanced Political Economies." In Streeck and Thelen, *Beyond Continuity*, 1–39.

Streeck, Wolfgang, and Kōzō Yamamura, eds. 2001. *The Origins of Nonliberal Capitalism: Germany and Japan in Comparison*. Ithaca, NY: Cornell University Press.

–, eds. 2003. *The End of Diversity? Prospects for German and Japanese Capitalism*. Ithaca, NY: Cornell University Press.

Tabuchi, Hiroko. 2014. "Japanese Begin to Question Protections Given to Homegrown Rice." *New York Times*, 9 January. http://www.nytimes.com /2014/01/10/business/international/japanese-begin-to-question-rices -sacred-place.html?_r=0.

Takahashi, Daisuke. 2013. "Nōchi Seido Kaikaku Wo Meguru Ronten Seiri to Kongo No Tenbō" [Review of the relevant points and outlook concerning the reform of the farmland system]. *Tochi to Nōgyō* 43:95–106.

Taniguchi, Kenji, ed. 2009. *Chūsan Chiiki Nōson Keieiron* [Rural areas managament theory in hilly and mountainous areas]. Tōkyō: Nōson Tōkei Shuppan.

Taniguchi, Nobukazu. 2014. *Nōkyō-Ron Saikō* [Reconsideration of the agricultural cooperative theory]. Tōkyō: Nōson Tōkei Shuppan.

Taniguchi, Nobukazu, and Yunmi Lee. 2013. *JA Chokusetsu Gata Nōgyō Keiei to JA Shusshi Gata Nōgyō Hōjin No Chōsen* [Challenges for JA direct farming enterprises and JA-financed agricultural corporations]. Tōkyō: JA Zenchū.

Tashiro, Yōichi. 2006. *Shūraku Einō to Nōgyō Seisan Hōjin: Nō No Kyōdō Wo Tsumugu* [Hamlet-based collective farms and agricultural production corporations: Establishing agrarian cooperation]. Tōkyō: Tsukuba Shobō.

– 2009. *Konmei Suru Nōsei Kyōdō Suru Chiiki* [Chaotic agricultural policies, cooperating regions]. Tōkyō: Tsukuba Shobō.

– 2010. "Izumo Chiiki Ni Okeru Shūraku Einō No Hatten to Daikibō Einō: Izumo-Shi Oyobi Hikawa-Chō No Jirei" [Development and large-scale farm management in hamlet-based farm cooperatives in the Izumo Region: Examples from Izumo City and Hikawa Town]. *Tochi to Nōgyō* 40:167–82.

– 2013. "Nōchi Hoyū Gōrika Jigyō Wo Tsūjiru Men-Teki Shūsekitai to Shite No Shūraku Einō" [Hamlet-based collective farms as farmland concentration bodies in farmland rationalization projects]. *Tochi to Nōgyō* 43:23–47.

– 2014a. "Korekara No Nōchi Riyō to Nihon Nōgyō No Hōkōsei" [The future direction of Japanese agriculture and farmland use]. *Nōsei Chōsa Jihō* 571:2–9.

– 2014b. *Sengo Rejīmu Kara No Dakkyaku Nōsei* [The departure of agricultural policies from the postwar regime]. Tōkyō: Tsukuba Shobō.

– 2017. *Nōkyō Kaikaku: Posuto TPP – Chiiki* [Nōkyō reform, post TPP, and the regions]. Tōkyō: Tsukuba Shobō.

– 2018. *Nōkyō Kaikaku to Heisei Gappei* [Nōkyō reform and Heisei mergers]. Tōkyō: Tsukuba Shobō.

Thelen, Kathleen. 2004. *How Institutions Evolve: The Political Economy of Skills in Germany, Britain, the United States, and Japan.* Cambridge: Cambridge University Press.

– 2012. "Varieties of Capitalism: Trajectories of Liberalization and the New Politics of Social Solidarity." *Annual Review of Political Science* 15 (1): 137–59. https://doi.org/10.1146/annurev-polisci-070110-122959.

– 2014. *Varieties of Liberalization and the New Politics of Social Solidarity.* Cambridge: Cambridge University Press.

Tōjō, Shinji. 1992. "Daikibo Inasaku Keiei No Nōchi Shūseki to Infōmaru Purōsesu No Igi" [The significance of informal processes for farmland consolidation for large-scale rice cultivation]. *Nōgyō Keiei Kenkyū* 30 (9): 1–9. https://doi.org/10.11300/fmsj1963.30.3_1.

Tokuno, Sadano, Tsutomu Yamamoto, and Masae Tsutsumi. 2008. *Chiiki Kara No Shakaigaku: Nō to Furusato No Saisei Wo Matomete* [Sociology from the regions: Seeking the revitalization of agriculture and hometown]. Tōkyō: Gakubunsha.

Toyama, Hiroko. 2012. "Shūraku Einō: Sono Gensetsu to Seisaku No Hensen" [Community-based farming in discourse and policy]. *Waseda Department of Law Bulletin Paper* 62 (2): 127–70.

Trading Economics. 2020. "Japan: Agriculture, Value Added (% of GDP)." https://tradingeconomics.com/japan/agriculture-value-added-percent-of -gdp-wb-data.html.

Tsai, Chia-Hung. 2005. "Policy-Making, Local Factions and Candidate Coordination in Single Non-Transferable Voting: A Case Study of Taiwan." *Party Politics* 11 (1): 59–77. https://doi.org/10.1177/1354068805048473.

Tsai, Kellee S. 2006. "Adaptive Informal Institutions and Endogenous Institutional Change in China." *World Politics* 59:116–41. https://doi.org /10.1353/wp.2007.0018.

Tsai, Lily L. 2007. *Accountability without Democracy: Solidary Groups and Public Goods Provision in Rural China*. New York: Cambridge University Press.

Tsukamoto, Takashi. 2012. "Why Is Japan Neoliberalizing? Rescaling of the Japanese Developmental State and Ideology of State-Capital Fixing." *Journal of Urban Affairs* 34 (4): 395–418. https://doi.org/10.1111/j.1467-9906.2011 .00591.x.

Tsunoda, Ichie. 2012. "Unique Community Farm Management in Kamiina District Shifting Focus from Owning to Using Farms." http://www.japanfs .org/en/news/archives/news_id031918.html.

United States Department of Agriculture. 2017. "Farms and Land in Farms: Summary 2016." https://usda.mannlib.cornell.edu/usda/current /FarmLandIn/FarmLandIn-02-17-2017.pdf.

Verdery, Katherine. 2003. *The Vanishing Hectare: Property and Value in Postsocialist Transylvania*. New York: Cornell University Press.

Voda, Petr, and Petra Svačinová. 2019. "To Be Central or Peripheral? What Matters for Political Representation in Amalgamated Municipalities?" *Urban Affairs Review* 2 (3): 1–31. https://doi.org/10.1177/1078087418824671.

Vogel, Steven K. 2003. "The Re-organization of Organized Capitalism: How the German and Japanese Models Are Shaping Their Own Transformations." In *The End of Diversity? Prospects for German and Japanese Capitalism*, edited by Wolfgang Streeck and Kōzo Yamamura, 306–33. Oxford: Oxford University Press.

– 2005. "Routine Adjustment and Bounded Innovation: The Changing Political Economy of Japan." In Streeck and Thelen, *Beyond Continuity*, 145–68.

Wank, David L. 1999. *Commodifying Communism: Business, Trust, and Politics in a Chinese City*. Cambridge: Cambridge University Press.

Wolf, Steven A., ed. 2014. *The Neoliberal Regime in the Agri-Food Sector: Crisis, Resilience and Restructuring*. London: Routledge.

Wood, Donald C. 2012. *Ogata-Mura: Sowing Dissent and Reclaiming Identity in a Japanese Farming Village*. New York: Berghahn Books.

Woodhouse, Philip. 2010. "Beyond Industrial Agriculture? Some Questions about Farm Size, Productivity and Sustainability." *Journal of Agrarian Change* 10 (3): 437–53. https://doi.org/10.1111/j.1471-0366.2010.00278.x.

Yamada, Kyōhei. 2012. "Municipal Mergers in Japan: How Did the Fiscal Incentives by the Central Government Affect Municipalities' Decisions?" American Political Science Annual Meeting Working Paper. http://ssrn.com/abstract=2107502.

Yamada, Kyōhei, and Kiichirō Arai. 2017. "Do Boundary Consolidations Alter the Relationship between Politicians and Voters? Evidence from Municipal Mergers in Japan." Annual Meeting of the Midwest Political Science Association, 2017.

Yamamoto, Kōhei. 2010. "Shakai-Teki Kigyō to Shite No Shūraku Hōjin No Keiei to Tenbō: Hiroshima-Ken No Shūraku Hōjin Anketo Chōsa Kekka Kara" [Analyzing the management and prospects of community-based corporations as a social business: A report on community-based corporations in Hiroshima Prefecture]. *Nōringyō Mondai Kenkyū* 179:201–6.

– 2011. "Shakai-Teki Kigyō to Shite Shūraku Hōjin Seturitsu-Go No Ishiki Ni Kan Suru Ikkōsatsu" [Considering the consciousness of community corporations as social businesses following their establishment]. *Hiroshima Keizai Daigaku Keizei Kenkyū Ronshū* 34 (1): 33–42.

– 2013. "Nōgyō, Nōson Ni Okeru Shakai-Teki Kigyō Ni Kan Suru Kiō Kanren Kenkyū No Seiri to Kadai" [Review and questions of previous research regarding social enterprises in agriculture and farm villages]. *Hiroshima Keizai Daigaku Keizei Kenkyū Ronshū* 35 (4): 93–105.

Yamashita, Kazuhito. 2005. "The Mistakes in Agricultural Policy That Have Hindered Structural Reforms and the Merits and Demerits of JA Agricultural Cooperatives." http://www.rieti.go.jp/en/papers/contribution/yamashita/06.html.

– 2008. "Issues in the Farmland System." http://www.tokyofoundation.org/en/articles/2008/the-issues-in-the-farmland-system.

– 2009. "The Agricultural Cooperatives and Farming Reform in Japan (1)." http://www.tokyofoundation.org/en/articles/2008/the-agricultural-cooperatives-and-farming-reform-in-japan-1.

– 2015a. "A First Step toward Reform of Japan's Agricultural Cooperative System." http://www.nippon.com/en/currents/d00169/.

– 2015b. "The Political Economy of Japanese Agricultural Trade Negotiations." In *The Political Economy of Japanese Trade Policy*, edited by Aurelia George Mulgan and Masayoshi Honma, 71–93. Basingstoke, UK: Palgrave Macmillan.

Yasu City. 2017. "Dai-Ni-Ji Yasu-Shi Nōgyō Shinkō Keikaku (An)" [Outline of the second Yasu City agricultural revitalization plan]. http://www.city .yasu.lg.jp/ikkrwebBrowse/material/files/group/60/5.pdf.

Yoshida, Kunimitsu. 2012. "Shūyaku-Teki Nōgyō Chiiki Ni Okeru Shakai Kankei Kara Mita Nōchi Idō No Tenkai" [The development of farmland tranfers in an intensive farming region from a social relations perspective]. *Human Geography* 64 (2): 103–22. https://doi.org/10.4200/jjhg.64.2_103.

– 2015. *Nōchi Kanri to Sonraku Shakai: Shakai Netwaku Bunseki Kara No Apurōchi* [Farmland management and village society: A social network approach]. Kyōto: Sekai Shisōsha.

Yoshida, Tadanori. 2016. "A New Crop of Farmers Is Revitalizing Japanese Agriculture." *Nikkei Asian Review*, 8 December. https://asia.nikkei.com /magazine/Fresh-ideas/On-the-Cover/A-new-crop-of-farmers-is -revitalizing-Japanese-agriculture?page=1.

Zenkoku Nōgyō Kaigijo. 2016. *Kōshū-shi Nōgyō Iinkai Katsudō Seiri Kaado* [Kōshū City agricultural committee activity report]. Tokyo: Zenkoku Nōgyō Kaigijo.

Zimmerbauer, Kaj, and Anssi Paasi. 2013. "When Old and New Regionalism Collide: Deinstitutionalization of Regions and Resistance Identity in Municipality Amalgamations." *Journal of Rural Studies* 30:31–40. https:// doi.org/10.1016/j.jrurstud.2012.11.004.

Zucker, Lynne G. 1991. "The Role of Institutionalization in Cultural Persistence." In *The New Institutionalism in Organizational Analysis,* edited by Paul DiMaggio and Walter Powell, 83–107. Chicago: University of Chicago Press.

Index

An italic *f* following a page reference indicates a figure.

Japan and Global Society